E PICNIC '82

ECT TO SEARCH

RAIN OR SHINE

STADIUM — CNE

BY GARYS&Q107

1982 5:00 PM

4   ADULT
        admission

6    $2.00

1982

19

JIAN GHOMESHI

82

VIKING

VIKING
an imprint of Penguin Canada

Published by the Penguin Group
Penguin Group (Canada), 90 Eglinton Avenue East, Suite 700,
Toronto, Ontario, Canada M4P 2Y3 (a division of Pearson Canada Inc.)

Penguin Group (USA) Inc., 375 Hudson Street, New York, New York 10014, U.S.A.
Penguin Books Ltd, 80 Strand, London WC2R 0RL, England
Penguin Ireland, 25 St Stephen's Green, Dublin 2, Ireland (a division of Penguin Books Ltd)
Penguin Group (Australia), 250 Camberwell Road, Camberwell, Victoria 3124, Australia
(a division of Pearson Australia Group Pty Ltd)
Penguin Books India Pvt Ltd, 11 Community Centre, Panchsheel Park,
New Delhi – 110 017, India
Penguin Group (NZ), 67 Apollo Drive, Rosedale, Auckland 0632, New Zealand
(a division of Pearson New Zealand Ltd)
Penguin Books (South Africa) (Pty) Ltd, 24 Sturdee Avenue, Rosebank, Johannesburg 2196,
South Africa

Penguin Books Ltd, Registered Offices: 80 Strand, London WC2R 0RL, England

First published 2012

1 2 3 4 5 6 7 8 9 10 (RRD)

Copyright © Jian Ghomeshi, 2012

Manufactured in the U.S.A.

LIBRARY AND ARCHIVES CANADA CATALOGUING IN PUBLICATION

Ghomeshi, Jian
1982 / Jian Ghomeshi.

ISBN 978-0-670-06648-3

1. Ghomeshi, Jian. 2. Iranian Canadians—Biography. 3. Popular music fans—Canada—
Biography. 4. Popular music—Canada—1981–1990. 5. Music, Influence of. 6. Nineteen
eighty-two, A.D. I. Title. II. Title: Nineteen eighty-two.

ML3534.6.C2G56 2012   780.92   C2012-905011-3

Visit the Penguin Canada website at www.penguin.ca

Special and corporate bulk purchase rates available; please see
www.penguin.ca/corporatesales or call 1-800-810-3104, ext. 2477.

ALWAYS LEARNING   PEARSON

FOR MOM AND DAD

CONTENTS

PROLOGUE

"Let's emphasize all the mistakes."

—DAVID BOWIE, ON SWEDISH RADIO, 1982

Nineteen eighty-two was a big year. Really big.

You might not think so. And you might wonder about my qualifications for making such a declaration. You might not think any single year is deserving of too much attention.

Then again, if you do want to champion one twelve-month period, you might contend that it should be some other year. I'm anticipating this. For instance, you might be all "Team 1991!" That's the year Nirvana released *Nevermind* and ushered grunge music into the mainstream and started a new generation of non-Canadians wearing plaid shirts (in Canada we already had the outfit). That was a big year. Or you might lobby for 1945, because that was the year of the final battles of the European theatre of World War II, as well as the German surrender to the Western Allies and the Soviet Union. Indeed,

1945 was also a big year. Mind you, I've never been so sure of that term, "theatre of war." Doesn't the word "theatre" connote artifice or entertainment? As a way to refer to scores of actual young dudes far from home, trudging around in shit and killing each other, it's a bit optimistic, isn't it? But the term sounds impressive. And it sounds smart to pick a year like 1945. It's got gravitas and the end of a war. Nineteen forty-five is definitely in the up-market aisle when shopping for a year.

So then you wonder, why 1982? There was no armistice or Nirvana. And you might chuckle at the idea that 1982 merits a book unto itself. The 1980s are still considered a bit of a joke dressed up in oversized shoulder pads. Even one of the most populist spokespeople of the era, the Bangles' Susanna Hoffs—is there a more sage authority?—has said, "The fact that the '80s are now a beloved era is shocking."

And you might think all of this 1982 business is an attempt at irony. You might be tempted to roll your eyes at the thought. But in case you think I'm kidding about 1982, I'm not. And actually, there's intra-'80s competition about this stuff, too. As time passes, self-satisfied observers of late-twentieth-century history continue to focus on another year: 1984. Well, damn that 1984. It's been fawned over for decades. There's no denying 1984 was huge. It had important Orwellian overtones and was the year Prince released *Purple Rain*. That was big. But 1982 came before 1984. And sometimes the opening act doesn't get as much credit as it deserves for warming up the crowd. Who will speak for 1982? I will.

The thing is, 1982 was a lot more than just the debut season of *Remington Steele*—although I know that impresses some of you enough for me to stop right there. In 1982, the

Commodore 64 computer was introduced, Ronald Reagan had survived being shot, poisoned Tylenol capsules killed seven people, the Falklands War started and ended, Michael Jackson released *Thriller*, Canada repatriated its Constitution, and the first compact disc was sold in Germany.

And that's not all. Over the course of 1982, I blossomed from a naïve fourteen-year-old trying to fit in with the cool kids to something much more: a naïve, eyeliner-wearing fifteen-year-old trying to fit in with the cool kids.

To be quite honest, this pivotal period of my teens doesn't seem so far away. I can still channel the angst over wanting a Clash T-shirt to help me fit in. Not that I haven't grown past that feeling. I have. I think. Okay, so maybe I feel the need to be wearing my old Clash T-shirt right now. It makes me almost cool. Stop staring. And in the immortal words of the unevenly talented '80s duo Tears for Fears (Roland was the talented one and Curt was just cute), the scars linger.

But I'm no longer a teen. And I'm beginning to learn that 1982 was a long time ago. It's sinking in every time some fresh-faced hipster asks me if I've ever heard of Kate Bush. These kids now don't get it. They either don't know the references or they think of them as vintage. There's even a whole world of young adults running around thinking of the 1980s the way we used to think of the '60s. Old. Well, actually, old but also fascinating, and a bit zany. It's just like the feeling you always get watching those black-and-white sex films from the 1920s. I mean, if those films exist. Like, in theory.

The '80s are now so long ago that those of us who were alive back then risk getting that glazed-over look of nostalgia in our eyes when we think about it. You know, the way older people get.

The way some very nice but earnest Boomers like to remember seeing the Beatles for the first time. These Boomers will familiarly reminisce about seeing the Beatles or Stones whether they actually saw them or not. And they probably didn't. But they will say things to each other in public as if they did.

"Oh, honey, remember the second time we saw the Stones and you got really stupid high with Julie?"

You see, Boomers will say these things because they know no one will ever check. And if you try to verify dates or details, they will tell you they can't remember, because they were stoned, or drunk, or too excited, or it was too long ago. And the point is just that. It's far off enough in history that no one cares if they were actually there to see "Ruby Tuesday" performed live. And then—and this is the important part—the Boomers will get a wistful look about them and mutter something about 1967. They might use the word "innocent." Boomers talk about the past and get nostalgic for a less confused time—an innocent time.

But the Boomers are just copying their parents and the generations who came before them. It must be that as humans get older, we believe that the previous era we lived through was more virtuous. It's like an aging disease and a survival mechanism rolled into one. So now those of us who were teens in the 1980s are starting our turn. But we're not there yet. The early '80s still don't really seem "innocent." Not quite. Not in the way that kind of language is applied to the '50s to remind us that everyone was happy then, and white, and there was no poverty, and women wore pearls and heels in the kitchen. Those 1950s. Only good times with rich people wearing hats.

I still remember the '80s too well. They certainly didn't seem very innocent when we were living them. In the early '80s, John Lennon was killed, the pope was shot, Iran had been taken over by the Ayatollah Khomeini, and Madonna was wriggling into her garter belt for her pop-culture debut. We had learned that racism was bad, porn had become mainstream, big hair was all the rage, and punk rock had emerged around the world. Not so innocent. But just because those of us who were alive in the '80s don't particularly think of ourselves as seniors doesn't mean things haven't changed. The world has evolved so dramatically in the past three decades that the generation gap might as well be a century wide. So much of what was hot in the 1980s has been updated and reformulated and upgraded. There are also essential international institutions today that weren't even invented in the '80s. There are crucial daily staples of our lives today with names we wouldn't even have begun to understand or recognize. Here is a list of words that did not exist in 1982:

- Google
- iPhone
- AIDS
- Wikipedia
- Radiohead

That's a pretty heavy collection of post-'80s reality. Let me say this again. None of those words even existed in 1982, let alone the life-changing institutions behind them. But I have more:

- same-sex marriage
- Facebook
- *The Simpsons*
- debit cards
- flat screens

Can you even remember a time before you were creeping photos of "hot" people on Facebook? Barely. Right? So maybe, as it turns out, the '80s *were* more innocent. Or maybe they were just harder to endure, because you had to actually get up and walk over to a shelf and pick up a book and flip to the right page to get a good definition of "innocent" rather than Google it on your tablet. And, yes, clearly, there was a lot we didn't have in 1982, including personal computers in our palms. But what we did have was New Wave. And New Wave music came from the UK. That meant it was already cool. And New Wave was exciting, and electronic, and serious, and futuristic, and cosmetic, and sometimes a bit dumb. And New Wave was effectively created by a guy named David Bowie.

You see, 1982 was also the year after Bowie released "Cat People" and the year before he released *Let's Dance*. It was two years after his brilliant *Scary Monsters* album and two years before he put out *Tonight*. Some people would go on to say that *Tonight* was a less than spectacular effort for Bowie, or, more specifically, a "crap record." But I'm one of the few people around that really appreciated *Tonight*. And I know all of this about Bowie because Bowie was my hero, my idol. In 1982, I wanted to be Bowie. And if I couldn't be Bowie, I would try to come close. Bowie was cool. Everyone agreed. If I could be like Bowie, I would turn out okay.

My dear Iranian-Canadian parents didn't really understand all of this. They were already pretty busy in damage control trying to explain that being from Iran didn't mean we agreed with those hot-tempered bearded guys who took fifty-two Americans hostage in 1979. When Khomeini consolidated the revolution in the early '80s, he really messed with those Persians in the diaspora still holding on to our "I love Iran!" T-shirts. So with this backdrop, my parents just wanted me to fit in. And in that quest, we were united. Except that for me, fitting in wasn't really working. I needed to be cool to fit in. And being cool might mean makeup and pointy boots and Bowie. This was not exactly the conventional middle-class prescription from Tehran.

And so it turns out 1982 was a pivotal year in my life. Nineteen eighty-two was the year I became New Wave. In my goal to be like Bowie, I acquired the black clothing, the hair gel, and some of the attitude to fit in with the punks and New Wavers. Or at least, I came close by the end of the year. And it didn't help that all the heroes in New Wave were white like Bowie—although I liked to imagine that Bowie had no race. He was too cool. And there were some cool black guys, like the ones in the English Beat or the enthusiastic bass player in Culture Club. He always wore a hat. They gave me hope.

But they weren't Iranian. No one was ever Iranian. I was probably the first Persian-Canadian New Waver. Well, maybe I was the only Persian-Canadian New Waver. The point is, there may have been significant changes happening in the world, but I had a more targeted idea of what was essential. I knew what was real when I was fourteen. I have made a list of the most important things to me in 1982:

- David Bowie
- black pointy boots
- fitting in
- red/blue classic Adidas gym bag
- sister and parents
- drum kit
- Theatre Room 213
- hockey
- Talking Heads
- fitting in
- Wendy

If you just read that list with care, you might have noticed that "fitting in" appears twice. This is not a typo. And I will explain. But you will also notice that the list is bookended by two names. Bowie and Wendy. And that's also no mistake. Because amongst all the other characters and events in 1982, this is the story of three people: me, Wendy, and Bowie.

And as much as he was my idol, I never met David Bowie. And as much as she was my dream girl, I'm not sure how well I got to know Wendy. But one thing's for sure, of the three of us, I probably understood myself less than I did the other two. I was only just developing a sense of who I wanted to be. And it involved a fair bit of hair gel.

1

"OUR HOUSE" — MADNESS

In 1982, I lived in Thornhill. That was part of the problem. Don't get me wrong. Life was quite reasonable in Thornhill. At least, for most people it was. It was nice. It was straight. It was normal. But David Bowie never chose to hang out in Thornhill. And it wasn't just because he was too busy being an inspirational androgynous musical genius rock star.

You see, in 1982, Bowie couldn't appear in Thornhill for more profound reasons than simple scheduling. It would have been impossible for Bowie to reside in Thornhill, even though he was white and English and financially secure, like many of its denizens. If Bowie were ever seen in Thornhill, and most especially if he'd fancied it, he wouldn't be Bowie. He would be a fake. He would be just another victim of homogeneity. And there would be headlines in trendy magazines calling him out. *NME* would do a front-page exposé: "Place Oddity: Thin White Duke Seen Hanging Out in Canadian Suburb! Bowie a Fake!"

But Bowie wasn't a fake. He was unique. He was Bowie. So he wouldn't be seen in Thornhill in 1982. He would never have fit in, for all the right reasons. And that's why Thornhill was a problem.

Let me be clear. I am not a Thornhill detractor. I was not a self-hating Thornhiller. I had many fine experiences growing up in the suburbs. I met my first real girlfriend, Dana Verner, in Grade 5 in Thornhill. We kissed. Twice. I think. Then she broke up with me. Years later, she told me she would've stayed with me had she known I'd one day meet John Cusack. I count that as a win. But anyway, Dana Verner was one of the most desirable girls in my Grade 5 class. And I would never have had the chance to kiss her if I'd not been in Thornhill.

Also, I once scored seven goals in a hockey game in Thornhill. Okay, maybe it was just road hockey. And maybe there were only six kids playing, and one of them, Little Charles, was wearing a cast on his arm and couldn't hold his stick properly. Little Charles had earned his name at Henderson Avenue Public School because he was small. And unrelated to that, he broke his arm in the summer of 1980. He still had his cast on the day I scored seven goals. I'd totally deked Little Charles and drove straight to the net, Lafleur style, to score my seventh tally. Little Charles later made the case that my excellent deke was only owing to him holding his stick with one hand, and also because the cast on his other hand felt heavy. I think that was a technicality. And I figure the goals still count in Thornhill history, because the word "hockey" is part of "road hockey," and also because it was a competitive game, and also because I scored them. But look, the point is, there was nothing exactly *wrong* with Thornhill. And that was also part of the problem.

Thornhill is a suburb of Toronto. It is in the province of Ontario in Canada. It is directly to the north of Toronto. If you pass Steeles Avenue, you leave the border of Toronto and enter into "scenic" Thornhill. Scenic Thornhill looks pretty much identical to the area just south of Steeles, with houses and streets and schools and cars, but north of Steeles it's called scenic. That is, except when it's called Markham, and parts of it sometimes are. Both Thornhill and Markham are in York Region. And they are also part of the GTA, or Greater Toronto Area. As you can see, it's all very sophisticated. I could never really keep track of all these names. I just know we called it Thornhill. I used to hang out at the Thornhill Square mall. And I played hockey at the Thornhill Community Centre. And in 1982, I was pretty much the only kid playing an instrument with a bunch of adults in the Thornhill Community Band. So, like it or not, I was deeply entrenched in Thornhill.

I joined the Thornhill Community Band as the new drummer in 1982. The insiders called it the TCB. You might think it was a real honour to be selected as the drummer. You might think it was an indication of my superior level of talent at the time. But the Thornhill Community Band was almost totally volunteer, and there was very little quality control.

I only got involved in the TCB because, in the beginning of Grade 9, Don Margison's father had inquired if I'd be able to play drums when the old percussionist, a retired gentleman named Reginald who'd been with the TCB since the late '70s, quit. Don had told his father that I was a very good drummer. This was probably a mistake. Mr. Margison was the lead trombone player in the TCB, and he was quite accomplished. He wore sweaters over collared shirts, and one of his sweaters had his name inscribed on it, along with a little picture of a trombone. In other words, he was good enough to have his own trombone sweater. Mr. Margison was in his fifties and he was balding. He was usually frustrated that other people weren't as good at their instruments as he was, and at TCB practices his face and his balding head would get red with irritation. He would also drink at some of the practices, and he would get red then, too. Sometimes it was difficult to tell if Mr. Margison was red from blowing hard into his trombone, or from drinking in excess, or from his mounting frustration over working with amateurs.

I had agreed to come in for an audition after Don Margison told me of his dad's request. Don was an acquaintance who was an excellent young piano player. He'd seen me playing "Tom Sawyer" by Rush on a drum kit in the music room after school. He thought I was good. He didn't know that I played "Tom Sawyer" well only because I had practised it over four hundred times, because in 1982 that's what aspiring drummers did. Don just knew I was a drummer who could play "Tom Sawyer." And that his dad needed one.

As part of the stringent audition process for the TCB, I met with two of the executive members—a nice bearded man named Jack and Mr. Margison. I was very intimidated at the audition. My father dropped me off, and he was waiting outside while I went in to the high school music room. The bearded man named Jack was also in his fifties, and had a big belly and wore corduroy pants and a flowery shirt underneath a vest. He greeted me by saying, "Hey there, man!" like bearded people talked in the 1960s. I think he might have previously been one of those guys that other musicians call a "jazz cat." He played

4

the bass saxophone in the TCB. On the evening they invited me to audition, he took a seat next to Mr. Margison in the music room and I stood in front of them. Mr. Margison sat upright and looked quite stern. Strangely, the audition involved no music performance but rather an "informal chat." I assumed this was a ruse. I was prepared for a minor interrogation to see if I was the right young man for the job. "So ... can you play drum kit well?" bearded Jack asked me in a friendly way to get things rolling.

"Um, yes," I replied, trying to sound confident. "I mean ... I think I can. I mean, of course."

"Well, that's very good, man. Right on." He turned to Mr. Margison and nodded with a satisfied look. "And what about percussion, then? Can you play percussion?"

"Yeah. That too." I didn't know exactly what they meant by percussion, but I could handle a tambourine and shakers and I had played bongos. Once, I played bongos on BBC television in England when I was five years old with a bunch of other kids. I'm not sure I knew how to play very well. But since I'd done it on TV, I must have been good enough.

Then it was Mr. Margison's turn to speak. He cleared his throat first to signal his intervention.

"Well, that's all very fine. Thank you for coming. But I hope you know this isn't a rock band, young man. Can you actually read music?"

As he said this, Mr. Margison turned his head sharply towards bearded Jack as if to suggest that this should have been the first question asked. Mr. Margison had worn a look of disappointment on his face since the moment I walked in. I'm not sure what Don had told him, but I wasn't living up to expectations. It seemed strange that he needed to clarify that the TCB wasn't a rock band. I was quite sure Mr. Margison wouldn't fit in with any rock bands.

"Um ... I'm okay at that. Like ... reading music, I mean," I responded.

Bearded Jack could tell I probably couldn't read music very well, but he didn't seem to mind. He was nodding along as if nothing about this conversation really mattered much. Mr. Margison was looking distraught.

But before I knew it, Jack had jumped up and was shaking my hand. "Well, okay then, man. Welcome to the band!"

Mr. Margison looked angry. His face was getting red. He had been out-voted by the bearded man named Jack. His balding head turned a shade of deep red that I had not witnessed yet. It was more like burgundy.

With this probing test over, I was in. There were about thirty members of the TCB, including trumpet and French horn players, clarinetists, a tuba-playing woman, and Jack the bass saxophone man. Most of the band members were older men, and many of them were balding and also had beards. The conductor was a kind lady named Amanda. During my first year playing drums in the TCB, we practised the theme from *Superman*, and I played a repeating marching drum roll at the start. This meant I was in the spotlight. I was also in the spotlight because I wasn't old. And I may have drawn attention because I was the only one with dyed and gelled and semi-spiked hair. I was never sure if Mr. Margison and the older, white, conservative people in the Thornhill Community Band ever really liked me. I was pretty sure they just needed a drummer and I was the only one available. We wore special blue shirts with a V-neck and white trim in the TCB. I got mine oversized and let it drape over my black New Wave pants. I was intent on being my own man, even though I was scared that most of them hated me. We met twice a week and practised a few songs that we considered our hits.

I have made a short list (or shortlist) of the biggest hits of the Thornhill Community Band in 1982:

- theme from *Superman*
- theme from *Star Wars*
- "How Deep Is Your Love"
- "William Tell Overture" (theme from *The Lone Ranger*)
- "New York, New York" (theme from *New York, New York*)

As you can see from this list, the TCB had an affinity for performing themes from famous movies and TV shows. Crowd pleasers. It didn't seem to make much of a difference that we almost never played for a crowd. The elderly trumpet player named Marvin declared that our *Lone Ranger* theme would "bring the house down!" There was much excitement about this at practice, but I'm not sure that it ever happened. Or that there were many houses we could bring down. We did do a few gigs, including a big Christmas concert at the Thornhill Community Centre. At the Christmas concert, we had some local high school tap dancers perform while we played the theme from *New York, New York*. That was our showstopper. Unfortunately, the community band never really sounded very good. The members were mostly very nice and earnest, but there wasn't much of what you might call "soul." Maybe that was fitting for Thornhill.

THORNHILL WAS THE quintessential suburb. I've never lived in any other suburb, but I imagine they all look like Thornhill, with people who act like they did in Thornhill. It was the kind of place where men watch sprinklers on their lawns. Have you ever noticed that men like to watch sprinklers? They do. Or at least, they did. But I think they probably still do.

When suburban men reach a certain age (let's say, north of thirty-five), they like to stand at the foot of their front lawns and watch their sprinklers distributing water on them. This seems to be a biological need. It may look like a banal exercise, but men take it very seriously. You might expect that these men are involved in another activity while they are watching the lawn—like thinking. But I'm not so sure they are. I think they're not thinking. Watching the lawn is like a middle-class, suburban form of meditation for men. It becomes more common as they age. Their heads are empty and they are just watching sprinklers. Sometimes men will rub their bellies while they watch their lawns. Perhaps these men are so tired from a busy week that this is their respite. Or maybe these men feel a sense of accomplishment and worth by looking at their lawns. Maybe, in the moments when their heads aren't empty, they're thinking, "This is MY lawn! Look what I've done. I've got myself a lawn with a working sprinkler! I don't have to think. My belly feels good. I am feeling my belly." Maybe that's what suburban men are thinking.

This suburban sprinkler-watching activity divides along gender lines, too. Women have never stared at lawns and watched sprinklers, not in 1982 and not now. Not with the same dreamy look. Not for hours at a time. Women are more proactive and productive. They would start weeding or planting or they would point out the names of flowers or they would think about how things could look better. But men are different. Men will spend hours watching their sprinklers.

In 1982, on my street and on the streets nearby, you could see dozens of Thornhill men watching their sprinklers on any given Sunday afternoon. Sometimes, the style of sprinkler would mirror the personality of its owner. There was the machine-gun-like, rat-a-tat-tat rapid-fire "pulsating" sprinkler that would sit in the middle of a lawn and aggressively shoot water in all directions. I would later learn that this was also sometimes called the "impulse" sprinkler. It was likely owned and run by the dad of a tough guy. It was often considered the most effective, because it would discharge water in a strong fashion and was close to the ground so it was wind-resistant.

Then there were the "stationary" sprinklers that would just blow some water from a hose onto an area of lawn that needed particular attention. These static sprinklers would generally be left unattended for hours and were regularly featured on the lawns of more passive families. And then there were the vertical-shooting "oscillating" sprinklers that were positioned in the middle of a lawn and gracefully waved a stream of water to the right and then to the left and then back to the right. My father had bought the oscillating kind for our house. He would stand at the end of the front lawn and watch our graceful sprinkler for what seemed like hours. The oscillating sprinkler was very slow. I often wondered if my father would get us one of the machine-gun-type sprinklers. They seemed cooler, and that would make my father tough. And then people would think I was tough. But we never had one of those. I asked him once, but he didn't seem very impressed with the idea.

I have made a short list of the lawn sprinklers that were available in Thornhill in 1982:

- stationary sprinkler
- rotary sprinkler
- oscillating sprinkler
- pulsating (impulse) sprinkler
- travelling sprinkler

As you can see, there were distinct and varied types of sprinkler to be utilized in the suburbs in the early '80s. But ultimately, the point was to watch the sprinkler as much as to water the lawn. And it was all the same, watching sprinklers, no matter the kind. The style of sprinkler seemed to neither heighten nor dampen the enthusiasm. Simply, this is what men in Thornhill did. And so you see, while the Clash were inspiring punks to resist Thatcherism in the UK and a revolution was being co-opted by mullahs in the streets of Iran, grown men in Thornhill were watching sprinklers. That was the problem with Thornhill.

I didn't choose for us to live in Thornhill. My parents did. They picked our new locale when I was nine, a couple of years after we moved from England. It was all their decision. When you're nine, these options are not exercised democratically. There was no negotiation. I didn't feel I had the power to say, "Okay, I respect your decision. You guys do the Thornhill thing, and I'm going to go to Montreal and rear myself in the centre of what will become a hot music scene that will eventually spawn the indie collective Arcade Fire and a bunch of other bands that sound like the indie collective Arcade Fire."

I didn't have the resources to make that case at the age of nine. And I wouldn't really have wanted to do so, anyway, because that would have meant leaving my family. And my parents had bought me a guitar and a drum kit, and I would have had to leave those things behind, too. And I was really skinny, but I got hungry a lot, and my mother is the best cook in the world when she's making Persian food, like *ghormeh sabzi*. *Ghormeh sabzi* is a popular Iranian dish often served when family members return home after being away. It's a herb stew with lots of greens (*sabzi*) and some kidney beans and lamb and other things that I can't identify because I've never made it. It's served over rice (*polo*) and with bottom-of-the-pot rice (*tahdig*) as well. You might think bottom-of-the-pot rice sounds like a mistake. But it's not. Persians love it. It's crunchy and has oil. And my mother is the best cook. So part of the deal with getting my mother's food was living in Thornhill. But as a training ground to become Bowie, Thornhill was a disaster.

If Bowie was about edge and platform boots and spiked hair and drugs and cross-dressing and cool riffs and distortion and impenetrable-but-profound lyrics and creativity, you could easily make the case that the inverse of Bowie was the town of Thornhill. I've tried to picture Bowie walking down my street in 1982. In my imagination he has platform boots on and looks a bit like a sexy woman and he's singing "Be My Wife" from his 1977 album, *Low*. But I can't truthfully picture that. Nor can I picture him on my street as another one of his characters, Aladdin Sane. Or even as the *Let's Dance* guy from the 1983 tour with the yellow suit and super-blond hair. I can't picture him even if he were wearing my old

North Star runners and hooded sweatshirt from Roots. Not in 1982. Thornhill wouldn't have understood what to do with Bowie then.

Thornhill was a safe and quiet suburb where conformity was coveted. No one really rocked the boat. The dwellings all looked relatively similar on our street, and most of the houses had big lawns and nice trees. The adults on my street in Thornhill usually referred to themselves as "middle class." I decided "middle class" must mean "the same." Differences were expressed only in subtle ways. For example, the Jones family used silver for their house numbers next to their front door, while we and the Mullers had black.

Of course, my family stood out because we were Iranian and the rest of the street was pretty white and old-school conservative. That is, with the notable exception of the Olsons. The Olsons were a black family at the far end of the street, and they were very successful and attractive and charming. They had kids the age of my sister and me, and they created unfair expectations. All of the Olson progeny would go on to be great thinkers and business people and a supermodel. So the Olsons stood out too. But they were like a superhero family. They were in a different league. Who lives in a family where someone becomes a supermodel? And anyway, they were black and not Middle Eastern. There were some occasions where my family may have been exceptional for reasons other than our ethnicity—but the cultural difference always seemed to be unavoidable.

For our first couple of years in Thornhill, our house was set apart from others because of a little exterior twist that involved lighting. My father would put red light bulbs in the lamps that stood on each corner of our porch. These lamps were very distinctive, especially by Thornhill standards. No one used coloured lights on their houses except at Christmastime. This was an unspoken rule. But my parents had a streak of creativity that was often at odds with their desire to have us assimilate. It was like the fact that we had Persian rugs all over our house. But it was okay to be more different behind closed doors. The red lights were on the outside. This was a problem in Thornhill.

If you drove up our Thornhill street on an evening in the late '70s, you could identify the Ghomeshi house because of the two red lamps holding down the fort. We would turn them on after 6:30 P.M. and then turn them off in the morning. In retrospect, it was rather impressive that my mother let my father get away with the red lamps when it would clearly set us apart. But she did. And the lamps became our trademark in the early days in Thornhill. I suppose I took pride in our red lights. They looked romantic and maybe a bit edgy. Even then, I had an instinct for all things unique. But I was foolish and young.

One day, my father came home in something of a panic and started unscrewing the red lights on the porch. He seemed upset, and he ran around looking for white light bulbs to replace the red ones. He said something to my mother, and then she looked very serious and concerned as well. No one would tell me what was going on. When I finally got an answer about what was happening, my father explained that Mr. Pile from a few houses down the road had pulled him aside and told him that the red lamps were problematic in Canadian culture. My father shook his head in frustration as he recounted the little neighbourhood confrontation about the red lamps.

"He ees telling me that the red lights are meaning bad thing," my father explained. "He ees telling me that red lights means we are running cathouse!"

I never found out if "cathouse" was my father's word or Mr. Pile's. And I wasn't sure what "running cathouse" meant. But I could tell it was something bad. And it probably made us less Canadian. And this wasn't good. And Dana Verner would probably break up with me again, and my mother would be upset that we were different, and people would talk about us. I wondered why "cathouse" was the cause for such alarm. I wondered if the problem was that our house was suspected of having an overabundance of cats. For a couple of years after this incident, I assumed that red lights must represent a form of feline insurrection within an otherwise tranquil home. And this was obviously a negative thing. But it still didn't make sense that my father had dashed home and changed the light bulbs in such a fluster.

One day, my sister, Jila, explained to me that "cathouse" was a term that meant whorehouse. Jila was three years older than me, so she understood these things. I knew what a whore-house was. I knew it was a place where hookers worked. It was probably a house full of sexy whores. I knew this because I had seen something similar on the Friday-night *Baby Blue Movies* on Citytv when my parents were upstairs. But no family in Thornhill would want to be known for running a whorehouse. And we never had the red lamps again.

My father was a highly regarded engineer who had done his schooling in Iran and the UK, but people didn't always think that, because he had a heavy accent. When you have an accent you are sometimes considered dumb. At least, that was the case in 1982. Then again, it also depended on the accent. If you had a French accent from France, you would be thought to be sexy in 1982. And if you had a strong German accent, like our neighbour Mr. Muller, you might be mistaken as gruff. English accents were considered cool, but I wasn't really aware of that when we first came to Canada and I was eight and spoke like a Londoner. I just knew I wanted to lose my accent so I would fit in.

But maybe the worst and most misunderstood accent was the Middle Eastern one. If you had a Middle Eastern accent in 1982, you might be thought to be dumb or confused or to have a natural facility for explosives. This hasn't completely changed over the last three decades, but people seem to have more reference points for brown people now. My mother had less of an accent than my father, and she was much whiter, but it was clear she was from somewhere far away, too. The fact that there were very few immigrants in our part of Thornhill at the time meant assumptions were made about my father and our family because we were Middle Eastern. For instance, the red lamp incident might really have been about contrasting ideas, but it got presented as my father not understanding "Canadian culture." I didn't know about the roots of stuff like this at the time. I just resented my family for being different and my father for his accent.

On another occasion we had gotten squirrels caught in our attic and my father had tried various methods to shoo them out. There were lots of squirrels in Thornhill in the '80s. It was like a squirrel epidemic at times. In the spring of 1981, when there had been a few squirrels living inside our attic for months and nothing had worked to shoo them out, my father and I had gone to a local Home Hardware store. My father had the idea that we might find a cage or trap to catch the squirrels so he could take them and release them somewhere away from our home. The point was to try to liberate the attic without harming the squirrels. When my father asked the guy in the baseball cap behind the counter about a trap of this kind, the man wagged his finger and said he wouldn't help us.

"We don't eat squirrels in this country," the guy behind the counter said.

I remember sensing my father's disappointment when the man accused us of eating squirrels. I saw his shoulders slump a bit, and then he motioned to me for us to leave. It all happened quickly. The man in the baseball cap probably had no idea how tasty Persian food like my mother's *ghormeh sabzi* was and that we wouldn't be so desperate as to eat squirrels. But that didn't matter. I was angry with my father. I was angry that he had a heavy accent and that people thought he was stupid. I wished I wasn't Iranian, even though I'd only known Iranians—or Persians, you can use either word—to be kind and loving and generous family-oriented people. I wondered why my father had not yelled at the guy or punched him like a tough dad would. I told my father he should have said something. My father replied, "Don't leesen to this man. There ees no point fighting with heem. He did not understand very well." My father was usually graceful in these situations. Just like the oscillating sprinkler. But sometimes I wished he would be more like the impulse sprinkler.

I was different in all the wrong ways in Thornhill in 1982. Rather than looking and acting like Bowie—which would be impossible, because then I'd be too cool to be seen in Thornhill—I was often distinguished from others because I was Persian. There were no other Iranians in Thornhill in the early '80s. None. Or almost none, anyway. And this is ironic, because the place is now teeming with Persians who've settled there and constructed a mini "Tehranto" just minutes from where I grew up. But they weren't there when I was young. Not when I needed them.

Beyond assumptions based on accents, the dearth of Iranians meant people didn't understand anything about our background. After Iran's Islamic Revolution and the tumultuous events of the early '80s there, people were still quite confused about who and what we were. This went beyond racism. Sometimes it was just confusion.

One day, Annie McMillan from down the street asked me about our ethnic background. I wanted her to like me, because she wore tight, faded jeans and would always tan the way pretty girls did. Annie was two years older than me and she was quite tall. She saw me playing road hockey alone and crossed the street and came straight towards me. I was excited that Annie wanted to speak to me. Then, after saying hello, she asked me if my family were Arabs. She didn't say it in a mean way. In fact, she said it in the way a pretty girl with a tan does when she's being nice.

"Are you guys Arabs?"

There was a genuine curiosity in her tone. I thought Annie might think we were exotic, the way Freddie Mercury was exotic in his spandex and moustache when he was onstage during the "Live Killers" tour with Queen. But I wasn't sure if she thought it would be a good or bad thing for us to be Arabs. So I decided to tell her the truth. We were not.

17

"No, we're Persians. Iranians. Like, from Iran," I said. There was an awkward pause and Annie looked a bit puzzled. I decided to continue. "It's in the Middle East. That's where my parents come from. But I'm not from Iran. I mean, I was born in London. Like, in the UK. But we're Iranian."

I tried to explain this as comprehensively as I could to cover all the bases. And I thought if I let her know I was born in England it might make me better in her eyes. She had pretty brown bangs and she could flip her hair like Kristy McNichol. And she had a very nice tan.

"Oh, okay," she said. "So, you're like Arabs, though?"

"Well, no. Iran is a separate country and the people are actually Aryans. That's our race. Aryans." I didn't know what that part about Aryans meant, but I had heard my uncle saying something similar. And I knew the point was that we were different from Arabs.

"So, are you from Arabia, then?"

"No. Iran. We're not Arabs. Like I said. We're not Arabs … at all."

Annie still looked puzzled. It was clear she would not be able to get her head around this.

"But your food is like Arab food, right?"

It went on like that.

This was not Annie's fault. She simply hadn't met any other Iranians. And she probably didn't know any Arabs. I always wondered what she was thinking of when she asked about "Arab food," but she probably didn't know either. And besides, she had tight jeans and she was very pretty. She had a nice tan. And Annie was like a lot of Thornhill: pretty straight ahead and relatively confused about what and who my family were.

Thornhill was certainly safe in 1982. It was clean and well-kept and what is often professionally called "livable." Kids would play on our street well into the night and there was never much concern about that. We generally left our houses unlocked and trusted our neighbours. But here again was another reason Thornhill lacked credibility. There were no dark alleys where gangs roved and ran cocaine importation businesses the way they did in *Scarface*. There were no "crack-whore" streets or red-light districts (well, except for our porch before my father changed the lamps). And even when a lot of the kids did drugs or drank behind the Golden Star restaurant or near the ravine, it was all still relatively harmless. Safe suburbs are the best places for raising kids, except for the kids who think they don't want to be safe. While Bowie was being spotted in the cesspools of underground society, Thornhill was pretty squeaky clean.

I wish I could say that this was nostalgia. I wish I could say that Thornhill has since devolved into a dangerous 'hood filled with hookers and crime-ridden back alleys. I wish I could tell you that my old stomping grounds have become bloodied and busted. That would be cred. But I can't. While Thornhill is a much more diverse and urban place than it was three decades ago, it still has a reputation as a nice burgh for upper-middle-class families to settle in. A recent survey of crime in Canada found that the region in which Thornhill is located is still one of the safest in the nation. So the Bowie who appears in the "Ashes to Ashes" video would still likely be unwelcome.

But there were some variations in different parts of Thornhill in the '80s. And one of the ways this played out was in the marked distinction between the two main high schools:

Thornhill SS and Thornlea SS. Our family lived in the zone that required me to go to Thornhill SS. It was generally considered a tougher school with a lower academic standard. It was more "old Thornhill." That meant less cool. My friend Toke told me that Thornhill SS was also more of a rocker school. His brother, Mitch, had gone there, and Mitch wore a leather jacket and listened to Black Sabbath.

Thornlea SS, on the other hand, was literally on the other side of a bridge. It had first been constructed in the 1960s as an open-learning experimental liberal school with socialist principles. I didn't know what that meant at the time, but I knew Thornlea was still considered cool. It was no longer experimental, but it was a more diverse place with greater breadth of courses and had a more racially integrated student body. It was known for its growing academic prowess and, most important, for its focus on fine arts. This was also cool.

My sister had successfully petitioned to transfer to Thornlea SS in 1979, because she was interested in theatre and because it seemed more glamorous than going to the "old Thornhill" school, which was closer to us geographically. With my growing affinity for theatre and music, I also petitioned to follow in my sister's footsteps. I got accepted into Thornlea, and in 1982 I started there in Grade 9. Going to Thornlea would become the biggest decision ever to affect my future. It was at Thornlea where I first became New Wave. It was at Thornlea where I started on my path to be Bowie. And, most important, Thornlea is where I met Wendy.

2

"ARABIAN KNIGHTS"
- SIOUXSIE AND THE BANSHEES

Wendy was like Bowie. Inasmuch as a diminutive sixteen-year-old blond girl from Thornhill could be like Bowie. To those who just didn't understand, she probably wasn't much like Bowie. But she had shoulder pads. And she smoked. And when she smoked, she held the cigarette between her index finger and her thumb like she was holding a joint. That's the way Bowie did it.

And Wendy had that early '80s short haircut with the long straight bit in the front. It was totally David Sylvian. David Sylvian was the lead singer of the band Japan, and he had dyed-blond hair that was long in the front and short in the back. He was very serious. He would flip his hair back sometimes, but usually it was parted on the side and covered one of his eyes. And that's the way Wendy had her hair, too. And David Sylvian got that from David Bowie. So, you see, Wendy was exactly like Bowie. And she was punk. Or, no, she was New Wave. Wait. No. Punk. Okay, I'm still not sure which. But she was almost seventeen. And she barely spoke to me.

In fact, she barely looked at me. Wendy was my dream girl. Female Bowie.

You probably know what I mean when I say that Wendy was cool. Or you think you do. You probably have an idea of what cool is. But there's a subversive trick to cool. Cool can be fleeting. And what is cool in your head this minute might not be cool in a couple of years from now. It will stop being cool if it lacks substance, or if it has too much substance, or if it *is* a substance. It might also stop being cool if it becomes too popular. Pop success is often at odds with cool. But then, if you hang on, you'll be cool again in a couple of decades. Longevity is another trick. Cool can change.

Remember vinyl? Vinyl records were cool when Zeppelin put out *In Through the Out Door* in 1979. That album was so cool it had a few different jacket sleeves that you could colour. Then vinyl became near extinct as people started collecting CDs and throwing out their ELO albums. In the mid-'80s, vinyl records were seen as antiquated and inferior. Then, fifteen years later, everyone got iPods. And after a while, some people got tired of their music only coming out of tiny plastic rectangles with a digital list of songs. These people yearned for large black discs of music that they could scratch. And so now, vinyl is cool again.

The same is true of eggs. When I was a little kid in the 1970s, my mother would make me eat lots of eggs. My mother would say that eggs were an important part of the daily diet. Then, in the '80s and '90s, my mother started instructing me to stay away from eggs because of cholesterol or fat or bird flu or something. She was not alone in this capricious attitude towards eggs. Eggs became so uncool that people started to eat only the white bits. Some people went even further than that. In the '90s, some people resorted to eating fake stand-in eggs with funny names—anything to avoid real eggs. But cool can change. And now my mother thinks I should eat eggs again. They provide protein, she says. Even Starbucks sells eggs, in elaborate Starbucks packaging. And Starbucks is cool. Or wait, no, Starbucks isn't cool. But it was once cool. And eggs were cool and then not cool—and then cool again. Just like Joan Jett. Totally like Joan Jett.

I have made a short list (or shortlist) of things that were cool and then not cool and now are cool again:

- vinyl
- eggs
- cigars
- *SNL*
- Joan Jett

As you can see, this short list demonstrates that our idea of cool can change. But not Wendy. I knew Wendy would always be cool.

Wendy went to my high school, Thornlea SS. She was an older woman. She was already in Grade 11. She was totally New Wave. Or punk. I was still fourteen and in the midst of a rapid transition from acoustic-guitar-wielding folkie—and ethnically inappropriate "Ebony and Ivory" duet singer—to aspiring New Romantic. I had been gradually building my black wardrobe for months to accomplish this mission. My skinny legs looked even skinnier in black pants. I had started dyeing and gelling my hair. Actually, I had started dyeing and gelling and then blow-drying and gelling (again) my hair. The colour of my hair would change every few weeks. It was alternately jet black or highlighted with blond streaks or, in one ill-fated stint, rusty orange. I had not yet discovered crimping. That was a year or two away.

Of course, I did all this hair business without the blessing of my very professional Iranian father.

"Why you are wearing your hair like thees? You are wanting your hair to be orange like thees?"

My dad's thick Iranian accent would get a bit thicker when he was upset. His tactic was to ask questions to demonstrate his displeasure.

"You are thinking it ees looking good, thees orange hair?"

"That's the way cool people do it now, Dad. They colour their hair and use gel." My replies had an appropriate teenage tone of exhaustion.

"Why you don't want to wear new clothes?"

My father would always continue to the next question if he didn't get a good answer to the first. He was usually exasperated with the whole thing before we even started talking. Sometimes, he would deeply exhale when he saw me with a new hair colour. That's when I knew he was going to ask a question to demonstrate his displeasure. I was exasperated, too. We were man and boy pre-emptively tired of the same conversation.

"Vintage clothing is cool, Dad. Everyone knows that."

"You are wanting to look like beggar?"

It went on like that.

My dad would ask these kinds of questions because he really didn't understand. For example, it was obvious he didn't understand the haircuts or sartorial splendour of the Human League and Kajagoogoo. Well, okay, most people probably never understood the band Kajagoogoo. Or why they used that name. But that included my dad. He didn't understand that being New Romantic often meant dressing in exaggerated counter-sexual or androgynous clothing. And he definitely didn't understand my growing affinity for second-hand stores. He didn't come to North America for his son to dress in used clothing.

My mother, on the other hand, would not ask any questions. She just made statements. She would state facts.

"Oh, you've decided to put the black pointy boots on again. Those are the ones you got from the second-hand market at the Palais Royale last month. You've decided to wear those boots a lot."

See? That's an example of three very factual sentences. My mother had devised a cunning way of expressing her negative opinions by simply stating facts. I would later learn that this is called passive-aggressive. But at the time I had no idea anyone else had this ability. I just knew that my mother would calmly say these things like she was reading out the details of a court case. She would speak them slowly to allow the stenographer to keep up.

Sometimes my mother would helpfully point out facts about others, too. She did this to draw a comparison for the sake of underscoring an idea.

"You know, that Chris from across the street doesn't dye his hair. He has a very nice haircut. He looks like Mark Hamill."

This was my mother's way of expressing disapproval of me. She wanted me to wear more normal shoes and be more like

That Chris, who was around my age and lived across the street. My mother figured if I were more like That Chris, I would somehow fit in and not get teased or something. She seemed to overlook the minor detail that my name was Jian and I was the only ethnic kid on the street, other than the Olsons. And the Olsons were black. And black wasn't really ethnic.

My mother never expressed her disapproval directly. She was generally very polite. And, ultimately, she may have known her efforts would be futile. Even if I'd wanted to, I could never actually be Chris. That Chris. He was physically bigger than me and had straight blond hair. It was like Wendy's hair. Except That Chris didn't look like Bowie. But That Chris did mow the lawn.

"Oh, look, that Chris is mowing the lawn again."

This was another statement of fact from my mother. She would say this as if That Chris deserved a medal or an extra cup of Laura Secord chocolate pudding. And, yes, That Chris was mowing the lawn. Actually, he seemed to be in a perpetual state of mowing the lawn. That is, when he wasn't watering the lawn. I became convinced That Chris took such meticulous care of his family's lawn with the sole intention of reminding my parents that they had a son with pointy shoes who was less attentive to the yard. Chris would go on to own a profitable landscaping business after high school. That Chris had a nice haircut. Just like Mark Hamill.

I looked nothing like Mark Hamill or any of the *Star Wars* leads. My style was a combination of New Wave aspiration and early '80s obligation. Sometimes the clothing and the hair required accessories to accompany the outfit. In my desire to keep up with the trends, the summer before high school I used the money I'd saved by working in the backroom at SAVCO Pet Food and Supplies to buy myself a coveted Adidas gym bag. This was no ordinary bag. If you were a young denizen of suburbia in Canada in the late '70s and early '80s, the fake-leather Adidas gym bag was all the rage. It was my prized possession going into Grade 9. It was the kind with the stripes and handles and the shape of a small hockey-gear bag. It had a really simple design featuring one zipper and no pockets in any form. It also had a small area to put your name with the Adidas logo on the side. I had written my name on the label in authoritative upper-case black marker: THIS BAG BELONGS TO JIAN GHOMESHI. THORNHILL, ONTARIO.

Now, to be clear, the Adidas gym bag wasn't really New Wave. In some ways it was quite the opposite. The bag had a universal appeal and was embraced by various cliques. But then, there was no consistent aesthetic to my style at the time. And my Adidas bag was the envy of a lot of kids in my class. Everyone who was anyone had an Adidas bag. I began to carry mine with me everywhere. My friend Toke had gotten an Adidas bag of his own in the summer before Grade 9. His was brown with white handles. Mine was red. Actually, mine was red with blue stripes and handles.

Here is a short list of the colour combinations that were available in the Adidas gym bag in the early '80s:

- red/blue
- blue/dark blue
- yellow/blue
- brown/white
- green/blue

Sometimes, when Toke and I walked down to the Mac's Milk corner store on Henderson Avenue on a lazy summer afternoon, we would bring our Adidas bags. There was nothing practical about this exercise. We usually had no reason to carry our bags, but we liked the idea of being seen with them. Even when high school started, I rarely had enough books or papers or gel or lunch to merit bringing the Adidas bag. But that didn't matter. I would still carry it along. Everywhere. The following school year, when faced with having to purchase a new bag, I would opt to accessorize with a black briefcase. It was more in line with my New Romantic style. But for now, I had my red-and-blue Adidas bag. My dyed gelled hair, my tight black pants, my pointy shoes, and my red-and-blue Adidas bag.

My odd fashion combination was not entirely my fault. There's only so inventive a kid watching early Spandau Ballet videos can be. I didn't have the stylists or money or friends to know how to do New Wave properly. But I knew I liked Bowie. And he wore eyeliner. Wendy wore eyeliner, too. I decided I would be more New Wave if I wore eyeliner as well. In a serendipitous moment during the middle of Grade 9, I found an eyeliner pencil that had been left in Room 213, the theatre room. The eyeliner looked practically new! I decided to liberate it from the theatre room and make it mine. I stashed it in my Adidas bag. It was a fine acquisition, but there was a small hitch with my new eyeliner. When I pulled it out at home, away from the dark lighting in Room 213, I realized the colour wasn't ideal. It was purple. Purple eyeliner. I knew that black was probably better than purple. But I had no idea how to acquire black eyeliner. And purple wasn't too far off. I couldn't ask any guy friends for black eyeliner. And I wouldn't ask a girl. Bowie certainly didn't ask girls for his eyeliner. He just … had eyeliner. I was sure no one talked about where they got eyeliner.

One day, towards the second half of Grade 9, I woke up early and meticulously put on my new purple eyeliner. It didn't seem to be making much of a noticeable mark, so I leaned my face in close to the mirror and liberally applied the eyeliner to make sure it looked good. I went to school that day convinced I was cooler than I had ever been. I was convinced I bore a striking similarity to Phil Oakey from the Human League. He wore eyeliner all the time. He probably wore eyeliner at home. Thick eyeliner. Sadly, my latest style coup was short-lived. I had been at school for less than an hour when Jane Decker saw me at our lockers in the second-floor hallway. She stared at me for a moment and then pointed at me with her arm straight and her index finger inches from my face.

"You're wearing eyeliner! Why are you wearing eyeliner?"

She said this at a volume loud enough to echo down the hall. Jane Decker obviously didn't understand. Just like my father. But I had not put enough thought into those who didn't understand cool, and I was utterly unprepared for this moment. There were no other aspiring New Romantics to be found to rally support. Instead, there was now a group of preppy kids and science nerds and jock types gathering around the lockers to see the evidence of the eyeliner, and the guy wearing the eyeliner. There was a pause before the floodgates opened. Jane Decker was the star yearbook editor and a future successful lawyer. She was turning this into a public inquiry and felt the need to pursue the truth by pointing out the facts, just like my mother would. Louder. Again.

"You're wearing eyeliner!"

The crowd was growing larger. I saw what seemed like dozens of peers, enemies, and curious onlookers assembling. In my defence—and with the integrity of all self-respecting punks in mind—I said the first thing that came to mind upon being accused of wearing eyeliner: "I am not! I'm not ... wearing ... eyeliner."

Now, let this be a lesson to all you fourteen-year-old boys out there who may find yourselves in this situation. If you ever happen to be wearing very noticeable thick purple eyeliner to school for the first time and someone calls you on it, denial may not be the most effective response. My voice sounded less convincing with each word. This was trouble. Jane Decker smelled blood.

"Yes you are! Look! I can see it. You're wearing eyeliner! And it's ... purple. I can clearly see it. Purple eyeliner!"

The growing mob was now joining in with various helpful contributions to the outing of the eyeliner boy:

"Yeah!"

"He's wearing eyeliner!"

"You totally are!"

It was hard enough to manage being the ethnic kid with the unpronounceable name trying to look like a white UK New Waver. Now, somehow my version of wanting to fit in had led me to a thick heap of purple eyeliner and an unwelcoming audience at the lockers. I needed to do something. Fast. The crowd had turned on me, and Jane Decker, as their leader, was feeling empowered. What would Bowie do? I couldn't think. I resorted to the only action an aspiring glam-rocker could take: I denied it again.

"No. I'm not! And it's not purple!"

Okay. So that last bit was a problem. Even as the words left my mouth, I realized that "it's not purple!" was an awfully unnecessary detail for a guy supposedly not wearing eyeliner. And I *was* wearing eyeliner. And it very clearly *was* purple. There was another pause as the crowd waited to see how this would play out. I felt overwhelmed by the implications of what might happen if I started to cry. I imagined the way the tears would smudge my thick purple eyeliner. That would really exacerbate things. I wondered if there was any chance the running eyeliner would make me look like Alice Cooper. Like a younger, more ethnic Alice Cooper. Alice Cooper always seemed to have eye makeup streaming down his face back in the '70s. Cool kids had liked Alice Cooper then. Maybe it was still cool to have smudged eyeliner. Maybe that would be rock. Or punk. But my streaming makeup would be purple. And purple probably wouldn't count. And denial would be impossible if the eyeliner began running. It was all a disaster.

I needed to end this. I quietly closed my locker and clicked the lock without looking up. Then I ran down the hall with my red-and-blue Adidas bag. I could hear laughing. I didn't talk to Jane Decker for a couple of weeks after that. And I didn't wear the purple eyeliner again.

THE EYELINER AND THE SHOES and the hair were all about being cool. I knew that Bowie was cool. And if I could just be more like him, I would be okay. And Wendy would probably start to notice me as well. It really came down to music in those days, and the divisions were profound. The rift was particularly strong between the rockers and the punk/New Wave kids. The preppies had long made themselves irrelevant with their indiscriminate tastes. The preppies were into sugary pop stuff like REO Speedwagon and Air Supply, and that was just embarrassing. Some preppies liked Bruce Springsteen, and I secretly appreciated that, because I had liked Springsteen and I'd learned to play "Hungry Heart" on acoustic guitar in Grade 7. But now I didn't really tell anyone I liked Springsteen. Springsteen may have been a working-class hero from New Jersey, but I didn't know that. I just knew that the preppy kids liked him. Joel Price had gone to see Springsteen in Grade 8, and he was definitely a preppy, who would never wear second-hand clothes or pointy boots. Our gym teacher, Mr. Manly, made me wrestle Joel Price once in gym class in Grade 8. Joel pinned me right away and looked at me and laughed. I decided I didn't like wrestling. And after that I wasn't sure I liked Springsteen much, either.

If you were a New Wave kid or a mod in 1982, you liked the Jam, Siouxsie and the Banshees, the English Beat, and Bowie. In contrast, if you were a rocker, you wore a Zeppelin T-shirt with a "Zoso" logo that represented Jimmy Page, and you blasted AC/DC and you probably had a keen appreciation for Journey guitarist Neal Schon. I had empathy for the rockers, because I was a big fan of Rush. Rush was a legitimate rock band. And also, Toke had gone to see Ozzy, who was also a real rocker, and Toke told me about the concert in such detail that I pretended I'd been there and recounted the show to others. But now I was more New Wave. In fact, Rush was also trying to be New Wave, but no one was really buying it. There was no cross-pollination between the rockers and New Wavers. Still, amongst all the divisions, the one thing that united all of us was a bitter disregard for any kind of manufactured-sounding stuff: corporate pop and rock, man. No one liked a rocker who became a commercial sellout. Joan Jett fell into this category. Her omnipresent song "I Love Rock 'n Roll" was a number-one hit in America in 1982. That would qualify as too popular. Her song was getting played in the wrong stores at the mall. She was definitely not cool.

In our teenage world, you were defined by the concerts you attended. I was intent on building my live music repertoire to establish my credentials. I had started going to rock concerts when I was eleven, and I'd got off to a bad start by alternative standards. The first real concert my parents took me to was Billy Joel. He wore a suit jacket and sneakers and sang "Just the Way You Are." Later in life, I would decide that Billy Joel was a real talent. But at the time he didn't seem very cool. Then, to really set back my reputation, my parents took me to see the noted Canadian singer-songwriter Dan Hill at the Ontario Place Forum. He was the "Sometimes When We Touch" nice guy. "Sometimes When We Touch" was a sensitive song that featured the following lyric at its dramatic conclusion:

I wanna hold you till I die
Till we both break down and cry
I want to hold you till the fear in me subsides.

You probably know that song and that end part. And that sentiment would strike a very poignant chord in therapy sessions a couple of decades later. But at the time it didn't seem very cool. This massive hit had led Dan Hill to pretty much define the middle of the road in music. He was very real and organic. He had a bushy beard and no gel in his hair. He wore baggy trousers, the kind that allowed for "room to breathe." He also performed with bare feet. He probably didn't have any pointy boots. Dan Hill was not very punk.

My father was impressed that Dan Hill could perform a whole concert of songs by himself. "The Dan Hill! He ees on stage for two hours! He ees playing all of the songs heemself! For two hours! Honestly, it ees great!"

My father called him The Dan Hill. He didn't really know any Dan Hill songs. I'm not sure he had heard much of Dan Hill before the concert. My mother had told him that Dan Hill was a very nice new singer and that with admission to Ontario Place we wouldn't have to pay extra to see him—so it became a family outing. But my father was clearly impressed with Dan Hill's stamina. The Dan Hill. I saw my dad's point, and I decided Dan Hill was impressive, too. But when I told Toke about Dan Hill and how he had played for two hours, Toke told me his older brother said Sabbath had played for longer. And regardless of his stamina, I would soon renounce any appreciation for Dan Hill. He was not New Wave. He was not cool. Of course, many years later, I would decide Dan Hill was a very good songwriter. Just like Billy Joel and Joan Jett. Cool can change.

When I turned thirteen, I finally graduated from going to concerts with my mother and father. I knew it was important to curate my personal gig calendar. It was simple: if I went to cool shows, I could tell other kids that I had gone to cool shows. Part of the trick was to try to always smell like smoke. If you had a jean jacket or a mod army shirt that smelled like smoke, and especially if you were a non-smoker, other kids would know you went to a lot of concerts. I was not a smoker, but in the early '80s all concerts were filled with older people smoking cigarettes and pot and hash. Mostly they smoked cigarettes. This was cool. Smoking meant that you understood music better and that you had a carefree but serious vibe. It was also sexy. Bowie was holding a lit cigarette on the cover of *Young Americans* for precisely this reason. And so, even though I was an asthmatic and didn't smoke, I tried to smell like smoke.

It was impossible to go to a show in the early '80s without getting caught up in wafts of cigarette exhaust. Even in big places like Maple Leaf Gardens, the whole concert would be blanketed in clouds of smoke. This was not just manufactured by machines onstage the way it is today, it was the power of the collective, sucking on their cigarettes and blowing. If you were a young teen who wasn't savvy enough to sneak into bars, concerts were the main place to go if you wanted to come home reeking of smoke. This was an aspiration. Two decades later, smoking would be banned at live shows for health reasons. This made sense. It was much better to go smoke free for health reasons and for unimpeded sightlines at gigs. But it never felt the same as when everyone was lighting up and being unhealthy. That was real cred.

I started going to concerts with my friend Murray Foster, who was playing in our band, the Wingnuts, in Grade 8. I was the singer and drummer of the Wingnuts and Murray was the guitarist. Rob Mundle was the third member of our band, and he also played guitar. He was a year older, so he had a good amp. We didn't have a bassist, because both Murray and Rob wanted to play guitar and refused to play bass. In a strange twist, Murray would go on to be an excellent bass player. But back then we were confined to the guitar-playing roles for Murray and Rob. Two decades before the Black Keys and the White Stripes, the Wingnuts were unwittingly the first band to feature only a drummer and electric guitars. The big difference was that we really didn't sound very appealing. But Roxy Anslow and another girl from Mr. Mackian's class named Katie made Wingnuts T-shirts and wore them to our gig. We only ever played one gig. That didn't matter. It was a big one at the school gym towards the end of Grade 8. And we had girls wearing T-shirts with the name of our band on them.

Murray was really not very New Wave in junior high and Grade 9. He had nice blond hair that was parted in the middle and he wore large, white-ish running shoes and shorts and athletic socks. But Murray was a bit taller than me and he had older brothers, so he was less timid around the tough punks. Murray's mom made really good chili, and lots of kids made regular trips to Murray's house to have some of his mom's chili. She seemed to always have chili ready. Murray's house became known for his mom's chili. Murray was well liked, but his mom's chili made him even more popular.

Murray and I started accumulating our concert credentials by going to as many shows as we could afford. We saw New Order one night, the Jam a few weeks later, and then the punk female-led British band Siouxsie and the Banshees. Siouxsie and the Banshees were getting a lot of spins amongst the coolest New Wave occupants of the theatre room at school. Their song "Happy House" had become an anthem for some of my sister's friends in Grade 12. I had a sense that Wendy was probably a big fan of Siouxsie and the Banshees. This was an important concert to attend.

Not surprisingly, the Siouxsie and the Banshees show was a particularly challenging affair. Murray and I were clearly the youngest kids there. In retrospect, we were probably the only kids there. Siouxsie and the Banshees had dark lighting and ripped clothing and everyone in the audience was crammed close to the stage and smoking. The Siouxsie and the Banshees drummer's name was Budgie. It was cool to have a name like Budgie. Everything about Siouxsie and the Banshees was cool.

The last song Siouxsie played was called "Arabian Knights," from their album *Juju*. It's a goth-ish, New Romantic classic. It features a catchy chorus refrain that repeats the line "I heard a rumour." Then, after Siouxsie sings about hearing a rumour a few times in each chorus, she refers to a girl and asks what has been done to her.

That night, Siouxsie had been onstage for only about forty-five minutes when she decided to end the show after that song. I wasn't sure why. I concluded that playing for only forty-five minutes was what real New Wave artists with integrity did. But Siouxsie didn't seem very happy with things. As I remember, while Siouxsie was walking offstage, she sneered into the microphone and said, "Yeah, I heard a rumour. I heard a rumour that we played here tonight. We didn't. Fuck off!"

Siouxsie had screamed that last part into the mic. It seemed quite antagonistic. But a funny thing happened when Siouxsie told us all to fuck off. The crowd cheered in appreciation. I started to cheer, too, because all the older punks in their twenties were doing it. But it didn't seem like a very nice sentiment. In fact, it seemed like the opposite of what you're supposed to do when you're saying goodnight to an audience that's paid hard-earned money to see you play.

We'd never thought of telling people to fuck off when we did our Wingnuts gig at the junior-high gym in Grade 8. And Dan Hill hadn't told us to fuck off at his concert the year before. The Dan Hill. He had been onstage for at least seventy-five minutes longer than Siouxsie.

But Siouxsie was cool. And she wore a lot of eyeliner. I probably could've worn purple eyeliner to the Siouxsie and the Banshees gig and been accepted. Jane Decker wasn't at the Siouxsie show. I imagined myself telling Jane Decker to fuck off when she pointed at my purple eyeliner in the hallway. Then I imagined the audience cheering. I was finding my crowd.

3

"I LOVE ROCK 'N ROLL"
— JOAN JETT AND THE BLACKHEARTS

The prized concert to go to at the end of my Grade 9 year was the Police Picnic at the CNE Grandstand in downtown Toronto. The headliners of the Police Picnic were a band called the Police. You probably know the Police. You know them because they've got a formidable back catalogue of massive pop hits like "Every Breath You Take." And you know them because they acrimoniously split up and after that only talked to each other through lawyers. And because the lead singer, Sting, became a big solo star and started saving rainforests. And because guitarist Andy Summers began taking interesting photographs. And you know them because Stewart Copeland is one of the best drummers ever. And because they reunited twenty years after they split up and did a heavily promoted world tour and charged $250 a ticket and then acrimoniously split up again. Now people say they only talk to each other through lawyers once more.

You probably know the Police for all of these reasons. But at the time, the Police were a ska/reggae/New Wave band from the UK that had become alternative music sensations. They were not yet global megastars. They had just released their fourth album. The previous year, they'd started an annual multi-band show in Toronto called the Police Picnic. It would end up taking place for three summers in a row.

I had first learned about the Police when Jasmine Leung gave me their second album, *Reggatta de Blanc*, as a gift for my thirteenth birthday. It was a gift that would have a major impact on me. But I didn't know that at the time. I really didn't know much about the Police, either. But I pretended I did. I thanked Jasmine Leung the way you thank people when you've received something you really wanted. "No way! This is great!" That's how I responded. I knew to say "This is great!" even though I wasn't sure it was great. You see, beyond getting the sense that I should know who the Police were, and that this was a cool gift, it was important to act thankful and polite. I learned this from my mother.

My mother was always very polite. She would react with enthusiasm when she was the recipient of a gift or kind gesture regardless of what she actually thought. For instance, when we got a yearly Christmas basket of jams and biscuits from the Polish people next door, my mother would act surprised. It was strange that she acted surprised, given that the basket was an annual gift that we anticipated. But my mother said it was important to be polite.

The Capetskis were the family who lived directly to the west of us on our suburban street in Thornhill. There was a hedge that ran between our houses, and my father and Mr. Capetski would take turns trimming it. Mr. and Mrs. Capetski had come to Canada from Switzerland many years earlier, but their families were originally from Poland, so my father called them "the Polish people next door." He called them this even though he knew their names. My father would often identify people this way. Perhaps he thought it was helpful. For instance, when I was in Grade 3, he called my best friend, Aris, "the Greek boy." Or he would refer to the friendly lady who ran the Mac's Milk store near us as "the good Chinese woman." He didn't seem to say these things in a derogatory way. I assumed it was just the way his generation identified others.

When my sister, Jila, and I got older and more sensitive to these things, we would question my father about his unnecessary need to take note of everyone's race.

"Dad! Why are you pointing out that she's Chinese? What is the relevance of the lady at Mac's Milk being Chinese?"

My father never quite understood the problem.

"But she ees Chinese. You say she ees not Chinese? She ees! You want me to say she ees Greek?"

The thing is, technically, my father's answer was totally logical, even if we knew it was an excuse. This was a debate we would never win. In an interesting twist, sometimes my father referred to people from England in a more omnibus way as "*kharejee-ah*." That's the Farsi word for foreigners. This was an odd moniker for my dad to use for English immigrants, because we probably fit the profile of foreigners more closely than they did. And anyway, we had also come from England, although our background was Iranian, and my father proudly made a point of identifying himself as Canadian. But usually the labels were related to the country of origin. And so the Capetskis were "the Polish people next door." They had two kids about the age of my sister and me.

My mother was very polite, and she demonstrated her politeness each year with the Polish people next door. Not that she had to try. It came naturally to her. My mother was very nice. The Polish people next door would deliver us our annual Christmas basket of jams and biscuits. They would do it in person. They would gather as a family on our porch and my mother would act surprised, because that was polite. Maybe they all came to the porch just to witness my mother's ersatz surprised response.

"No way! This is great! We love these biscuits!"

My mother's appreciation always sounded very genuine. But some of the biscuits had orange bits in them, and no one in our family really liked those. My mother would subsequently bundle up the jams and biscuits in new wrapping paper and give them to our relatives who lived in Don Mills. I would later learn that this was called "re-gifting." We didn't tell the Polish people next door about the re-gifting. In fact, we would reciprocate with a Christmas basket for them as well. It never quite made sense that we were exchanging baskets of items we weren't sure our neighbours liked instead of buying ourselves our own baskets full of things we knew we'd want. But it was nice to receive presents. Just like the present I got from Jasmine Leung. I didn't re-gift my first Police album. It quickly became one of my favourites.

Reggatta de Blanc had a blue-tinted cover photo featuring the three members of the Police looking cool. They also looked remarkably similar with their dyed-blond hair. It didn't take me long to become a big fan of the Police. A year after Jasmine Leung gave me that album, I started a new band with Murray (ex–rhythm guitarist for the Wingnuts) and we did a cover of

"Roxanne" from the debut Police disc, *Outlandos d'Amour*. I was the singer in our new band and sometimes I also played drums. This group was much cooler than the other ensemble I was playing in, the Thornhill Community Band, led by the stern lead trombone player, Mr. Margison. Our new Grade 9 rock band with Murray was democratic. We were called Urban Transit. And amongst other material, we did Police songs.

Even at the age of fourteen, I was too much of a baritone to reach the high notes that Sting could hit. "Roxanne" probably wasn't a very smart song for us to try to cover. But I had found a green army jacket at a second-hand store that looked like the one Sting wore. I had seen Sting wear it in a live concert video from Japan on *The NewMusic*. I figured that at the very least I looked like Sting when I sang "Roxanne." One problem was that Sting had straight blond hair like Wendy and That Chris from across the street. He also had a small perky nose. It would have been very hard for me to actually be Sting.

I've constructed a point-form list of things I would've needed to do to become more like Sting when I was in Grade 9:

- play bass
- sing higher
- dye hair blond and straighten blond hair
- stay out of sun (become whiter)
- wear green army jacket
- get nose job

Aspiring to be like Sting in Grade 9 was almost as challenging as trying to be Bowie. None of this was easy.

Many of the older New Wave kids at Thornlea SS hung out in or near the theatre room. The theatre room was a large, carpeted space that was room number 213 at our school. It had theatre-type lights on dimmers and it was very dramatic. Fluorescent school lights were rarely on in Room 213. This was because Room 213 was cool. Room 213 was referred to simply as "213" by its regular inhabitants. If anyone actually called it the theatre room, they would betray themselves as outsiders. It had become my destination between classes, and I was accepted by most of the older theatre kids there. I sensed the older students considered me a curiosity and liked the fact that I had pointy shoes and played guitar and drums. Besides, I had lineage. My sister, Jila, was a major star of the 213 scene, and she was now in Grade 12. Wendy, the female Bowie and the object of my affections, was often hanging out near 213. She was the younger sister of Jila's friend Paul. Sometimes I would find myself in Wendy's proximity because she was with Paul and he was talking to my sister. I began to understand where I needed to strategically locate myself. I learned that if I stood near my sister and she was near Paul, I would be near Wendy.

Over the course of Grade 9, I became a legitimate member of the 213 crowd, and I got involved in several after-school theatre groups. I saw Wendy at least once a day. Like, I witnessed her somewhere at school once a day. Wendy and I barely ever said anything to each other. I was a bit scared to look at her. I was pretty sure she never looked at me.

There was an unofficial dress code and set of practices in 213. No one talked about it, but everyone abided by the code. For one thing, the drama teachers who taught inside 213 were only called by their first names. This was cool. Obviously. There was Sue and Jim, and also Grace. Grace wasn't a drama teacher, but she hung out in 213, so we still called her by her first name. Grace was renegade that way. Everyone in 213 wore mostly black, including my sister, the teachers, and Paul and Wendy.

I have made a short list of (unofficial) basic items that were required in 213:

- black baggy theatre pants or black tight skinny jeans
- black jacket
- prominently displayed New Wave band pin
- black shoes, boots, or ballet-type slippers
- black flowing scarf
- cigarette pack
- Siouxsie and the Banshees tape
- black eyeliner (girls)

You will note the inclusion of cigarettes on this short list. As I have explained to you, I didn't smoke, and in 1982 I was terribly aware that my non-smoker status was a liability. Smelling like smoke meant you attended a lot of concerts, but smoking also looked cool and it made people in 213 more intellectual and thoughtful. The rockers who hung out downstairs at our school also smoked, but that was for different reasons—they did it because smoking made them tough and badass. In 213, smoking was a sign of depth. Sometimes, a theatre student in 213 would hold a lit cigarette in their index and middle fingers and put the bottom of their palm on their forehead. It was like their palm was holding up their head.

Then they would rest their elbow on a table or on their knee. This "palm on the forehead" smoking position was an indication that they were thinking and that the world was not an easy place.

My choice not to smoke was mainly because I was an asthmatic. Doctor Salsberg had told me when I was twelve that I would die if I smoked. I wondered if he was exaggerating, and I was often disappointed with myself for not taking up cigarettes. All the teachers who used only their first names, like Sue and Jim and Grace, smoked. They were thoughtful and introspective. My sister smoked, and so did Wendy. I wondered if Wendy would notice me more if I smoked and put my palm on my forehead.

Everyone was talking about the Police Picnic scheduled for the summer of 1982. The multi-band lineup had been announced, and it would include the Beat and Flock of Seagulls and a really artsy rock band called Talking Heads. By the time June arrived, I'd realized I needed to do something to get Wendy's attention or she would forget about me over the summer. It might seem strange to worry about someone you've never really talked to forgetting about you, but I held out the hope that Wendy had noticed me hanging about—even if she never looked at me. I had been trying to build my confidence to make my big move and talk to her. Finally, I devised a cunning plan. I would tell Wendy that I had gotten Police Picnic tickets and invite her to come along with me. I didn't actually have tickets, and I had little hope that the plan would actually work. But I was in for a surprise.

One afternoon in the second week of June, I saw Wendy standing near the lockers on the second floor at Thornlea. This was the same location as the purple eyeliner incident a couple of months earlier, but most of the older 213 kids didn't know about that. I was counting on Wendy not having heard about the purple eyeliner. Even in 213, I couldn't take any chances about how people might react.

Wendy was emptying the contents of her school bag into her locker. She was alone. This was a rare chance for me. I summoned up all my confidence and adjusted my black jacket on my skinny shoulders. I was wearing my black pointy boots and I had my Adidas bag in my right hand. I acted as if I were just innocently walking down the hall. When I got near Wendy, I stopped about three feet away from her side. I tried not to appear terrified. Wendy turned and looked at me. She was shorter than me. She was cool. She was like Bowie. She flipped that bit of blond hair in the front that was longer than the rest of her hair, just like David Sylvian. Sylvian had gotten that from Bowie. Wendy stared into my eyes, waiting for me to say something. I finally did.

"Hey. So, are you going to the Police Picnic?"

I had found the courage to speak to Wendy. Barely. My voice sounded like it was forming words for the first time. But I had spoken. This was no minimal feat. I looked down immediately so I wouldn't have to look into her eyes for any hint of judgment or rejection. Her beautiful, cool, girl eyes. Bowie eyes. After a few moments, there had been no answer to my question, so I re-asked it a bit louder.

"Yeah, so, are you going to the Police Picnic?"

This time she answered. "No. I wish."

Wendy looked a bit uninterested in speaking to me. But that's the way cool people were. And this was progress. We were having a conversation. I hadn't planned past this point. I struggled to think of the next line and to make it sound natural. Now I was improvising.

"So, like, you didn't get tickets?"

Wendy momentarily turned to her locker and then looked back up at me. "No. I wish," she said again. Then she added, "Talking Heads are playing at it, too."

I nodded. I didn't really know much about Talking Heads. But I could tell they were cool from the way Wendy said their name. All I really knew was that they had that song that sounded like it had the word "fuck" in it, but it didn't actually have the word "fuck" in it. I had been to a house party at Rosanna Dray's place with some of my Grade 9 friends, and when they played that song, everyone sang "fa fa fa fuck" at the chorus part that sounded like "fuck" even though that wasn't the lyric.

Wendy was still looking at me. She had not turned away. This was my moment.

"Well, I got tickets. So, maybe ... well ... do you wanna come to the Police Picnic? Like, with me?"

"Umm. Okay." Wendy smiled.

Just like that, I had a date. I was going to the Police Picnic with Wendy, the older woman. I would be attending the most anticipated summer concert of the year with a teenage-girl version of Bowie. So maybe our "date" wasn't exactly a romantic or salacious trip to the drive-in. I couldn't drive. I was barely fifteen. But the agreement was to meet at Finch subway station and head down to the CNE. That was good enough. I was the king. I called and got tickets. They weren't cheap by my standards. It didn't matter.

As the weekend of the concert approached in early August, I did a lot of planning for what I was going to wear. It was a month since I'd asked Wendy to go, but I called her once in July to confirm that she was coming. To tell you "I called her" might sound like an innocuous bit of information. But it isn't. Calling Wendy was no simple task. These kinds of phone calls were not easy in 1982. We didn't have text messages or Facebook or IM-ing or DM-ing or BBM-ing in the '80s. Communicating with someone you liked involved high-stakes exposure and risk. To get in touch with Wendy, I had to call her house. This left me vulnerable on all fronts—to the other residents of her house, and to anyone at my house who might hear me. The chances of being discovered, judged, or ridiculed were massive.

We didn't have mobile phones in 1982. You probably guessed that. But we also didn't have any kind of cordless phones at all. Not yet. Not in my house. In other words, telephone receivers were attached to wires that went into a box with a dial pad on it, and that box had wires that came out of it and went directly into the wall underneath the box. The wire that was attached to the telephone receiver was called a "phone cord." That's right: phone cord. If you are a teenager today, you may not have ever seen those two words together. But I can assure you that these phone cords once existed. Almost all phones had phone cords in 1982. These cords were usually curly. I'm not sure why. Perhaps they were curly so that when people were on the phone they could try to uncurl the phone cord as a game during boring parts of the conversation. That's what people did. But the point is, the phone cord meant that you couldn't make a call or answer one just anywhere you wanted. You had to be near the phone box that the phone cord was attached to in order to speak on the telephone.

By the 1990s, even before everyone had mobiles, many families had multiple telephones in their house or a cordless phone or two that they shared. So, by the '90s, when there was an incoming phone call, people began saying things like, "I'll get it and take it into the downstairs family room, Dad!" But this wasn't possible in my house in 1982. You spoke where the phones were. At our house, we had two primary phones attached to the wall. One was in the main hallway at the top of the stairs. The other was in the hallway at the bottom of the stairs. Both were in the middle of the house so everyone could hear every phone call that was being made. Both had curly phone cords.

I knew I had to call Wendy to confirm our date at the Police Picnic. To maintain a semblance of privacy when speaking to my dream Bowie girl, and to minimize my exposure and embarrassment, I had to be careful. I had to time my phone call just right so that no snoops in my house heard me *and* so that Wendy would be at home and available to take my call. This was near impossible to do. We didn't send messages to make appointments for phone calls in the early '80s. The phone call *was* the message. And also, most people didn't have answering machines, and there was no such thing as voice mail. So, if the intended target of your phone call was not home or unavailable, messages had to be communicated directly through humans. This was terrifying and fraught with potential pitfalls. The objective was to find the perfect sweet spot when various factors in play would lead me straight to speaking with Wendy. A goal that would prove too difficult to meet.

The first time I tried Wendy, things ended fast. It was in mid-July, and I had waited for an afternoon when no one was home and I could use our upstairs phone. A woman that sounded like Wendy's mother answered. I panicked. I did the instinctive thing to do when the mother of a girl you're infatuated with picks up the phone—I hung up. Fortunately, there was also no caller ID on phones in 1982, so you could hang up on someone with impunity. Complete discretion. Wendy's mother probably thought it was some hooligan playing games. She would never know it was me and that this was no game.

The second time I called—the next day—I crossed my fingers and prayed that Wendy would answer the phone herself. On this occasion, thankfully, it was not her mother's voice at the other end of the line; instead it was her older brother, Paul, who picked up. I decided not to hang up. Bowie would not have hung up. He probably wouldn't be intimidated. Besides, Paul was Jila's friend. He was nice, and I thought he might be an easier conduit to Wendy. It turned out he wasn't necessarily intent on making things so simple.

"Hello?" he answered, with his older-guy voice. Paul was three years older than me. He was my sister's age, and he often wore a silver-grey vest over a white shirt at school. He had chest hair that you could see peeking out from the top of the shirt that was underneath his silver-grey vest. The chest hair was an indication that Paul was older. Also, his shirt had puffy sleeves the way pirates have those flowing sleeves. Pirate-type white shirts were worn by two kinds of people in the early '80s: pirates and theatre students. Paul was not a pirate. He was quite theatrical. He dressed like Adam Ant. He also wore form-fitting black pants and boots. And he was cool. Of course, he was Wendy's brother, so it only made sense that he was cool.

I cleared my throat and tried to sound very mature as I started to speak to Paul while I fiddled with the curly cord on our phone.

"Oh. Hi, Paul. Um ... this is Jian. I'm Jila's brother, from school? You might remember we've met, and ... well, anyways, I was wondering if ..."

"Yeah"—Paul didn't even let me finish; he was laughing—"she's here."

I suppose my affections for Wendy were more transparent than I'd thought. Paul had somehow discovered I was smitten with his sister. Maybe he had figured this out independently, because he was wiser and older and wearing a pirate shirt with a vest. Or maybe Wendy had told her family about the Police Picnic. Maybe they had laughed about it over Sunday family dinner. Maybe they were laughing at me right now. I could hear Paul chuckling as he put down the receiver and called Wendy's name. I was convinced I heard a tone in his voice that suggested he knew I was taking his sister to a concert, and that he knew she was two years older than me, and that he knew she was like Bowie and out of my league.

After what seemed like ages, Wendy came on the phone. I was worried that she might cancel on me. Maybe she had only agreed to come to the concert with me as a joke. Maybe she never meant it. Or maybe she had forgotten about our impending date and made other plans for August. I still had my fingers crossed while holding the phone when Wendy began speaking. Then, with one opening line, she made it all okay.

"Hi, Jian! The Police Picnic is going to be rad!"

Wendy sounded like she was actually excited. This was excellent news. Things were still on. My July phone gambit had been a success.

As I've suggested, the outfit was important. Always. But it was especially important at cool concerts. I had learned as much. I needed to look really New Wave so that I wouldn't embarrass myself or, more importantly, embarrass Wendy. On the morning of the Police Picnic, I decided on black pants, pointy ankle boots, a silver belt, and a black, short-sleeved, button-up shirt … and my Adidas bag. I had lots of gel in my hair and it was puffy and feathered like one of the members of Spandau Ballet before they changed their look and became preppy.

I fastidiously packed my Adidas bag with all the essential items I figured I needed for my trip to the Police Picnic with Wendy. I decided to bring my brand new Sony Walkman with portable headphones. Walkmans had only just started to become common in the summer of '82. I was proud I had one, and I'd already made some mix tapes specifically for my Walkman.

I have jotted down a short list of the items I packed in my Adidas bag that morning:

- Sony Walkman with Police mix tape inside
- portable headphones
- extra mix tapes featuring the Beat and Heaven 17
- jean jacket
- hair gel
- sandwich bag of mixed nuts

You may be wondering why I didn't bring any bottles of water along. I would have brought bottles of water if the Police Picnic were being held now. That's what you bring to outdoor concerts these days. That would seem like a natural inclusion amongst the items in the Adidas bag. But water didn't come in bottles in the 1980s. It came from taps. And things seemed just fine that way. Paying for a plastic bottle of water would've seemed like something a comedian would dream up. So I didn't have any bottles of water.

I met Wendy at Finch subway station and we got to the CNE Grandstand downtown at about 3 P.M. The subway ride was about thirty minutes long. Between the Sheppard and Rosedale subway stops I let Wendy listen to my new Walkman and to my mix tape with the Beat. I had purchased general admission tickets on the "floor," so when Wendy and I arrived at the Grandstand, we headed to the field and pushed our way forward. We reached a point about fifty rows from the stage, and I told Wendy we should push even closer. She said, "Okay!" and smiled. It turned out Wendy was actually very nice. Even though she was cool, she wasn't very much like Siouxsie from Siouxsie and the Banshees, who had told us to fuck off at her show. I was suddenly feeling a new sense of confidence. There were around forty-five thousand punters attending the Police Picnic in 1982, and most of them were bigger and older than me. But I had Wendy. Who else could claim to be there with the female Bowie? Soon, we were almost twenty rows from the stage.

The Police Picnic show started with a local New Wave band called the Spoons. They were dressed in white and they played an admirable set, even though they had some sound trouble. We were close enough to get a good look at their faces, and I could tell that the guys in the band were all wearing makeup and eyeliner. The Spoons had started as more of a progressive rock band, but they were now fully New Romantic. They looked and sounded like they were from the UK. They were actually from an industrial suburb of Toronto called Burlington. But that didn't matter. They had gelled hair and cosmetics and angular shirts and drum machines. The Spoons had a single called "Nova Heart." The video for the song featured a glowing egg. Eggs were still cool at this point. Many years later, I would become friends with a couple of former members of the Spoons. They no longer seem to wear eyeliner.

There was no alcohol sold at the Grandstand in those days, and quite a few people around us had snuck some in. The floor was getting really crowded, and I was having trouble figuring out where to place my red-and-blue Adidas bag when I wasn't holding it. I had decided to put it safely on the ground between my feet. Wendy was getting offers from some of the older New Wave guys to our right to share drinks with them. They had stubble and they were smoking, and one of them had a cut-off English Beat T-shirt. I could tell they thought Wendy was pretty. Wendy declined their offers, although she did let one of them light her cigarette. I think she was being considerate of my feelings by passing on the drinking part. I wished I had snuck in some booze so I could offer it to Wendy too. I hadn't really thought of that. I didn't have a lot of experience with alcohol, except for the vodka coolers I had drunk a few times at John Ruttle's house. One night, I had vomited in the bathroom near John Ruttle's parents' bedroom. I had had one too many Rockaberry coolers, and I had single-handedly consumed two bags of corn chips as well. I learned that vodka coolers didn't agree with me. But I wished I had some alcohol to offer Wendy.

A Flock of Seagulls were next up, featuring front man Mike Score. He had that "seagull" hairdo that would soon become a 1980s punch line. Flock of Seagulls played a relatively proficient half-hour gig that included their hit song "I Ran." Midway through their set, my sightline to the stage became slightly obscured in the jostle of the crowd. A very large punk guy decided to position himself directly in front of Wendy and me. His name was Forbes. At least, I think his name was Forbes. I learned this through deduction. A voice from a few rows behind us yelled, "You're an asshole, Forbes!" during a break in the Flock of Seagulls music, and the large punk guy turned around and grinned and gave the finger to the voice a few rows back. So we learned that the large punk guy was Forbes. I'm not sure if that was his first name or his last name.

Forbes was probably about six feet tall, but he seemed even taller because he had a spiked mohawk hairdo atop his six feet. He had army pants on and a white tank top. In later years, this kind of shirt would be referred to as a "wife beater." But at the time it was just a tank top. Or "white shirt with no sleeves." The tank top allowed Forbes to showcase his muscles and his underarm hair. Forbes also had very impressive combat boots on. They were impossible to miss. They were huge and they went up almost to his knees. I checked that my Adidas bag between my feet was secured safely away from Forbes's combat boots.

Next onstage were the Beat. This was the first big musical highlight of the day. The Beat were called the English Beat in North America. They were a multi-racial ska/New Wave band that was unquestionably cool. They were big in alternative circles along with other 2 Tone label bands like Madness and the Specials. It probably worked out for the best that their name had become the English Beat, because in the Canadian New Wave world, anything "English" was coveted. At the house party at the end of Grade 9 at Rosanna Dray's place, everybody had danced to the Beat for most of the night. Rosanna had long black curly hair that she teased and hairsprayed, and she was New Wave and everyone knew she was a good dancer. When she had a house party, all of her friends attended expecting to dance.

Throughout the party, Rosanna kept going back to her turntable and putting on "Mirror in the Bathroom." No one complained at these repeats in programming. "Mirror in the Bathroom" had been the big Beat song at the beginning of the '80s. Rosanna yelled at John Ruttle at one point during "Mirror in the Bathroom" because he was dancing too close to the stereo and making the needle skip. It was never easy negotiating enthusiastic dancing and a turntable at a party in 1982.

The English Beat had a profound effect on New Wave fashions. The Beat—along with the Specials—had made the wearing of little fedora hats and vests cool. Ranking Roger, one of the lead vocalists from the Beat, often seemed to have a hat and a vest on, and his energetic style and Jamaican-influenced vocals had become the enduring centre of the Beat's image. Everyone wanted to be Ranking Roger. A lot of Beat fans had started wearing vests like Ranking Roger. A case in point was Wendy's brother, Paul. Mind you, Paul wore his vest over a pirate shirt, because he was demonstrating that he was theatrical. Beat fans didn't wear pirate shirts. But it was still a similar vest. And in your vest you would do a ska dance by swinging your arms in the air one at a time and moving your feet in the same direction. This dance looked even better with a fedora. Or you could pogo. Lots of mods liked to pogo as well. The point is, the English Beat were about dancing. And most important, the Beat had groove. It was infectious. It seemed like everyone loved the Beat.

The Beat only ever released three studio albums. By the mid-'80s, two of the main members had moved on to form General Public, and two others had gone on to form Fine Young Cannibals. But neither of these bands would ever trump the Beat. And only the Beat had a senior Jamaican saxophone player named Saxa. You might think it was silly that the sax player was named Saxa. But it wasn't. He was cool, even though he was old. Black musicians with beards and hats were already cool, and they looked even cooler when they were old. They got better. Not like Mr. Margison in the Thornhill Community Band, with his balding head that became red when he was angry. Saxa was still performing with the Beat in 1982. And '82 was probably the best year for the English Beat. It was that year that the Beat released their third and final album, *Special Beat Service*, featuring the song "I Confess." It was also that summer that they were playing for the last time with their original lineup.

The Beat were dazzling fun at the Police Picnic. Lead singer Dave Wakeling caught a Frisbee during "I Confess" and threw it back without missing a lyric. Ranking Roger was hopping around the stage, and Saxa was waving his arms between sax lines. Wendy really liked the Beat. We were dancing and pogo-ing with our hands in the air. Forbes the punk was jumping around like a madman with his arms in the air, too. His flailing had the effect of exposing his hairy armpits. His armpits came very close to my head at times. He was tall. He was giving the finger to people in what seemed like a form of affection or appreciation, much like the way the punters had cheered for Siouxsie when she told us to fuck off. The fun was widespread and the mood in the stadium was undeniably unified. For a little while during the English Beat's set at the Police Picnic, with the sun shining brightly and Wendy at my side, it really seemed like things couldn't get much better. But events were about to take an unfortunate turn.

At some point, the promoters behind the second annual Police Picnic had thought it a good idea to include Joan Jett and the Blackhearts on the bill. After all, Joan Jett had a hit song and had come from some cool musical roots. She might sell tickets. She was a legit rocker when she formed the Runaways as a teenager in the 1970s, and she had worked with members of the Sex Pistols and X. But what the promoters misjudged was that Joan Jett had become very popular in the mainstream. And that was not cool. Not with this crowd.

Let me try to explain. There was a strong divide at the time between those who fancied themselves alternative and those who followed mainstream music. The alternative music lovers were really into the innovation and changes that were happening in music. They were strongly influenced by what was coming out of England or New York. There were sometimes noisy and harsh sounds. This new music would at times also incorporate many non-rock sources and influences. The enemy was the mainstream, the corporate American acts. They were seen as being stuck in the past, manufacturing airbrushed "meat and potatoes" commercial radio songs, albeit with electric guitars. Joan Jett had been an alternative original, but after her slick, radio-friendly "I Love Rock 'n Roll" became ubiquitous that year, she was regarded as part of the mainstream. The enemy.

When Joan Jett hit the stage, the reaction wasn't pretty. From the moment she and her band emerged from the wings, the crowd was less than welcoming. The New Wave and punk audience started booing her mercilessly. And even before Joan Jett played the first chord on her guitar, a banana peel came shooting out of the crowd and just missed her head. The band tore into their opening song and Joan Jett began singing, but the crowd reaction just got worse. Wendy and I were laughing at first, but within minutes we stood silent and alarmed as we watched everything and anything get thrown at Joan Jett. T-shirts, paper cups, smuggled-in beer bottles, Frisbees ... Apparently, nothing was off limits or too good to be thrown at Joan Jett.

Forbes was pushing anyone in his vicinity and acting like a madman. He clearly took it very personally that Joan Jett had been allowed to take the stage. He was cursing and spitting and jumping up and down with his middle finger in the air. He was not alone. There were punters loudly booing all around us. The stubble-faced older guys to the right of Wendy had lost their warm disposition from when the Beat were onstage and were now screaming uncomplimentary words at Joan Jett. One of the stubble-faced guys threw his lit cigarette at the stage. This was a problem, because lit cigarettes don't travel very far, and we were at least fifty feet away from Joan Jett. The cigarette landed on a girl with dyed-green hair two rows in front of us. She turned around and gave us all a dirty look. But the stubble-faced guy's point was to express anger at Joan Jett. And that's what the lit cigarette did. At the end of Joan Jett and the Blackhearts' first song, it was clear that things might escalate. The audience was in a violent mood. Wendy looked at me and said, "This is crazy. She's going to get hurt." I agreed and felt scared inside. But I didn't let Wendy know I was scared.

When Joan Jett launched into a second song, the crowd went berserk and a new shower of items was thrown at the stage. I promise you, I'm not exaggerating this. I'd never seen anything like it, except for when referee Bruce Hood called an outrageous penalty against the Toronto Maple Leafs in the playoffs against the Islanders in the late '70s. My dad took me to Maple Leaf Gardens to see that game. When the crowd started throwing debris on the ice at Bruce Hood, I also threw some popcorn—much to the disappointment of my father—but I was actually afraid of people throwing things at the ref. And that was just a hockey game. This was real life, where things were getting much more aggressive with Joan Jett.

Given that Wendy and I were relatively close to the stage, things that were being tossed from behind us were now landing near us or on our heads. Forbes was grabbing anything he could find and throwing it at Joan Jett. A bottle landed close to us, and Forbes picked it up off the ground and threw it, almost hitting the Blackhearts' second guitarist. I had a feeling that something bad was about to happen. I wasn't wrong.

When Forbes was scouring the ground to find things to throw at Joan Jett, I could see he'd spotted my red-and-blue Adidas bag. It was still between my feet, but it was sticking out in front, quite close to Forbes's combat boots. Forbes looked at me and then looked back down at my Adidas bag. I didn't want to allow myself to fathom what could transpire here. I had bought this Adidas bag with my saved-up money from SAVCO Pet Food and Supplies when I was in Grade 8. I had carried it with me everywhere. Toke and I used to take our Adidas bags when we walked to Mac's Milk and saw the "good Chinese woman" behind the counter. I'd been carrying my Adidas bag when I asked Wendy to come to the Police Picnic. And now it was at my feet, holding my brand new Walkman and my mix tapes and my jean jacket and my portable headphones.

Forbes looked back up at Joan Jett and the Blackhearts and started to scream "Fuck you!" along with the rest of the crowd. Just when I thought Forbes had become distracted, he twisted his body around to face me. In one motion, he bent down, grabbed my Adidas bag, then stood up and held it over his head, King Kong style. I was panicking. I looked up at Forbes and he looked down at me with my Adidas bag above his head. The bottom of my Adidas bag was touching the tips of his mohawk.

"Please don't do that," I said as firmly as I could.

Using the word "please" might have been a particularly diplomatic form of negotiation with a crazed punk gorilla, but I didn't feel in a position to be any more aggressive with him. Wendy tried. She grabbed Forbes's arm and said, "Hey, c'mon, stop it. That's his bag!" I was terrified at what Forbes might do but excited that Wendy was sticking up for me. We were a team.

Forbes was having none of it. He looked at Wendy and started to show his teeth like an ape. It was clear the mission to stop Joan Jett was much more important than saving either the Adidas bag or the feelings of a confused young suburban boy aspiring to be a New Waver. Forbes pulled his arms back the way you'd prepare to throw a soccer ball back into play from the sidelines. Everything was moving in slow motion now. Then it happened. Forbes lunged forward, pumped his arms, and launched my Adidas bag into the air.

The music stopped. Everything stopped.

Or at least it seemed to. Of all the things the crowd had witnessed being catapulted at Joan Jett and the Blackhearts, this was clearly the most valuable so far. The Adidas bag flew through the air, and I could feel the collective gasp of forty-five thousand onlookers anticipating where it might land. In that split second, I could see Joan Jett registering the incoming Adidas missile and sidestepping it to avoid impact. The red-and-blue projectile flew directly in Joan Jett's direction and just missed her, heavily hitting the stage next to her amp. It landed right side up. From my vantage point I could see the name tag on the bag, now sitting prominently onstage. In fact, the whole crowd could. It was very clear, in black, upper-case letters: THIS BAG BELONGS TO JIAN GHOMESHI. THORNHILL, ONTARIO.

Suddenly, everything was back at regular speed and events were moving ahead without any regard for the Adidas bomb that had just been launched from the audience. Other things were being thrown. Forbes had pushed forward a couple of rows to make his human-rights case even closer to the stage. The crowd was still loudly booing the Blackhearts. I looked at Wendy and she put her arm around my shoulder. She knew I had just lost my Adidas bag forever.

After their second song, Joan Jett threw her guitar on the ground and motioned to her band to abandon the stage. They fled the onslaught and headed into the wings. As she left, Joan Jett held her head up and sneered with a kind of tragic look on her face, the way someone's face looks when they're feeling quite upset but want to appear tough so no one will know. That's what Joan Jett looked like. Except everyone knew it had not gone well. Joan Jett then gave us all the finger. This time there were no cheers the way there had been when Siouxsie told the audience to fuck off at her show a few months earlier. An MC came on to chide the audience, stating that Joan Jett would not come back out unless the avalanche of debris stopped flowing. There was general confusion for a little while after that.

In the midst of all this, my Adidas bag could still be seen on the stage. Wendy had her arm around me, and I could tell that she was looking directly at me, trying to gauge my reaction. I just kept staring straight ahead at my bag. I wondered if the impact of the landing had knocked my new Walkman on inside the Adidas bag. Maybe my new mix tape was playing with the Heaven 17 song "Let Me Go" blasting in the portable headphones.

The stage crew began collecting everything that had been thrown on the platform and tossing it into a big pile at the side of the stage. A crew guy with a ponytail and a jean jacket and lots of official laminates around his neck grabbed my Adidas bag and threw it out of sight into the wings. That would be the last I would see of it. Wendy now turned so that she was standing in front of me with her back to the stage and the crowd in a commotion all around us.

"Are you okay?" She looked concerned.

I tried to keep my composure for Wendy's sake. "Yeah. I'm fine. Umm ... that was crazy what Forbes did."

"Yeah. Totally crazy. But I'm glad you're all right. You know, he shouldn't have done that."

It was the first time I could tell that Wendy was a really caring person on top of being like Bowie. It was exhilarating and kind of romantic. In fact, this probably would have been my favourite moment ever if I hadn't been thinking about all the stuff I just lost. Wendy continued to talk to me in an effort to make sure things were okay.

"But it's just a bag, right? And it was pretty funny." She was changing the tone so I could move on. "You can get another bag. Maybe you can get a black briefcase type."

"Yeah. It's just a bag," I said. "I don't use it that much. Not a problem."

I bit my bottom lip. Wendy would never know the significance of the Adidas bag. She had no sense of its history and how big a deal it had been when I got it, and of the different colours it had been available in. She didn't know that the red-and-blue kind of Adidas bag was a bit more rare. At least, I thought it was when Toke had gotten the other, more regular, kind. The bag wasn't ultimately that cool. It certainly wasn't New Wave. It had never fitted in with the rest of my outfit or with the 213 crowd anyway. And if I was going to lose it, it was strangely poetic that it should happen with Wendy. Maybe this was what it meant to become more of a man. I was dealing with a lot of adult stuff on this day. What I didn't know was that before the Police Picnic and my date with Wendy were over, my world would change further.

4

"UNDER PRESSURE"
— QUEEN AND DAVID BOWIE

The UK was always cool.

Before Joan Jett hit the stage at the Police Picnic in the summer of 1982, the lineup of bands had all been British. That is, except for the Spoons—and they were a Canadian band trying to sound British. Everyone wanted to sound British. Even British bands wanted to sound British.

It's no secret that in Grade 9 my favourite artists were from the UK. Bowie was from England. So were the Police, and the Clash, and the Beat, and just about every other cool band, starting in a previous generation with the Beatles, the Stones, and the Who. In the '80s, Britain was where real New Wave style and substance were centred. I'm not really sure why. Maybe it was because the UK was better at starting cultural trends. Maybe it came out of a more pronounced class war and politicized youth. That's what my sister told me. But maybe it was because most English people had straight hair (much easier to crimp) and pale complexions (much easier to make paler), and that naturally made them more punk. And also there were lots of reasons to be unhappy in England. Or at least, Brits would find reasons to complain. They might be unhappy about smaller food portions, or fewer TV channels, or more Thatcher, or less sunshine. They could often be bitter and miserable. And being miserable was cool. And New Wave music sounded better in a miserable or defiant English vernacular.

Billy Bragg wouldn't have been as successful if he'd sung working-class protest songs with a Californian accent. He would've sounded like a surfer, and surfers have no reason to be angry. So Billy Bragg would have sounded like a liar. But he had a British accent. And so he was believable. And that was cool.

Besides, for me it made even more sense that I had an affinity for all things British. I was born in London and spent my first seven years in the UK. If only I'd known how to harness that lineage, I would have been more successful in Thornhill in Grade 9. I could have retained my English accent and peppered my sentences with "y'know wha-I mean?" and said about my friends, "They're my best mates." And then Wendy probably would have thought I was more special and punk and unique. But I was a different kind of unique. When I was in England, as much as I had friends and loved supporting Arsenal Football Club, I didn't really fit in. And then I didn't really fit in when I got to Thornhill. My search for appropriate role models often came up empty. And being myself didn't seem a very appealing option.

WHEN I WAS A little kid in England in the 1970s, the boys I hung out with at primary school called me Blackie.

Blackie.

This is a fact. It became my label. And some of those kids who called me by that name were my friends.

"Hey, Blackie!"

That's how they would greet me. This term was apparently based on my parents' ethnic background and the way I looked. My parents had moved from Iran and settled in England before my sister and I were born. And we were the only ethnic family around. But I didn't really understand what that meant at the time.

I didn't take offence to being called Blackie. It didn't bother me as a little kid, because I didn't recognize any of the broader societal implications or any sort of power dynamic. I figured Blackie was just another nickname. There was Paulie and Nicker and then there was me, Blackie. Most of the good football players in the English Premier League had nicknames, too. In England, soccer was called football. And the footballers all had catchy monikers. Just like me.

You might wonder if I'm making this up. You might be surprised to learn that I was called Blackie. That's because it was stupid. It never made any sense. I wasn't black. My skin wasn't even a particularly dark shade of brown, unless I'd spent too much time on the beach at Brighton. But in the suburb of London where I grew up, almost everyone was white. Like, pasty, pinky white. There were no black kids or brown kids or yellow kids—at least none that I remember. So I became the de facto ambassador for all of them. And clearly, "Brownie" or "Olivie" just didn't have the same ring as "Blackie." I don't know why. I didn't realize how insulting it could be to be singled out for my race until a few years later. But I did start to get the message that I was different. Confusion about my ethnicity began right then. And it never really ended until well after high school.

When my family first arrived in Canada from England, we settled in an area called Don Mills. Don Mills was in the middle of Metropolitan Toronto, somewhere that was neither downtown nor the suburbs. Don Mills was an area that featured Fairview Mall and the Ontario Science Centre and a hamburger place my parents took me to on the weekends called Big Boy. I was seven. This was long before I knew Wendy existed. This was long before cool electronic music made by British people wearing eyeliner who called themselves the Human League. This was back in the mid-'70s, when I thought of Bowie as a kids' performer because of his ditty "The Laughing Gnome." My mother had taped that song on our Panasonic cassette recorder when we were still in the UK. It was my favourite track on the mix tape she'd made with me.

More than anything, upon arriving in Canada, I felt a sense of liberation. Well, not at first. At first I felt terror. Terror then liberation. I'd been scared about going to Canada because some of the kids in London had warned me about all the spiders. They repeatedly made the case that I would have to fight legions of spiders in my new country.

"Blackie, you're gonna be covered in spiders in Canada, mate! The spiders will eat you!"

"No, they won't!" I valiantly replied.

But I wasn't really sure if the spiders would eat me or not. And I wondered why my parents were taking me to a place that was swarming with them. That didn't sound very safe. And the spiders weren't the only problem. By the time we arrived on Canadian soil, I'd accumulated a number of other fears. These worries included snow. I'd never witnessed giant snowflakes the like of which were falling the night we landed at Toronto International Airport. My father met us at the airport, and it was a particularly snowy evening. He'd moved to Toronto a few months earlier to set up our new apartment and settle into his new job. He had to drag me outside to the taxi that was waiting for us, because I wasn't at all sure I was ready to leave the airport when I saw the mounds of snow. The Canadian outdoors looked daunting. And it also looked beautiful. And cold.

The thing is, in the 1970s, air travel to a new place was pretty much a guessing game. You couldn't predict what you might encounter when you landed. It was like those old Cracker Jack popcorn boxes with the "surprise" inside. You never knew what you would get. That was the difference between travelling in the 1970s and travelling now. Now, you can Google the weather at your destination. Now, you can look at up-to-date videos of your intended new homeland before you step on board the flight headed to your intended new homeland. Now, you can Skype with someone for free and ask questions like "How's the weather?" And also, "Is there a military coup going on at present?"

But in the 1970s, it was all in our imagination. I had no idea what Canada would be like, except for a postcard my father had sent from a weekend trip he'd taken to Montreal. That's all I had to go on, other than a book I had about polar bears. And I had been told about the snow. And I had been warned about all the spiders. And I had overheard our next-door neighbour in England, Mr. Boggart, telling my mother that Canada was a "vast land." That sounded scary as well. I was afraid all of these things.

I have made a short list of things I was scared of finding in Canada before arriving in the 1970s:

- spiders
- snow
- vast land
- slippery ice
- bearded father

As you can see, there were a number of things to be scared of when anticipating an inaugural trip to Canada at the age of seven. You may be wondering why "bearded father" is on that list. That item has to do with my father's absence from the family for a few months. He had travelled to Canada in advance of the rest of us. In our time away from each other, I grew very worried that my father would become unrecognizable to me and that when I saw him again in our new Canadian home he would look like a foreigner. I worried that he'd be angry and mean. I decided that this unfriendly and foreign demeanour would find expression in my father having a beard. That made sense to me. Fortunately, when we got to Canada in December of 1974, I realized that there were no swarms of spiders, that the snow was actually fun, and that we had moved to another city that wasn't as daunting as the term "vast land" implied. And also, to my great relief, I found that my father did not have a beard.

But most important, after the fears, coming to Canada meant liberation. It was liberation from the homogenous nature of our previous community in Middlesex, England. I very quickly felt like I belonged in Toronto. I felt a sense of belonging more than I had in any other place. It was like I had walked into a first-generation immigrant dreamland.

Upon settling into Don Mills, I made new friends immediately. And my posse was a veritable mini–United Nations. It included Aris, who was Greek; Roy, whose parents were Indian; David, who was black; and Umar, whose Pakistani-German family, the Jans, became our best friends. I was no longer Blackie. I didn't stand out at all. Not for my skin colour or background. We were in a region full of people who had just come from other parts of the world. I decided I loved Canada. Everyone was like me. No one called me anything other than my own name. I didn't even mind that I had an English accent, because many of the other kids had funny accents, too. I soon had a girlfriend. She was Korean. Well, okay, maybe she wasn't a real girlfriend—it was Grade 3. But her name was Nina Chee, and she was cute and we had a bond. Our bond involved me running away from Nina Chee even though I had strange butterflies whenever I saw her. I had strange butterflies and then she would talk to me and then I would run away. It usually happened in that order. That was the extent of our relationship. But I never really noticed or cared that she was Korean. It all felt comfortable. My friends and my surroundings were very diverse. I had a glorious moment of childhood when I didn't really question my identity or that of others. Not much.

Then things changed. Two years later, when my parents decided to move us to a conservative part of old Thornhill, my world was dramatically altered. We were now living in an established suburban area of note. It was supposedly a move upward. We had a big new home. But we were alone in our new-immigrant status in this community. And we stood out. And I was skinny. And then the revolution happened in Iran. And I began to fight a turf war against my own ethnicity. I knew I was different. And I became quite sure that was not okay.

BY THE TIME I ENTERED Grade 9 at Thornlea Secondary School in the fall of 1981, I had become resentful of my Iranian background. It was all very annoying. Other kids in Thornhill had families that had been in Canada for generations. Their parents didn't have accents or weird rituals. Besides, there were no Iranian New Wave role models. Being Iranian was a liability if you wanted to be New Wave. Can you imagine the members of Duran Duran being Iranian? No, you can't. You can't because they wouldn't have been. Not in the '80s. They were all white and had perfect noses and straight hair.

If the members of Duran Duran had been Iranian, they would have looked less out of place when they made "exotic" videos like the one for "Hungry Like the Wolf" in 1982. The premise for that video was that the members of Duran Duran were white English guys stuck in a foreign land. In fact, they were so emphatic about their bleached Caucasian appearance that the keyboard player of Duran Duran wore white makeup so he'd look even whiter. That meant he didn't look very Persian.

Besides, Bowie wasn't Iranian. Neither was Wendy. And neither was Sting or Stewart Copeland or any of my heroes. And movie stars looked like Robert Redford or Clint Eastwood.

Not like me. My aspiration became the denial of my ancestry. I was just doing what I needed to do to survive.

Don't get me wrong. I wouldn't forgo our Persian traditions or values or my mother's cooking. Not behind closed doors. A significant proportion of my body already consisted of basmati rice and saffron by the '80s. I couldn't just give that up. And I loved my family and wanted to respect our roots. But I didn't like the public baggage that came with being Middle Eastern. It had never been easy to explain our culture to those who knew nothing about Persians. Then, after the Islamic Revolution of 1979, Iran had gone from being a somewhat glamorous curiosity for Westerners to being seen as an evil enemy of everything from capitalism to civility to rock music to America.

Clearly, the regime was despicable. But the line grew too blurred between the way Westerners saw the oppressive new Iranian theocracy and the generalizations they would then make about Persian people. We were all tainted. The proud history of Iranian creativity and culture was ignored. There was little information about the legacy of ideas and technology and poetry and dance that had been spawned in Persia. To the West, Iranians were summed up in one big dangerous stereotype. People assumed we were all hairy and angry, like the ayatollahs they saw on TV.

It wasn't until I was in university and a racist film called *Not Without My Daughter* received wide theatrical release that I would decide to take action. In this Sally Field movie, the caricature of all Iranians as barbarians is so ridiculous it would be laughable if it weren't so offensive. Yet there was no outcry at the time, because the Persian community in North

America was still too small and too timid to speak out. That was 1991. It was only then that I truly realized I took pride in my Iranian heritage and should not succumb to stereotypes about us.

At that point, I became very public in accepting my background. I wrote an editorial about the film and the negative depiction of Iranians for the York University newspaper *Excalibur*. And I didn't shy away from my identity during my campaign to become president of the student federation at York that year. By then, I was an activist. By then, I had some confidence. And I would never forgive Sally Field. But that was after the 1980s. That was after many years of hiding in the cultural closet.

Before 1979, things had been much better for the few of us of Persian background that had immigrated to Canada. Even if I was ethnic, I was seen more as exotic than terrorist. I only had to deal with people like Annie McMillan on our street in Thornhill, who wondered if we ate "Arab food." Annie didn't mean to offend. Besides, she wore tight jeans and she looked like Kristy McNichol. She had a nice tan. Most people just didn't know much about Iran. And when they did, Persians generally had a good reputation. Iran had been, after all, a staunch ally of the West.

In the late '70s, when I was in Grade 5, I'd seen pictures in a newspaper of Farrah Fawcett and Colonel Steve Austin visiting Iran. They were a glamorous Hollywood couple. I took the newspaper clipping from the Henderson Avenue Public School library and brought it home to show my parents. Steve Austin was the star of a TV show called *The Six Million Dollar Man*. He was a real action hero. Well, actually, he had bionic limbs.

That made him even better than a real action hero. And it was a triumphant moment for many Iranian kids when he visited Iran with his beautiful wife from *Charlie's Angels*. Everyone thought Farrah Fawcett was sexy, and she had layered blondish hair that flowed from high on her head, and she wore bikinis. Colonel Steve Austin and Farrah Fawcett were on their second honeymoon, and they spent it in Tehran. They were so in love they needed two honeymoons. Everyone talked about how they chose to go to a Middle Eastern country to express their love. Iran was considered a modern and exciting foreign place to travel to.

Apparently, the shah's son was a fan of *The Six Million Dollar Man*, and he had convinced his father to invite the couple to visit. The actor who played Colonel Steve Austin was actually called Lee Majors, but that seemed a silly name to use when you could be called the Six Million Dollar Man and you had bionic powers. It was clear that Colonel Steve Austin thought Iran was cool. I remember being proud of my background that day with the newspaper clipping, even if we were different from the white families on our street.

But all this changed after the revolution in '79. In the months after the shah was ousted, fundamentalist Iranian students took fifty-two innocent American workers hostage and an old bearded guy wearing a turban named Ayatollah Khomeini consolidated power with some other bearded guys wearing turbans. You probably remember this if you were alive at the time. It was big news. And in this case, being bearded really did mean you were scary. Khomeini always looked stern and angry. He wasn't like my Persian uncles, who were sweet and generous and had big, friendly personalities.

Khomeini was fierce. And he sat on the floor eating and meeting and talking and making revolutionary statements and looking even fiercer. He was always sitting on the floor, that Khomeini. I was never really clear why Muslims were no longer supposed to use chairs. Chairs seemed like too practical an item to suddenly dismiss in the name of religion. Why couldn't we be Muslim while sitting on chairs? But Khomeini sat on the floor. I assumed that chairs had become an example of the excessive materialism of the West. And Khomeini soon said that contemporary music and university and any kind of modernism were all anti-Islamic, too. He was the new symbol of Iran.

My father originally held high hopes for the 1979 Iranian revolution. He even supported it in the first few weeks, along with workers and women and students and others. It began as a popular revolution that inspired Iranians of all walks of life. My father had previously opposed the shah for his excessive and iron-fisted regime. But the revolution hadn't turned out the way liberal nationalists like my father expected. Now he would simply shake his head with dismay each night as we watched the evening news from Tehran on CBC.

"The whole world now ees theenking we are savage," my father would say. "I don't know why thees must happen like that. It ees, honestly, terreeble."

It was all very sad. My father grew bitter about the plight of his former homeland. He was outraged that the new regime was executing democratic activists in the name of Islam. But beyond the emotions we experienced inside our home, there were other implications for us, too. After the revolution, I was consistently reminded that my ancestry was somehow problematic and that North Americans didn't seem to like Iranians very much. At the Home Hardware store, there was the guy in the baseball cap behind the counter who accused my father of wanting to eat squirrels. And on the radio there was a new version of the old Beach Boys song "Barbara Ann" with the lyrics changed to "Bomb Iran." That was supposed to be funny. But it didn't feel funny. Not with my relatives still living in Tehran.

None of my extended family in Iran had long beards or religious robes or any kind of relationship with the new regime. But people seemed to want to bomb them. And by the time I was at Woodland Junior High, kids at school were starting to make jokes about me being a terrorist. They would ask where I was hiding my turban and my machine gun. I wondered what a turban would feel like on my head if I ever got to wear one. I wondered if hair gel would be necessary if I were to regularly wear a turban. Bowie would end up wearing a turban in his video for "Blue Jean" a few years later. But he never looked like Khomeini. His turban was more bohemian than Islamic Republic. And anyway, that video would not come out until 1984.

Of course, even before the revolution I'd been well aware that I had a different lineage than most other kids in Thornhill. But I really didn't understand the implications or the significance of coming from a Muslim family or having our background. My parents had brought up my sister and me to be quite assimilated in the hopes that we would avoid the difficulty of being singled out. But this only meant I knew less about who or what our ancestry was.

I certainly didn't know much about organized faith and the

way the world divided itself along religious lines. My parents had told me we were Muslim. I knew that part. But I wasn't always sure what it meant. I knew my father prayed a few times a day. Sometimes, I watched him as he prayed, and I tried to figure out what he was saying in a whispered tone. And I knew that when we went on long trips, my mother would make us kiss the Koran before we left. But that was pretty much it. That's what I'd learned about being a Muslim. We never visited a mosque or engaged in any other religious activities. We simply weren't a very observant family when it came to religion. In fact, we celebrated Christmas and Easter, and I'd learned to say the Lord's Prayer at school in England. That was the one prayer I had memorized, and it was a Christian one. Later on in high school, most of my closest friends would be Jews. I just had no idea how separated we were all supposed to be.

Sometimes, my ignorance of religion led to some unfortunate confusion. In Grade 5 at Henderson Avenue Public School, Kim Coughlin approached me one afternoon at the end of class with a very serious look on her face. Kim Coughlin had long brown hair and rosy cheeks and was very pretty and a good soccer player. I liked Kim Coughlin but never felt I could talk to her. I was too afraid that she might laugh and that I wouldn't know if she was laughing at me or not. She was too pretty. When you're that pretty, you get to laugh at people. And she seemed to laugh a lot. And she was usually surrounded by a few adoring fans.

But on this day, Kim had a very serious look on her face. She was wearing a sweatshirt with a hood when she walked up to me after class. Her cheeks were rosy. There was little in the way of any introduction. She just launched right into her query.

"Hi. So ... I have a question. Are you Protestant?"

The request landed like a thud on my head. It sounded very important, and I desperately wanted to answer correctly. Kim Coughlin had obviously noticed me and felt the pressing need to sort out some crucial details about my character. I wanted Kim Coughlin to like me. I would have done anything to fit in. But I had no idea what "Protestant" was. It sounded like an attitude or a physical disposition or a cheese. I had no idea. I realized I had a fifty-fifty chance of answering this unexpected quiz correctly.

"No," I answered, "I'm not."

I waited for the verdict. I'd made sure not to repeat "Protestant" in my reply to Kim Coughlin. I was still sounding the word out in my head and wasn't even sure how to say it.

"Oh, okay!" Kim Coughlin replied enthusiastically. "Good!"

Kim Coughlin then skipped away to join her friend who was waiting for her by the classroom door. It seemed I had done well. Mind you, it didn't mean that Kim Coughlin would spend much more time with me for the rest of Grade 5. But she had nodded and laughed warmly, as if my reply had been the acceptable one. I watched her immediately recount my response to the girl who had been waiting. They looked at me and smiled. It would be years until I properly understood what "Protestant" meant. Until then, I just knew I had answered the question correctly. And whatever it was, I knew I didn't want to be Protestant. Kim Coughlin didn't want me to be Protestant.

Then again, by 1980, most people could guess I wasn't Protestant. Even Kim Coughlin wouldn't have asked me that question by Grade 7. I had a Middle Eastern look, and now everyone was curious about my ethnicity, especially with world events being the way they were. Maybe it had to do with the size of my nose. My issues were compounded by the size of my nose as I hit my early teens. The sheer real estate of my nose was quite outstanding. My nose had grown disproportionately larger than anything on an average human face. My snoot seemed to develop and mature much faster than the rest of me. By Grade 7, I was a skinny twelve-year-old with the body of a boy but the beak of a man. And it was a significant one. It was an industrial-sized nose. It was a nose that could house its own little factory. And the big beak combined with the brown skin made me look more ethnic. There was no getting around it. Throw in my odd name and the pistachios in my lunch bag, and it was hard to make the case that I was another white kid like my friend Davey Franklin or That Chris from across the street. But my mother kept telling me I was the same as everyone else.

It became increasingly hard to suggest, somehow, that I wasn't Iranian. But after the revolution it was also hard to tell people that I *was* Iranian. It was a trap. My parents became very quiet about our background in public. This was true of many in the Iranian diaspora. In fact, many Iranians started to call themselves "Persian" to avoid being connected to the backward regime of old bearded men in power in their former homeland. Sometimes, I would use the word "Persian" and I could tell that a person who knew nothing about the cultural origins of Iran would think I had said "Parisian." Parisian would mean I was from Paris. I didn't bother to correct them. I hoped they would think I was French. My first name already sounded French-ish. And it was better to be thought to have come from France than from Iran. And, technically, they'd decided that without me having to lie. My desire for denial ran deep.

Sometimes, I would even hurt the feelings of others to save myself from ridicule. There was another kid in my grade named Ebrahim. He was a Muslim from Africa. We were friends, but I distanced myself from him when people asked if we had the same religious background. He had darker skin and sometimes got teased. I would abandon him to protect my own interests. It was shameful. But I lived with the hope that no one would find out I was Iranian.

My family collectively got its Canadian citizenship in a sweet ceremony in 1978. We had all studied hard and we'd aced the questions. It was a great day for us. My father was now able to tell people he was Canadian. He would thereafter maintain a tremendous pride in choosing to live in Canada and called himself a proud Canadian citizen. But there was no mistaking that he was an immigrant with an accent that originated somewhere else. And no matter how hard they tried, my parents couldn't will me to look whiter than I was.

Here's the thing you need to know about Iranians. Many Iranians like to think they're white. This is because some of them are. Or at least, they're almost white. And they certainly fancy themselves that way. And to be technically correct, Persians are actually members of the Aryan race. They are not Semites. You may be surprised to learn that I come from an Aryan race. Stop laughing. It's the truth. As you know, "Aryan" usually implies "white" in the popular imagination.

And Iranians like that. That's why Persians will often make a point of identifying themselves this way. "No, leesen, you know … vee are not Arab … vee are Auree-an," some will say. You will hear some Persians saying this, or something like it. They will insist on telling you they are Aryan. There's even a popular music group in Iran named Arian. That's Aryan spelled slightly differently, in case you didn't catch it. And on top of that, Persians have always had a predilection for things Western. In the '80s, most Iranians loved the United States and its people. It was a great irony that Iranians were often depicted as anti-Western, because there was so much affection in Iran for the West and interest in the trappings of modern American culture. Being considered white meant being more Western. And middle-class Iranians liked that. But I didn't know the historical background to all of this in 1982. I didn't even know what "Aryan" meant. I just knew my mother wanted me to consider myself white.

There's a problem with Iranians insisting on being considered fair-skinned. The problem is that many Iranians are brown. It's a nice shade of olive brown for the most part. Some are browner than others. But few are very white. They just want to be. At least, they did back in the 1980s. So, to put this in some context, while most of the world population was going out of its way to bake in the sun and become browner in the '80s, Iranians wanted to be whiter. This was always an issue for me at home. My friends would aspire to a suntan. They considered a tanned look to be sexy and healthy. Everyone wanted brown skin, unless they were goths or really New Wave or aspiring to be really New Wave. Even my Grade 5 girlfriend, Dana Verner, who had kissed me twice and then broken up with me, liked to go "tanning." And that was when she was ten. Some preppy people liked to suntan so much in the '80s that they started going to salons with electronic caskets that they would lie in so they could become browner. Being brown was so important that people would risk zapping themselves in caskets. But this did not happen amongst the ranks of my family. My mother always wanted me to avoid the sun. She would get very angry if I spent too much time outdoors in the summer.

"Why do you insist on going in the sun like this? *Vah-ee.* You're going to be black!"

That's what my mother would say. Often. *Vah-ee* is an alarmist Farsi expression meaning, "Oh, dear!"

I'm not sure if my mother really thought I would become black. I think this was a bit of an exaggeration. I could never really be black. But that's the way my mother talked some-times. This was her form of protection-speak. For instance, she said something similar when any member of my family went outside in the winter without a proper heavy coat on. My mother would say, "*Beeroon lokht nar-oh!*" This trans-lates to "Don't go outside naked!" Again, this statement may appear excessive. It seems odd to accuse a fully clothed human of being naked. But this was my mother's code for "Put on a winter coat!" And in the same way, when my mother said, "You're going to be black!" she actually meant, "Don't get too much of a tan, because then you will be even more brown, and you will stand out more and everyone will know you are ethnic and you will be made fun of and you will be sad, or, more specifically, I will be sad." My mother was trying to protect me. And she could say a lot in a few words.

Here is a short list (or shortlist) of things my mother did not want me to be in 1982:

- noisy
- ethnic
- punk
- naked
- late
- non-white

As you can see, my mother worried about many of the potential ways I might acquit myself when I was fourteen. For example, as I've noted, she did not want me to leave the house naked. But I could control that. I could put on a winter coat if I had to. Unfortunately for my mother, I couldn't control the final item on that list. No matter how many ways my mother tried to deny this reality, I wasn't white. I've always had a brownish tint to my skin. And this was why I was "Blackie" in England. And this was why I couldn't properly be New Wave. And this was why it was hard to look like Bowie. Bowie almost never had a tan. He was pale. Super pale. So was Wendy. And so were the goths that listened to Bauhaus. And so were the members of Duran Duran.

By the time I was in Grade 9 and had fully embarked on my New Wave transformation, I hated that I was brown and that I had a funny name and that my family was Iranian and that I had a huge nose and that people made terrorist jokes. But I also found it difficult that my mother wanted me to deny all those differences. It was as if my mother never wanted to fully accept the way I appeared. It doubtless came from an instinct to protect. But I was never going to have the complexion she had. I took after my father. He was brown. And I couldn't change the colour of my skin, even if it would make life easier for me.

Besides, in case I ever forgot I was brown, I'd get reminders of it from other kids. Even if I was no longer being called Blackie, I had to deal with some unsavoury substitutes. I would learn about other names I might be called during my time as a hockey player.

Hockey was a game I always loved playing. It is a sport I still obsessively watch. Being a hockey fan is a constitutional requirement of being a citizen in Canada. Or at least, it should be. It's like drinking tea in England or eating food that is high in saturated fats in the USA. It is part of who we are. As soon as my family arrived in Canada in the mid-'70s, I became a hockey fan. I got Toronto Maple Leaf Darryl Sittler's autograph at Ontario Place in 1979. He wore number 27 and he was my favourite. He signed my autograph book, "Darryl Sittler #27." There was another blond guy that signed my book, too, that day. I didn't really recognize him, but since other kids were getting him to sign things, I did as well. He turned out to be Wayne Gretzky. Later on, I pretended I had known that all along. I had Gretzky's autograph just before he really became Gretzky and broke every hockey record and married a blond Hollywood actress and started to do car ads.

I could rhyme off stats about hockey when I was a kid and had no shortage of enthusiasm. But playing hockey on ice didn't always produce the friendliest of memories for me. Much of that had to do with Jim Muffan. Muffan wasn't very nice. And in the change room for our Thornhill house league hockey team, Jim Muffan made no bones about identifying me as being different. On a few occasions he called me a Paki. I don't think he meant it in an affectionate way, either. Not like the way people may now call each other "homie." It wasn't exactly a celebratory experience for me. I was quite sure the whole team hated me. Muffan set the standard in the locker room. And it didn't help that I was a lousy hockey player.

By Grade 9, I had become one of the lousiest players in our Thornhill house league. I'm not being modest. I was truly lousy. I was certainly one of the least talented on my team. And I got worse as I got older. When I was eight, and I started playing hockey after arriving from England, I was in the middle of the pack as far as ability went. I wasn't bad. But as we got older and other guys got much bigger, the fact that I was an average skater became a liability. I had trouble evading body checks. As competitive as I was, in due time I was getting clobbered on the ice. I was the kid that got confined to the bench for the final three minutes of the game to prevent the other team from scoring. There was nothing more demeaning than knowing you were not getting called out on the ice because the coach thought you weren't good enough. Even my parents recognized how deficient I was, and they didn't totally understand the game. My mother once said, "I see they don't put you on the ice in the third period." That was a fact. My mother spoke in facts. Mind you, sports weren't all negative for me. My revenge would come with soccer in the summer. I was a big goal scorer and usually one of the fastest and best players on the team. But that was summer. In wintertime, playing hockey became an albatross. And a couple of kids made it about the colour of my skin. That was another way I understood I was different.

Jim Muffan was one of the bigger players on our team in 1981–1982, and he sometimes wore the coveted C on his chest. That meant he was captain. All the other kids wanted to be respected by Jim Muffan and laughed at his jokes in the locker room. Often they were dirty jokes. He was tall and had short brown hair and a grimace on his face most of the time when he wasn't telling jokes. He had muscles like a Grade 11 kid, even though he was only a Grade 9 kid. Muffan ruled the roost, and it was apparent early in the season that he'd decided he didn't like me. On one occasion on the ice, he looked at me after a stoppage in play and said, "You should go back where you fucking came from." That didn't seem the kind of thing you were supposed to say to a teammate. And I deduced that he probably didn't mean he wanted me to return to my house in Thornhill. Or London. Then, after another game where I was less than spectacular on the ice, Muffan looked directly at me across the locker room and said, making sure to speak loud enough for everyone to hear him, "Why are you even playing hockey, Paki? You're a stupid Paki."

I knew this had to do with how lousy I was. But it didn't help that I was an immigrant. And I wasn't just a Paki, but a stupid one, too. It never made sense that being less than a star at hockey made me stupid. I was a good deal smarter than Muffan in classes at Thornlea. But that didn't matter. If you looked different, you needed to at least know how to play well. There was another brown guy on the team, but no one called him racist names. His name was Randeep and he had much darker skin. But he was an excellent player who scored lots of goals. He was a team hero. So he was considered acceptable. But I was a Paki. I didn't ever bother explaining to Muffan that

Persians were not from Pakistan. I was ethnic, no matter what my mother said. By the winter of 1982, I had played my final season on the ice.

The truth is, as much as I adored hockey, I knew it wasn't my future to be a player anyhow. If I were going to star in any sport it would be soccer. I had always been a big fan of Arsenal from the English Premier League. And soccer leagues in Canada were full of immigrant kids, so I was a good player and one that didn't look out of place. But I was more artsy in general, and I had aspirations to be a rock singer. I wanted to be Bowie. Bowie didn't mess around with hockey sticks and pucks on ice. No one in New Wave did. And there weren't any Persian heroes playing hockey. And my dream girl, Wendy, didn't seem to care that much about athletes. And most important, unlike in hockey, in rock music there was one shining example of an ethnic counterpart I could aspire to: Freddie Mercury.

Freddie Mercury was the lead singer of Queen and he was a killer vocalist. He was one of the greatest rock singers of all time. He was also Iranian. Well, that's not true. He was Zoroastrian. But Zoroastrianism has its roots in Persia. And the technicalities didn't ultimately matter, because Iranians claimed Freddie Mercury as their own. Not very many others knew Freddie Mercury was Persian. Even now, most people couldn't tell you that. They might consider him British. Or European. Or exotic. But we always knew the truth. Iranian. And when I was nine, my cool older cousin Farid, who lived in America, had given me an eight-track tape of the double album *Live Killers*. It was the first proper album I owned. Farid looked intently into my eyes and delivered an important message upon handing over the eight-track: "You must become a fan of this music. This band is called Queen. The lead singer of this band is Freddie Mercury. He is the best. And he is Persian."

It was a moment of great pride. And Freddie Mercury would be a hero of mine thereafter.

As I hit my early teens, I began collecting Queen albums and trying to emulate Freddie Mercury. When I turned twelve, I had a birthday party at my house and put the first side of the new Queen album *The Game* on repeat on my turntable. Toke and Dana Verner and a few other kids attended the party. We pumped our fists to the catchy new song "Another One Bites the Dust." We had no idea that some Queen purists considered this a sellout "disco pop" turn for the band. We revelled in *The Game*. And Toke always approved of Freddie Mercury as well. "Dat guy Freddie ... ee's great!"

There were few musical things Queen did that I didn't love. But 1981 brought an event that would never find its parallel in music history. Not for me. In 1981, Freddie Mercury and Queen released a new song called "Under Pressure." And if new Queen material wasn't reason for excitement enough, the song was a duet with Bowie. My fantasy musical worlds collided. Bowie. And Queen. This could not have come closer to a personal paradise. It was as if the song were written and performed for me. Legend has it that Bowie had dropped into a Queen recording session in 1981 with the intention of singing backups on another song, and then they collectively wrote and recorded "Under Pressure." Many of the vocal parts were improvised, and the whole thing was done in one day. The results were remarkable. It was an avalanche of creative splendour all happening in one simple tune. There was Bowie and Freddie Mercury and amazing hooks and passion and an anthemic refrain. "Under

Pressure" became my theme in 1982. It lived on my turntable, but I carried it with me in my head everywhere.

"Under Pressure" has the distinction of being one of the few recordings in music history that no one hates. Trust me on this. It's too good. No one hates the song "Under Pressure." Think of the most famous song you can. Think of "She Loves You" by the Beatles or "I Will Always Love You" performed by Whitney Houston. Those songs have millions and millions of fans. But they have detractors, too. For every song, there is someone who for some reason hates that song. But no one hates "Under Pressure." It is gold. Ask anyone. They may not consider it their favourite. They may not love it the most. But no one hates "Under Pressure."

I have made a short list (or shortlist) of the six best moments of "Under Pressure" and the times at which they appear in the song:

1. 0.01—The top of the song features the iconic two-note bass line that may have been written by Bowie or by Queen bassist John Deacon. There is disagreement on who wrote it, but it's unforgettable, and it would later form the basis of a sample by rapper Vanilla Ice that would lead to another, less interesting and slightly ridiculous, hit called "Ice Ice Baby."

2. 0.57—This moment in the song is the first time Bowie sings his dramatic line about the terror of being aware of what the world is about in the pre-chorus. Few lyrics have been sung with such authority and power. This is Bowie playing Bowie.

3. 1.22—The beginning of the backup oohs that Bowie sings behind Freddie in the second verse. I imagine that Bowie winked at Freddie when he sang this part.

4. 1.30—Freddie's improvised musical "bee bap" nonsense words heading into the second chorus. Freddie is singing with abandon. It's so clear that this could not have been planned. It is one of the few moments in any modern rock song that features scatting.

5. 2.22—Freddie's melodramatic climbing note on the word "why?" with Bowie echoing "love!" in the background. More drama will not be found in most epic films.

6. 2.50–3.32 The final crescendo with Freddie singing "give love" and Bowie pleading into the microphone about this being the last dance. Gold.

"Under Pressure" was a one-off masterpiece. By the spring of 1982, it was number one in the UK and had climbed to number three in Canada. It was also my personal theme song. That's what I decided. To be fair, I didn't know at the time that others had personal theme songs. I thought I had discovered the idea. In fact, I didn't realize anyone else knew about personal theme songs until the emergence of Ally McBeal. You may remember there was a popular TV show in the late 1990s called *Ally McBeal*. It was the story of a quirky young lawyer and her adventures being very thin. Well, actually, the stories were about other things, but all everyone ever talked about was that she was very thin. So that was really pretty much what the show was about. But anyway, Ally McBeal had a theme song. A song she would have in her head that would get her through the day and shore up her self-confidence. For instance, one of her songs was "Hooked On a Feeling." That was an upbeat 1968 tune performed by B.J. Thomas. I had a theme song just like Ally McBeal, long before that show even existed. And I was also thin. But my theme song involved Bowie. And Queen. And being "Under Pressure."

It made sense that "Under Pressure" became my anthem. It was my theme because of the pressures I felt caused by my ethnicity. It featured my idol and a great singer who was Iranian. There was never an official video made for "Under Pressure" that included Bowie and Freddie Mercury. So I always just imagined myself in it. Freddie Mercury could also be androgynous and would sometimes dress in tight outfits and effeminate garb just like Bowie. Jim Muffan would have probably called Freddie Mercury names in the hockey locker room as well. But Freddie was handsome. He didn't have a particularly large nose. And he was a rock star. He was a role model.

Freddie Mercury seemed to know who he was. I didn't have that luxury. I was confused in Grade 9. I wanted to be New Wave, but I wasn't pale. I wanted to be accepted, but I was too different. I was told I was Aryan, but I was reminded I was brown. As I stood at the Police Picnic with my dream Bowie girl, I fought the inclination to believe I didn't deserve to be there. Wendy had supported me against Forbes the punk. She had agreed to come to the concert with me, and she was showing signs of believing we were a team. But now, after the Joan Jett debacle, I had lost the comfort that came with toting my Adidas bag. I was unsure how I would recover.

5

"Straight to Hell" – The Clash

The loss of my red-and-blue Adidas bag was traumatic. It certainly wasn't expected. And it was the speed of its disappearance from my life that made things all the more intense. Within seconds, the deed had been done. My Adidas bag was gone.

Let the record show that in August of 1982 a punk named Forbes threw my Adidas bag containing my new Walkman, my mix tapes, my portable headphones, my hair gel, and my jean jacket onto the Police Picnic stage. And let it further show that after Forbes pelted my Adidas bag at Joan Jett, I never saw it again. It was gone forever. In fact, I knew it was gone forever, because not too long after the incident, Wendy said, "It's gone forever." I wouldn't doubt Wendy.

The thing is, I never really blamed Forbes for the unsolicited appropriation of my bag. His actions were taken, I suppose, in the name of punk rock. He was an angst-ridden young man who needed an outlet for his rage. An outlet might involve beating up another kid or, in this case, throwing a bag. I would later learn that these actions were understood as "cathartic expression." I didn't really know it as that at the time. I just knew he was punk rock. And given that Forbes was not a fan of the creative pursuits of Joan Jett, his behaviour was further understandable as "artistic protest." So, I didn't blame him, even though it had been my most prized possession. That is, even though my Adidas bag and I had been inseparable since the end of Grade 8.

You might think I should've been angry at Forbes—that I might've taken some kind of recourse. You might think I was too soft or forgiving. I know you might think that. Jane Decker probably would have started a lawsuit against Forbes. And Toke would have had his older brother, Mitch, turn up and kick Forbes in the teeth. And maybe it would have been wise to be tougher in front of Wendy. But I was developing a sense of the cultural order of things. I really didn't know Forbes. And more importantly, he was a punk. He was a large punk. Actually, he was a large gorilla punk with a mohawk and combat boots. And he had prominent underarm hair. Basically, he was like … a real punk. And so, he was *supposed* to do things like steal a neurotic skinny kid's Adidas bag and angrily throw it at a hit-maker pop star. That was his gig, even if it wasn't very nice.

And surely I had given Forbes tacit permission to command my property by being foolish enough to stand next to him at a concert. I might as well have offered him the Adidas bag and given him my blessing. "Here you go, Forbes. Throw this!" Who did I think I was to expect any different? And what kind of punk would Forbes have been if he'd returned the bag to me and apologized? Forbes had to live up to his billing. I wondered if I'd be more popular if I were more like Forbes. I wondered if I could ever be a real punk. I knew I'd probably never be a real punk if I was scared of real punks. And I was. This was a dilemma.

Forbes looked like a member of the Clash. Well, no. Wait. Forbes looked like an ugly member of the Clash. Or maybe he looked nothing like a member of the Clash. But he brought them to mind. And the guys in the Clash didn't exactly have the matinee-idol features of Harrison Ford or Mark Hamill. Or Sting. Sting had a perfect nose and straight blond hair. And Sting had a high voice that could be pious and angelic. Sting had been a schoolteacher. In one of the Police videos, Sting appeared dressed as a schoolteacher. This was to remind us all that he had been a schoolteacher.

The Clash didn't sing or look that way. The Clash borrowed heavily from classic outlaw imagery to position themselves as rebels. I didn't know much about the Clash, but I knew that being in the presence of Forbes reminded me of the first time I'd seen them on *The NewMusic* on Citytv. They were wearing military garb and they looked angry. My mother had been in the room when the Clash appeared on *The NewMusic*. My mother had made a loud *tsk* sound and said *"Vah-ee"* in my direction. In this case, that was shorthand for: "Attention: This is your mother speaking. These shaved-headed political punk gentlemen don't seem very benevolent. You should not be modelling yourself after them. Please stay away from these types and don't get any ideas. Oh, yes, and another thing ... why can't you look more like Mark Hamill?"

See? My mother could say all that with *"Vah-ee."* Okay. I just threw in the part about Mark Hamill. But she was probably thinking it. My mother was quite efficient with her communication sometimes.

The Clash were a punk rock band from the UK, and they were very important. In many ways, they were the definitive British punk rockers, righteous and uncompromising about their left-wing ideology. Their fiery and idealistic outlook was in contrast to the nihilism of the Sex Pistols. And the Clash were more musically adventurous than most punk outfits that preceded them, mixing elements of funk, reggae, and rockabilly into their punk rock sound. But mostly, by the beginning of Grade 9, I knew the Clash were important because lots of mods and New Wavers had begun wearing Clash T-shirts, sometimes featuring cut-off sleeves. Clash T-shirts were popular among the theatre students hanging out near Room 213 as well. And there were Clash T-shirts being worn by punks at the mall. New Wavers appreciated the Clash, and many hard rockers begrudgingly admired them. Punks worshipped them, and almost everyone else who mattered understood that they were symbols of musical ferocity fused with integrity.

Wearing a Clash T-shirt was cool. So it followed that if you wanted to be cool, you wore a Clash T-shirt. In fact, wearing a Clash T-shirt was so cool that on some occasions members of the Clash wore Clash T-shirts so they would be cool, too. I had seen their lead singer, Joe Strummer, wearing a Clash T-shirt on *The NewMusic*. I later learned that the expression for this occurrence is "meta." You see, you might catch the Clash wearing Clash T-shirts on TV or onstage or in a photo, and it was unclear if they were cool because they were the Clash or because they were wearing Clash T-shirts. But Clash T-shirts also looked cool when the Clash were sporting them because … they were the Clash. I think this is what they mean by meta. It might be another word for "confusing." But the point is, that's just how cool the Clash were.

Here is a short list of some Clash T-shirt designs that were available for purchase in 1982:

- *London Calling* album cover T-shirt
- "Revolution Rock" T-shirt (white images on black)
- "Straight to Hell" T-shirt (featuring freaked-out monkey icon)
- white star with circle featuring "The Clash" T-shirt
- *The Clash* debut album T-shirt (various colours)
- "Clash City Rockers" T-shirt (yellow, red, and white on black)
- *Sandinista!* T-shirt (black and red)

As you can see from this short list, there were many sartorial options for Clash gear—options exercised by members of the Clash as well. This practice of wearing one's own T-shirts was quite anomalous. It was very punk. Who else could get away with such shameless self-promotion? Maybe the Clash were being ironic or cheeky, but they seemed too angry and political for that. Most artists look ridiculous or opportunistic if they're donning their own merchandise. Not the Clash.

Let this be another lesson in cool: If you are considered groundbreaking and hip and on the leading edge in contemporary pop culture, you can get away with things that others cannot. In fact, these things may become a trend. But you will stop getting away with them when you are no longer cool. And everything becomes uncool eventually. That is, unless you experience a premature end or a tragic death. Endings and death help maintain cool. In 1983, the Clash broke up acrimoniously after just six years (even if there was a new lineup that soldiered on until 1986). Basically, the band came to a premature end. They never became uncool.

If the Clash wore their own T-shirts with aplomb, very few others could. Can you imagine the guys in REO Speedwagon wearing REO Speedwagon jerseys while they sang their corporate hit ballads? No. You can't, because they wouldn't. They wouldn't, because wearing an REO Speedwagon T-shirt as a member of REO Speedwagon would be even less cool than actually playing in REO Speedwagon. They had a special REO logo that looked like an airplane brand, but they still wouldn't have worn their own T-shirts. The individual guys in REO Speedwagon were probably cooler than their band.

The same is true of Gowan. If emerging 1980s Canadian New Wave-ish singer Gowan had worn a Gowan T-shirt onstage, it would have been considered desperate, or at least goofy. Gowan was a pop-rocker who was born in Glasgow, Scotland, but had grown up in Scarborough, Ontario, and was tapped in the early '80s as a new Canadian star. His full name was Lawrence Gowan, but he just went by Gowan. Later, he would put out an album entitled ... *but you can call me Larry*. So, later, he wanted to be called Larry. But in 1982, he just wanted to be called Gowan. I'm not sure why. Maybe it was catchier. I once told my father about Gowan, and he repeated Gowan's name back to me as if I were making up words.

"Gow-van. I do not understand thees name. Why he has thees name?" My father grew tired of such things sometimes.

Gowan released his debut album in 1982, and by the mid-'80s he would score a couple of hit songs, including "A Criminal Mind" and "(You're a) Strange Animal." He was a very fine musician, but New Wave tastemakers were not at all convinced of Gowan's merits. And Gowan had an odd habit of doing karate kicks in the middle of performing his songs. I wasn't sure why he did these kicks and chops. Presumably, Gowan had mastered karate in his youth and had thereafter decided to make the martial arts a part of his rock show. Use what you've got, they say. But his propensity for the kicks was a bit uncool. Add to this his overblown pop anthems, and the tastemakers were really on the fence when it came to Gowan. The punk and New Wave elite of 213 were not wearing Gowan T-shirts. And so, if Gowan had worn a Gowan T-shirt, it probably would not have been a very successful career move. Gowan would later go on to be the singer of the re-formed '70s band Styx. Now, he is Larry Gowan. He is very nice and talented. But it would still be strange if Larry Gowan wore a Gowan T-shirt onstage. And it would make even less sense now that he is singing with Styx.

In contrast to REO Speedwagon and Gowan, the Clash could get away with overt self-promotion because they had musical and aesthetic credibility. And they were tough. And then they came to a premature end. During our subway ride heading towards the Police Picnic, Wendy had told me she really wanted to see the Clash play live. That was one of her ambitions. I decided at that moment that I needed to get a Clash T-shirt with cut-off sleeves. I also decided that I might need to start doing push-ups so my arms would look less skinny. These Clash outfits came with significant collateral implications.

The Clash had released their third album in 1979, an iconic rock record called *London Calling*. *Rolling Stone* magazine would later declare it the best album of the 1980s, even though it came out in 1979. That is how good the record was. In the early '80s, the Clash had gained an international cult following for their raw punk sound, defiant lyrics, and undeniable melodies. By the end of Grade 9, I had become a true fan. Unfortunately, my big fandom was a bit late for the cool crowd. I caught on to the Clash in the spring of 1982, when they released *Combat Rock*. It was an album that sold very well, but many purists considered it lame and sellout pop by Clash standards—especially because it garnered hit singles like "Rock the Casbah" and "Should I Stay or Should I Go." Hit singles were not cool. But I was captivated by the sounds on *Combat Rock*, and I eventually worked backwards through their previous albums until the Clash became one of my favourite bands ever. Still, at the time of the Police Picnic, I didn't know the music of the Clash very well. I had been too young when *London Calling* came out, and I had been busy attending concerts by performers like The Dan Hill with my parents.

For the most part, in 1982 I reacted to the Clash the way I reacted to most things punk when I was in my early teens: with a mixture of admiration and terror. I had a deep desire to meet the Clash, if I ever had the opportunity, but I imagined they might punch me in the head if we ever met. They would likely realize I was a comfortable suburban kid with the wrong hair and a lack of knowledge about class warfare in England. They might find out I knew the lyrics to Andy Gibb songs about love being higher than mountains and thicker than water. They might also discover that I did fairly well in school and liked my parents and didn't smoke cigarettes, even though I sometimes tried to smell like cigarettes. It was clear I had it all wrong. The Clash would probably hate me in Grade 9.

Still, I wondered if the heroic leader of the Clash, Joe Strummer, would have actually thrown my Adidas bag at Joan Jett. Probably. He was a punk. But maybe he would've shown mercy towards me. He had integrity and seemed smarter than Forbes. Maybe he would have pitied me because I was an immigrant and immigrants had it tough. Maybe he would have had an intuitive sense that three decades later "Spanish Bombs" would become the fourth most-played song ever on my iPod. It is impossible to know what Mr. Strummer would have done. But surely, for some other punks, it is a given that my Adidas bag would be fair projectile fodder in taking a stand against corporate rock. Jello Biafra, of the San Francisco punk band the Dead Kennedys, would probably have thrown my Adidas bag at Joan Jett. Mind you, he would also go on to become a prominent member of the Green Party of the United States. So it's hard to imagine that he would throw the bag at Joan Jett later in his life. That doesn't seem like something a member of the Green Party does. As you can see, there are many issues and nuances when it comes to judging who might throw my Adidas bag on the day of the Police Picnic.

I have made a short list of well-known punks who likely would have thrown my Adidas bag at Joan Jett in 1982:

- Johnny Rotten
- Joe Strummer (maybe)
- Joey Ramone
- Jello Biafra (pre–Green Party membership)
- other members of the Sex Pistols
- Forbes

One thing I was sure of: Bowie would not have pelted my prized possession. Can you imagine Bowie throwing a kid's carrying sack? No. You can't. Bowie would not have thrown my Adidas bag, because Bowie would have had more important things on his mind, like writing lyrics that are difficult to deconstruct, or the perfection of a synth sound, or trendsetting ways to hold his cigarette. And you see, the wondrous magic of Bowie was that while he was more elegant than the Adidas-throwing punks, he still had their respect and admiration. All of these things were possible in one person. The goal was, as ever, to be Bowie.

After the initial shock of my loss, I've often contemplated what happened to my red-and-blue Adidas bag. You probably think it was disposed of in the garbage. That's likely what you've decided. But sometimes I imagine other possibilities. I imagine that Joan Jett spotted my stray Adidas bag and decided to keep it. Maybe it would be her consolation for getting booed by the New Wavers at the Police Picnic. The more I think about it, the more I believe she did keep it. That Joan Jett. She probably ripped the name tag off it and adopted it. Maybe she still has it. Maybe she uses it to store old VHS copies of her videos, like the one for "I Love Rock 'n Roll," which was a number-one hit in 1981 and got her booed at the Police Picnic. Maybe she has it labelled the way I used to have it labelled, but now with her own words: "JOAN JETT'S BAG OF VIDEOS."

Or maybe she takes it to the gym and stores her workout clothing in it. And maybe now, when Joan Jett takes it to the gym, she gets compliments for having that shiny fake-leather bag:

Random gym member #1: "Hey, Joan Jett, nice bag!"

Joan Jett: "Thanks!"

Random gym member #2: "Hey, wow, where did you get that vintage fake-leather bag, Joan Jett?"

Joan Jett: "Oh ... I got it back in '82."

Random gym member #2: "Sweet. I've always known you were the coolest. Especially because of your red-and-blue Adidas bag, Joan Jett!"

You will note that people call Joan Jett by her full name. Both words. I'm quite sure that's because it seems wrong to call Joan Jett anything other than Joan Jett. "Joan" cannot sufficiently communicate her rock star value. And "Jett" alone is just weird. Her name is like Boy George. You have to use both parts. And now Joan Jett has cool cred because of the Adidas bag that she earned by getting angrily received by a Toronto crowd that included Forbes the punk. And she has me to thank.

Of course, all of this is speculation that has occupied my mind in the years after that day at the Police Picnic with Wendy in 1982. I didn't think of these things at the time. At the moment that my Adidas bag was thrown at Joan Jett, events occurred in slow motion the way they do in the movies when someone is taking a big fall or getting shot. As my bag sailed through the air, I looked at Wendy and then at the bag, and I experienced a zillion flashback thoughts which will be played in soft focus in the movie version of this story. Most significantly, I came upon an image of my friend Toke. He and I had gotten our Adidas bags around the same time in the summer before Grade 9. The loss of my bag was like a final chapter in my relationship with Toke. In the hours after the Adidas bag incident, I would have a tremendous revelation and a coming of age with Wendy. But long before my infatuation with Wendy, my comrade-in-arms had been Toke. Toke was nothing like Bowie. But I secretly wondered if Wendy could ever really replace him.

6

"DIRTY DEEDS DONE DIRT CHEAP"
- AC/DC

The tennis ball came flying at Toke's face off the stick of Rick Bolton, who was shooting from the middle of his driveway. Toke was taking his turn in net just in front of Rick's garage door. It was a slapshot from little more than a car length away. Rick was far too good a hockey player for this to be anything other than precisely aimed. He was four years older than us, and he had a mean streak when it came to playing with kids on the road.

It was the fall of 1982, and it was late afternoon on a cold day. Tennis balls absorb the cold in Canada. They get hard. This was less of a friendly green Dunlop and more of a missile. Toke never really stood a chance. He was a little chubby and slow to move as it was. And on this day he was bundled up in his regular green duffle coat with his hood on over a Habs toque. His clothing usually looked a size too small on him. It was probably restricting his movement.

The impact of the shot was inevitable. And when it hit, it hit hard. Road hockey had always been one of the meeting points for Toke and me. This is the last time we would play together. We had been drifting apart anyway as a result of us heading to different high schools and pursuing new interests. We shared an unspoken bond that couldn't be extinguished when Mitch came to seek justice in Toke's name. But it did feel like the end of an era.

BETWEEN GRADE 5 and Grade 9, Ron Toker was my best friend. That was his name, but this is the first and last time I will refer to him that way. From the moment I first met him at the age of ten, I called him Toke. It was a term of neither disrespect nor endearment. And it didn't have anything to do with drugs. Many people would make that mistake later on. But that reference was beyond me in Grade 5. It was simply his name. Toke. Most people ended up calling him Toke in junior high. I'm convinced I started it.

Toke was a bit of an oddball. Well, most kids are oddballs in one way or another. But Toke was unique. He had brown curly hair that morphed into something of an Afro when it grew long. Toke spoke with a very precise and slow rhythm. And he was generally prone to periods of silence followed by grand and polemical statements like, "The players on the Boston Bruins are all WEASELS!" Toke gravitated towards competitive wrestling in high school, and he would later become a body builder. But that was years after he had been my best friend. In 1982, Toke was still my accomplice.

Toke and I spent a lot of time together. He was the same age as me. We both went to Henderson Avenue Public School after my family moved to Thornhill in Grade 4, and then we went to the same junior high. We played road hockey, we watched TV, we made regular trips to the Golden Star burger joint at the top of Doncaster Avenue, and as we hit our early teens, we increasingly kept each other apprised of events happening around the world. Toke was a source for me. On some occasions, Toke was such a good source that I'd pretend to others that I'd witnessed things based on his detailed accounts—like when Toke went to see Ozzy. The only problem was that I probably didn't smell enough like smoke for people to believe I'd gone to the concert. That was often the problem. But in the early 1980s, you needed human sources to know what was going on. As a kid, these sources often took the form of other kids.

The '80s may not seem like that long ago to some of you, but they were prehistoric if you're counting in technology years. As I've explained, in 1982 there was no internet, or Facebook, or texting, or even email. You would have to actually receive breaking news verbally from your friends if you hadn't caught the story on TV or radio. And even on TV or radio, you'd have to catch the news at the appointed time. There were no PVRs or PDAs or any of the fancy gizmos with three letters. And if *you* were the source, you would have to track down your friends to personally communicate news of big things that had occurred. Years later, we would refer to the popular points of discussion on Twitter as items that were "trending." But in 1982 we called it "talking with your friends." This was only done in person or sometimes on the telephone.

It was a Tuesday morning in the middle of Grade 7 when I found out on 1050 CHUM that John Lennon had been killed the previous night in New York City. The man on the radio who made the announcement was very sombre, and between his announcements they were playing John Lennon music continuously. Within a heartbeat of finding out, I rushed to call Toke to see if he'd heard. It was at least an hour before we were to go to school, and that he'd want to hear this info right away. I was his source. I anticipated that he'd be surprised to hear my voice at this hour and that he'd know something was up. His older brother, Mitch, answered the phone when I called.

"Hello?" It was early. That's probably why he sounded a bit angry. But then, Mitchell Toker was always a bit angry, because he was tough. He wore a brown, tight-fitting leather jacket. And tough guys were not supposed to be too friendly.

"Oh … hi, Mitch. It's Jian. Is Toke there? I mean … is your brother there? I mean … Ron?"

Mitch dropped the phone. I could hear him shouting Toke's name. He sounded annoyed that he had to summon his brother on my behalf. Mitch was not very friendly sometimes. Perhaps he was wearing his leather jacket.

Toke picked up the line. "Hallo?"

"Toke! John Lennon got shot! Did you hear? John Lennon got killed by a guy!"

I shouted this into our rotary phone at the top of the stairs in the main hallway of our house. The receiver was army green and had a curly green phone cord attached to a green phone box. I'm not sure why my parents had decided to get a green-coloured phone. I breathlessly delivered the news about John Lennon before Toke could say anything.

Toke was silent. Sometimes he would pause before reacting to things. But maybe he hadn't heard me properly.

I raised my voice even louder to let Toke know this was important. "A guy killed John Lennon! Did you hear me?

Toke! John Lennon, who used to be in the Beatles!" Now I was really out of breath.

I could hear Toke processing the information on the other end of the line. Finally, he spoke. His words came out quite softly.

"Wow. Dat John Lennon. Ee's great," Toke said.

Oh, yeah, I should explain another thing. Toke would never say the *h* in "he's." It wasn't really that he had an accent, because Toke would comfortably use the *h* when saying other words, like "health" or "happy" or "heap." But not with "he's." It was just something Toke did. Toke would also say "dat" instead of "that" and "hallo" instead of "hello." Again, these were Toke-isms that had little consistency with the rest of his speech patterns. Toke was unique this way. And when Toke didn't like a guy, he would call him a "weasel." It was just like the name he had given all the players on the Boston Bruins hockey team. Toke was a Montreal Canadiens fan and had a toque with the Habs logo on it.

Often, when Toke was in the process of calling a guy a weasel, especially if he was agitated, all of his verbal idiosyncrasies would conspire together in one sentence: "Dat guy ... I don't like dat guy ... ee's a weasel!" This was one of the things that made Toke lovable and strange. But it also made him the target of some less-than-kind impressions. When other kids in our circle imitated Toke, they would simply say, "Dat guy ... ee's a weasel."

Toke had said "ee's great" about John Lennon as if John Lennon was not dead. But he was dead. And it was big news. Neither of us truly knew the cultural implications of John Lennon's murder in 1980, but we had a sense that this was essential information we needed to share, because adults were taking it very seriously. We knew how epic the Beatles had been, and I had seen a Beatles movie on TV way back when my family lived in England. Besides, I already had two Paul McCartney and Wings albums on vinyl, including *Wings Greatest*. I also had *Back to the Egg* on eight-track. Eggs were cool in the '70s and early '80s. And I had a Paul McCartney poster in my room that I had gotten with the greatest hits album.

As you might conclude from the contents of my fledgling record collection and the poster, I was more of a Paul guy as a kid. That is, in the inevitable question of "Who's your favourite Beatle?"—a question that was still being asked in the '80s—I would side with Paul. I remember wishing I could look like Paul McCartney when I saw him singing "With a Little Luck" on TV. But this predilection for Paul would not endure. By the end of high school—and forever after—John Lennon had emerged as my favourite Beatle. It was all about his facility for songwriting, his gorgeous, yearning melodies, and his darker-themed lyrics. Besides, cool girls would more likely be fond of guys who were into John Lennon, even though they secretly preferred George Harrison, because he was "the quiet one." I would later go back and discover all of John Lennon's solo records from the 1970s. They would occupy a special place in my collection. Not that I didn't love Paul. I still love Paul. But now he's number two in my Beatle affections. Here is a short list of my favourite Beatles, in descending order, when John died, followed by a short list of my favourite Beatles now:

1980

1. Paul McCartney
2. John Lennon
3. George Harrison
4. Ringo Starr

Now

1. John Lennon
2. Paul McCartney
3. George Harrison
4. Ringo Starr

As you can see, John and Paul are on top and George Harrison comes in at number three on both of these lists. This might suggest that I was not a big fan of George Harrison, since he seems to be scoring very low. But that's only because John and Paul were members of the Beatles as well, and they were musical geniuses. George Harrison was also brilliant, and his 1970 triple album, *All Things Must Pass*, is a masterpiece. He just wasn't better than John and Paul. So, if we included, say, John Oates from Hall & Oates and Andrew Ridgeley (the other guy from Wham!) on the same list with the Beatles, George Harrison would appear much higher. I'll show you. Look at the list now:

1. John Lennon
2. Paul McCartney
3. George Harrison
4. John Oates
5. Ringo Starr
6. Andrew Ridgeley (the other guy from Wham!)

See? George is now in the top three out of six. Of course, if Bowie were on this list, he would always appear at number one. As iconic as they were, the Beatles didn't stand a chance with Bowie. But I will admit that my Bowie mania may have led to some casualties of information in the early '80s, too. One of my favourite Bowie songs had been "Across the Universe," a recording that appears on *Young Americans*, released in 1975. I later learned that this was a John Lennon composition and a famous Beatles song. Even Bowie sometimes took cues from the Fab Four. Mind you, no one has really ever covered the Beatles better than Bowie. And he drew a significant and clear dividing line between the '60s and the '70s when he wrote in "All the Young Dudes" about his brother back at home still listening to the Beatles and the Stones.

The implications of the loss of John Lennon were evident to me everywhere. Later that morning, my music teacher at Woodland Junior High, Mr. Richards, started to cry in the middle of band class. It was obvious he was very sad about John Lennon. I had assumed my position behind the drums for band rehearsal, but Mr. Richards called off the practice and made us all take seats in a circle. He asked that we remain quiet while he played "The Long and Winding Road" on a large tape deck.

Mr. Richards was our music teacher in Grades 7 and 8. He was probably in his mid-thirties at the time, and he had sandy-blond hair, a beard, and a growing belly. He wore dark checkered shirts with dark checkered ties and dark corduroy slacks. This relatively dim sartorial streak had the effect of emphasizing how white Mr. Richards's skin was. Mr. Richards was very white. Like, I mean, even more white than normal white people. One time, the teachers agreed to play students in a basketball game in Grade 8, and Mr. Richards was playing on the teachers' side. That day he was wearing a dark T-shirt and a pair of purple shorts. It was the only time I would ever see his naked arms and his legs. They were very white—like, powdery white. I always wondered why Mr. Richards was so white. But now, on this sad day, his face was the whitest I'd ever seen it. He was very upset at the news of John Lennon's death.

At Mr. Richards's request, the AV lady, Mrs. Ellis, had brought in a hi-fi stereo on a trolley with a large tape deck. Mr. Richards dabbed tears from his eyes while "The Long and Winding Road" played on. His eyes had become very red, even though his face was so white. I remember exchanging glances with Murray, who played saxophone in music class and would later be my bandmate in the Wingnuts and then Urban Transit. Murray and I nodded at each other respectfully and lowered our heads, because we were upset about Lennon. Well, actually, we lowered our heads because Mr. Richards was upset. But we knew we ought to be as well. And the music was very moving.

Mr. Richards continued to cry, and then he rewound the tape and played "The Long and Winding Road" a second time in its entirety. This was clearly bringing back a lot of memories for him. I concluded that, if Mr. Richards had selected it, this song must also have been a very personal composition for John Lennon. I was well into my mid-twenties before I learned that John Lennon was not the writer of "The Long and Winding Road" at all. I'd fought others on this point for years, in the days before Google settled all debates, because I assumed John had written the song Mr. Richards played the day after he died. I was wrong. It was a McCartney song. I'm still not sure why Mr. Richards would play a McCartney song and cry about John. But the sentiment was very real. On the way home from school, I told Toke that Mr. Richards had been crying and that he played the John Lennon song "The Long and Winding Road." Toke pointed in the air and said, "Wow! Dat John Lennon. Ee was great!" I nodded. Sometimes Toke had a fine way of summarizing things.

Toke and I never actually declared that we were best friends. I'm not sure boys ever really do that. It just seemed too intimate and awkward for guys to look each other in the eye and declare best friendship. In contrast, girls often had a list of their best friends and the rankings they occupied. Robin Goldman was able to rhyme off the name of her best friend in Grade 6, and then her second-best friend, and then third, and so on. But with Toke, it was more organic. He and I just ended up together a lot.

Toke was a Sephardic Jewish kid who lived in a townhouse three streets away from me in Thornhill. He regularly wore brown corduroy pants and had a big, green, hooded coat. Toke was a bit chubby at the time, and I was a bit skinny. He had an Afro, and my hair was straighter. I was a non-practising Muslim, and he was a semi-observant Jew. We had all the makings of an odd couple, and we somehow complemented each other that way. Toke lived relatively modestly with his mother and his older brother, Mitch. In terms of social class, while my family was a little better off than his, Toke seemed fairly equal to me when compared to some of my other peers. And we both had brownish skin.

My previous best friend, Davey Franklin, was a champion young hockey player and an enthusiastic guy. He lived down the street from us in Thornhill. But his family and their house always reminded me of the things my family didn't have. Davey had a swimming pool. And his family had three cars. And he was the first kid on the block to have a giant TV screen. Davey invited me to watch the final of the 1979 Challenge Cup hockey series on his giant screen. In truth, the colours were not very good and the rear projection had lots of shadows. Besides, the Soviet national team defeated the NHL all-stars 6-0 that day. But still, I had not seen a screen that big in anyone's house before. It was very evident that Davey Franklin had things I did not. My family had a console TV in a fake-wood cabinet. It worked well, but it wasn't very big. Not like Davey's screen. I was becoming very aware of these differences. And most important, Davey and his family had Dixie cups. You could always tell the well-to-do families because they had disposable Dixie cups.

Dixie cups were small paper cups that came in a dispenser that you would secure on your bathroom wall. Prosperous suburban families in Canada always had Dixie cups in the 1970s. The concept was impressive: Each time you wanted to drink a bit of water in the bathroom or rinse your mouth, you would take a paper Dixie cup from the dispenser and then happily throw the cup away after its use. It was all very carefree. There was no sense in reusing a Dixie cup, since there were dozens more in the dispenser. And Dixie cups came with fancy pink-and-orange drawings on them sometimes.

You may think this is a dramatic example of over-consumption. You may think this is more evidence of the bizarre premium that was put on material excess in the early '80s. But Dixie cups were all the rage for those who could afford them. Even though they masqueraded as a "practical" idea, however, they were really stupid for the environment and didn't make much sense at all except as a measure of decadence. But most people didn't think about those things at the time. And none of this would stop me from wanting them when I was eleven years old.

My family didn't have Dixie cups. My family simply kept one plastic cup next to each sink that we would reuse each time we wanted water. Either that or we would just cup our right hand to scoop water to our mouths. This was old school. I would later learn that it was more environmentally friendly than throwing away paper cups, but that's certainly not the reason we didn't have them.

My father saw Dixie cups as a needless expense. Beyond an economic status that put us out of competition with the Franklins, both of my parents were always admirably frugal. I see this quality as sage and beneficial in retrospect. But frugality was a great disadvantage to a kid trying to fit in. For instance, between his bouts of mowing the lawn, That Chris from across the street would enjoy single servings of Laura Secord chocolate pudding for lunch each day. My sister and I never had that. My parents saw Laura Secord pudding in all those little containers as another needless expense. We never got the pudding. But nothing was as shameful as the dearth of Dixie cups.

I had been quite worried about the inevitable moment when Davey Franklin became aware of the lack of Dixie cups if he visited our house. And of course, to my great embarrassment, one afternoon he not only noticed our Dixie cup deficiency, but he pointed it out when he came out of our upstairs bathroom by asking why he couldn't find them. I had dreaded the question, and I tried to improvise a response. I told him we'd temporarily run out. He must've known it was a lie, because there wasn't even a dispenser.

I confronted my father about our notable lack of Dixie cups in the middle of Grade 5.

"Dad, we need to get a Dixie cup dispenser!"

"What is thees?"

"Dixie cups. We need to get Dixie cups like Davey Franklin's family! They have Dixie cups. Why don't we?"

"Why we should want thees Dixie cup?" my father had calmly replied.

"They're paper cups that you use in the bathroom and then throw out so you always have a clean one! Dad! How are we supposed to drink water in the bathroom?" I said this with some exhaustion. It was obvious that *everyone* needed Dixie cups.

"We have cup in the toilet room. You wash the cup and then use thees cup. Why you need all thees paper Dixie cup?"

My father was answering my questions with questions again. He clearly didn't understand. In these moments, I let myself imagine that my backward father was too rooted in the old country. Then I could make sense of things in my eleven-year-old mind. Of course they didn't have Dixie cups when they were wandering around on camels in Iran. I did this often. If I was angry at my father, I would jettison my knowledge of Iranians as a modern people and retreat to heinous stereotypes to explain his intransigence. Okay, so maybe these were the same stereotypes I would later deplore.

Not surprisingly, my mother felt the need to chime in about the Dixie cups.

"Honey, you don't need the Dixie cups. You know, Umar keeps his family's bathroom spic and span, and the Jans don't have these cups either."

The Jans were a family we became close to when we first moved to Canada. Umar was roughly my age, and he had been my first friend when we settled in Don Mills. His father was Pakistani and his mother was German. I would call them Uncle Munir and Auntie Karen, the way you call family friends who become very close. They were all very nice and dear allies. But Umar was tediously perfect in the eyes of my mother. Just like That Chris. Even when my mother was making a fair and reasonable point, she had to throw in a comparison to another kid who was doing something better.

If Davey Franklin had lots of fancy things that made me feel bad, the Franklins were also of Anglo background and were quite traditional in some ways. They were, to put it bluntly, white. Not as white as Mr. Richards, but they were Caucasian. In contrast to Davey Franklin and his parents, Toke and his family were more like us. Toke was also a relatively new immigrant and a Moroccan Jew. And when I met Toke, I found someone who didn't make me feel bad about not having a pool and a giant TV screen and Dixie cups. Toke didn't have Dixie cups either. But Toke was much more clear-headed about such things, or at least less neurotic. I once asked him whether he wished he had Dixie cups. Toke responded, "Dixie cups? Of course not." I liked my new friend.

Toke's older brother, Mitch, was a keen follower of rock music like AC/DC and Ozzy. In contrast to Toke's more cherubic features, Mitchell Toker looked like John Travolta with shorter hair like he had in *Saturday Night Fever*. Mitch clearly made regular trips to the gym. Mitch had a brown leather jacket, but he would often walk around the Toker family's townhouse topless. He would do this to show off his muscles while he blasted rock music. Early in 1982, Ozzy Osbourne had infamously bitten the head off a real bat onstage. Mitch recounted this story to us with demonic zeal, his arms waving in the air and his fists flying. I felt a bit afraid when Mitch got like this. I would never say anything to Toke or anyone else about my fear, but it was there. It might seem strange to be afraid of your best friend's brother, but Mitch could be an intimidating presence.

Mitch Toker carried a knife and had a reputation for being "wild." I had secretly hoped that Mitch would hook up with my older sister, Jila, when I was in Grade 7. That way, he would have to like me so my sister wouldn't break up with him. I tried to get them together on at least three occasions. But one day, when Jila came to meet me at Toke's house on our way to the mall, Mitch made the wrong move. Seems that as Jila was waiting outside, Mitch called down to her while hanging out of one of the upper windows with no clothing on. Jila did not witness his whole naked body, but she could certainly see his bare chest.

"Hey, Jila! What's up?"

My sister had dutifully replied, "Hi, Mitch. Just getting my brother." Then my sister looked away and started smoking a cigarette.

Jila told me about all of this later. She explained that she had not been impressed with Mitch's insistence upon "dangling

121

from the window and displaying his naked torso." She said the "naked torso" part with enough sarcasm that I could tell she was not seduced by such a sight. Jila was really good at sarcasm. Things didn't look too positive after that for a Mitch and Jila romance.

Still, whether wearing nothing on his torso or sporting his brown leather jacket, Toke's older brother became an important influence on us in learning about rock music and life. Toke was a regular source of information for me, but Mitch was the ultimate source. Mitch always had CHUM FM on in the house. Unlike 1050 CHUM, which just played the pop hits, CHUM FM had emerged as the more mature and cutting-edge progressive rock station in the late '70s. By 1982, I would discover CFNY, the New Wave and new music station. But until then, CHUM FM was a training ground.

Mitch particularly liked his hard rock. Because of Mitch, Toke knew lots of AC/DC lyrics. AC/DC were the massively successful Australian rock band that featured anthemic songs, loud power chords, screaming vocals, and a diminutive energizer-bunny guitarist dressed as a schoolboy. Of course, you already know AC/DC. Explaining who AC/DC were is like explaining what bread is. They became one of the biggest-selling bands of all time. AC/DC were the declared favourite of older rock guys in the late '70s, along with bands like Zeppelin and the Who. Toke would often slowly repeat AC/DC lyrics as if he were dictating to a child. Toke didn't sing. And Toke was already turning into a bit of a tough guy like his brother. Only sissies really sang. The fact that I sang would become a dividing line between us eventually, but for the most part in the early '80s I didn't sing very much in front of Toke, and definitely not in the presence of Mitch. Mitch had told Toke to always be proud and never let people tease him. Toke puffed out his chest when he walked and carried his Afro-laden head high. I think Mitch had taught him to do that, too.

Toke didn't have lots of friends beyond me, but early on he had gained some notoriety in being a renegade who would do crazy things. Toke would do these things in exchange for money. We had a group of kids who hung out on my street, including Pete Hickey, Randy Jones, Little Charles, and Toke. Back in 1978, the summer before Grade 6, Toke had declared that he would swallow anything if we collectively gave him fifty cents. His first challenge was to eat a raw egg. At the appointed time, we gathered in front of my house and watched while Toke broke a raw egg into a mug and then purpose-fully put the mug up to his mouth and quickly swallowed the contents. We gave Toke his fifty cents and he went home with his chest puffed out. The rest of us discussed how Toke was a real crazy daredevil.

The following week, Toke ate a pink pencil eraser for fifty cents. It was important for Toke to up the ante each time. Soon, word got out that if we could put together one dollar, doubling the purse, Toke was going to eat a "live guppy." Now, when I say "word got out," I mean Toke announced this with his right index finger in the air to anyone who would listen. "Hallo, everyone. I'm going to eat a live guppy. Dat's what I'm going to do. I will eat a live guppy on Wednesday afternoon for a dollar!"

I wasn't sure about the supposed importance of Toke's guppy victim being "live." It seemed like less of a shocking trick than swallowing a dead guppy. But I suppose Toke meant that the guppy would be uncooked and still squirming and therefore less than savoury. As rumours spread of Toke's intention to eat a live guppy, a group of kids once again gathered on the street in front of my house on the appointed Wednesday afternoon. Pete Hickey and Randy Jones were there, as well as me, Toke, and Davey Franklin. Toke showed up with some fanfare and a sandwich bag containing water and a guppy swimming in it. He made sure to collect his dollar first. We all pulled coins out of our pockets until it added up to the dollar we'd promised. Then Toke dramatically picked the guppy out of the bag, held it high over his head, and dropped it into his mouth and swallowed. Toke made a big production of swallowing the guppy. He made sure to make a loud *gulp* sound for our benefit. He then opened his mouth wide as evidence that the "live guppy" was well into his body. After he made it clear that he'd really swallowed the live guppy, Toke tried to make himself throw up. But he didn't. Still, there was no doubt Toke put some thought into these performances.

Here is a short list of items Toke swallowed for money in the summer before Grade 6:

- raw egg
- pink pencil eraser
- small bag of dirt
- sheet of paper
- live guppy

After each feat of public swallowing, Toke would put his right finger in the air and sing-speak the lyrics to the AC/DC song "Dirty Deeds." This was a song that actually dated back to the mid-'70s, but it continued to be Toke's anthem. Toke had become a fan of AC/DC's lead singer, Bon Scott, who was still alive at the time. Toke would say, "I like dat guy, Bon Scott ... ee's great." After eating the live guppy, Toke engaged in his standard ritual and went right into song. Again, when I say "song," I mean he would do the slow-speak Toke version of singing that included elongating the end of the word that came at the conclusion of each phrase. "Dirty deeds ... done dirt cheeeap. Dirty deeds ... done dirt cheeeap."

Sometimes I wondered if it would be a good idea for me to eat things the way Toke did—all daredevil like. I wouldn't do it for money, but I might do it to be liked. That would probably get me some attention and make me tough. Maybe then Dana Verner wouldn't have broken up with me. Like I told you, we kissed in Grade 5. Twice. I think. But then Dana Verner broke up with me. I wondered if it would make a difference if I was tougher. Maybe John Cusack was tougher when he was a kid. But I'm not sure he ate live guppies. And I'm not convinced Dana Verner would have stayed with me if I ate live guppies, either. Years later, by Grade 9, I had a good sense that eating live guppies was for kids. I knew that Wendy was too cool to be impressed by such foolishness. And Bowie probably didn't care about kids that could swallow a pink eraser.

Toke and I saw movies together and spent countless after-school hours playing road hockey or trading hockey cards. But as Toke and I grew older, we had less in common. I was in the school musical in Grade 8, *Joseph and the Amazing Technicolor Dreamcoat*, and that really wasn't Toke's bag. I was gradually getting into artsy girls and theatre and New Wave, and that was all very different from what Toke was interested in. Toke didn't really seem to understand Bowie. And Bowie was rapidly becoming my idol. If Toke didn't also become a fan of David Bowie, we were in serious trouble. CHUM FM was playing Bowie and songs like "Under Pressure" in 1981, but Bowie was probably too theatrical and androgynous for Toke. And though Bowie was respected, he wasn't hard rock. By Grade 9, Toke and I would end up in different high schools. I transferred to Thornlea SS, the "arts" high school my sister was attending. Toke went to Thornhill SS. He called it the "rocker" school.

Still, Toke and I remained very close until we were both fifteen. At the end of Grade 8, Toke and I had both gotten our Adidas bags. We didn't actually buy them together, but we had much to celebrate when we shared our cool acquisitions. We spent a bunch of time that summer walking around with our new Adidas bags and getting Lolas from the Mac's Milk on the corner with the lady my father called "the good Chinese woman" behind the counter. A Lola was a giant triangle of coloured ice with sugar. It came in flavours like cherry red or blue. We were never sure what flavour blue was. One time, Toke suggested that he would consume an entire Lola in one gulp if I gave him five dollars. Toke continued to think of dares that might make an impression. I didn't agree to give him the five dollars. That was a lot of money for us. You could get an album at Sam the Record Man on Yonge Street downtown for $2.99 if you got yourself in the 6 A.M. lineup on Saturday mornings. But also, the Lola just looked very large and potentially dangerous.

THE MOST COMMON ACTIVITY in our part of Thornhill from ages eight to fourteen was playing road hockey. I had gotten a net, and we usually had enough kids to form two teams. Our suburban street was relatively quiet, and most drivers knew that as they rounded the corner onto our road on any given afternoon there was probably some hockey going on, and so they gave us enough time to scream "Car!" and clear the way for passage. If other kids weren't around, Toke and I would just take shots. That would involve one guy playing net and the other guy shooting a tennis ball at him. In contrast to my less-than-spectacular on-ice performance in the winter leagues, I was a pretty good road hockey player. I was fast and I had a quick snap shot. I had scored seven goals in one road hockey game, although Little Charles claimed that I was at an advantage because he had a cast on and could only hold his stick with one hand.

Toke was a bit slower than the other players and was sometimes relegated to playing in net with his big green duffle coat and his Habs toque. One of the older kids on the street, Rick Bolton, was a junior hockey player with a chip on his shoulder and would play rough with us. He lived across the street a few houses down from me. Rick was a pretty nice guy overall, but not when he played hockey. He had lost a couple of fingers in his left hand, and he had to hold the top of his hockey stick with his elbow against his chest. Sometimes, when we played road hockey, Rick seemed to use younger kids as a way to get his frustrations out.

One cold day in the fall of 1982, around dusk, Rick summoned us from across the street to take shots with him. That really meant Toke and me taking turns in net while Rick took shots at us. Rick seemed to be having a harsh day, and he started shooting really hard at Toke. It didn't seem like Rick was trying to score, but rather that he wanted to target Toke and hurt him. Rick laughed each time he hit Toke, and I stood by helplessly as I saw the tension escalate. When Toke made the mistake of calling him a "weasel!" out loud, Rick Bolton took a blistering slapshot from the middle of his driveway and hit Toke directly in the face. Toke fell to the ground and started rolling around, holding his head. I had never seen him so vulnerable. I ran to see if Toke was okay, but he said nothing. He got to his feet and pulled up the hood of his green duffle coat and started running away in the direction of his house. I tore across the street to tell my mother that Toke had been hurt. Rick Bolton just laughed and continued to take shots at the net on his driveway.

About ten minutes after the slapshot incident, my mother, sister, and I saw Toke and his brother, Mitch, approaching. They were walking along the street in the direction of our house. As they came to our door, I opened it, with my mother standing next to me. Toke kept his head down, but we could see a red mark on his cheek.

Mitch Toker spoke directly to me. "Who did this to my brother?" Mitch had a stern look on his face, but this time I could tell his anger was not directed at me.

I looked at my mother and then across the street at Rick Bolton, who was watching events unfold from his driveway with his stick still in hand.

"Um ... well ... he did it." I pointed across the street at Rick. I imagined I would become known as a rat for telling on Rick. He had been prominent in Scouts as one of the older leaders and would probably never speak to me again. I worried that Rick Bolton would have me kicked out of Scouts Canada in revenge. But Toke had been my best friend. And even if he didn't understand Bowie, I needed to defend him.

Mitch was looking directly into my eyes. "That's what Ron said. Are you sure it was him?"

I nodded.

Mitch thanked me and turned to my mother. He said, "Hello, Mrs. Ghomeshi. I'm very sorry about this." It was all so civilized. I realized that Mitch was not always wild and crazy if he didn't need to be.

Toke and his older brother then walked across the street directly towards Rick Bolton. Mitch was wearing his dark brown leather jacket, the kind I figured John Travolta wore in *Saturday Night Fever*. Mitch said nothing as he walked up to Rick. Then Mitch Toker took Rick Bolton by the head and slammed his knee into his face. Rick crumpled to the ground. Mitch then put his arm around Toke and they began to walk away. Mitch was still looking back at Rick. He said, "Hey, asshole, don't you ever fucking touch my brother again." Toke was now looking at me. I was standing on the porch with my mother and sister watching the event transpire. Toke nodded as if to express some kind of solidarity. He said nothing. It was one of the last times we would hang out, but in that moment I knew that nothing would ever entirely shake our connection. We never really needed Dixie cups. We shared a history and a growing language of rock music. And besides, our passions would always remain united in our devotion to the band Rush.

7

"Subdivisions" – Rush

Before Toke and I went our separate ways in the fall of 1982, we spent a large portion of the summer on an unplanned musical pilgrimage. Bowie wasn't my only musical obsession in Grade 9. I swear. I had other rock heroes, ones that were closer to home, too. They even turned up in Thornhill. And we waited for them. And we hung out with them. Well, sort of.

Okay, I suppose I shouldn't overstate things. Bowie was the real obsession. And by the early 1980s, I wanted to be like Bowie. That's a fact. You know this by now. You know that I was striving to be New Wave. Or maybe even glam rock. Or at least I was aiming to be introspective and brooding and have a working knowledge of synthesizers and dyed hair.

It was my goal to adopt the fashions and attitude that would make me a young Persian-Canadian Bowie. Don't laugh. When I first encountered Wendy in Grade 9, I instantly saw where all my aspirations were leading me. She began to consume my thoughts and further confirm my interests. As you're aware, not only did I revere Bowie, I knew that if I were more like Bowie, there was likely a greater chance Wendy would be interested in me. It was pretty much a win-win, you know? In retrospect, perhaps it was strange that I liked Wendy because she reminded me of Bowie. It was circular. It was like the Clash wearing T-shirts with the Clash on them. And yes, maybe I was overly obsessed with Bowie. That's what you've already concluded at this point anyway. But if it seems like it was all Bowie all the time, it wasn't. I loved music. And my musical interests were by no means monolithic.

In 1982, I went to see the rock band Journey play at Maple Leaf Gardens. You may know Journey, because these days they're considered "classic rock." That means they get played on "classic rock" radio stations every hour or so. It's like a rule or something. "Classic rock" basically means music that is played incessantly on repeat without people being allowed to get sick of it. It means something like that. But the only problem with "classic rock" is that people do get sick of it. Except for the Boomers. They love "classic rock." And now Journey are "classic rock."

You may also know of Journey because everyone loves the song "Don't Stop Believin'." If you're at a bar or in a sports stadium or on a cruise ship, everyone will sing along to "Don't Stop Believin'." People today love the song "Don't Stop Believin'," even though it wasn't really a huge hit when it was first released in '81. Years later, everyone started to like it so much that it was used as the soundtrack for the final minutes of one of the best TV shows in history, *The Sopranos*. So, you probably know that song for sure. But back in 1982, Journey weren't "classic rock." They were just rock. They weren't old yet. When you're very popular and you get old, you get called "classic." And if you're a band, your music then gets played incessantly, the way you wish it might've gotten played in the first place. When I was fourteen, Journey were very different from Bowie. But I still liked them a lot.

I had gone to see Journey with John Ruttle and Valerie Tiberius and another girl named Jinjee. John Ruttle was my good friend, and he had gotten the tickets and arranged things. He was in Grade 10, so he was in charge. Valerie Tiberius was a very cute brunette girl who was in Grade 9 like me. She was smart and had excellent dimples and she wore skirts. John Ruttle wanted to ask Valerie Tiberius to go to the Journey concert, but he didn't want her to feel like it was too much of a date. He wanted her to think it wasn't a date, even though he wanted it to be a date. You see, if it felt too much like a date, she might say no. I learned that this was often the case with girls. They wanted to be taken out, but if it seemed like it was a date, it might create too much pressure and "expectations." So, you had to figure out how to take a girl on a date in a way that wasn't like a date, even though they ultimately wanted to go on a date. I knew girls liked dates in the end, because that's what happened in romantic comedy movies.

John Ruttle asked me if I would come along to the Journey concert to help give the outing a non-date veneer. I agreed. He also asked Valerie if her close friend Jinjee would like to come. Jinjee accepted, and so now she was paired with me. John Ruttle was already fifteen, a year older than me, so he got to make decisions like this. He was also good at determining who was paired with whom. Besides, he had sprung for the Journey tickets, so I wasn't going to complain. I didn't seem to have too much in common with Valerie's friend Jinjee. But I really liked her name. Jinjee. It was the kind of name you wanted to repeat as much as you could when you were talking to the person who had that name.

"Hey, Jinjee. Would you like more popcorn, Jinjee? Okay, Jinjee. I'll grab some for us, Jinjee."

Like that.

So I agreed to go to the Journey concert with Jinjee, along with John Ruttle and Valerie Tiberius, who were not on a date. Mind you, it's not like I wasn't excited to see Journey anyway. I appreciated watching Steve Smith on the drums and hearing Steve Perry's soaring vocals on songs like "Don't Stop Believin'" and "Open Arms" and "Who's Crying Now." Journey had released their hit album *Escape* the previous year. They had originally been more of a progressive hard rock band, but now they were embracing a more pop sensibility. This meant that as they became huge in '82, some rockers were abandoning them as sellouts. But we didn't know that. Besides, we were some of the youngest kids at the concert. We sat in the blue end-section of Maple Leaf Gardens. John Ruttle said he had "pulled some strings" to get us the tickets. This meant his dad helped. Mr. Ruttle was a TV executive, so he probably had a hand in getting us good seats. I bought a Journey *Escape* T-shirt with long sleeves after the show. Jinjee didn't want the *Escape* T-shirt with long sleeves.

The fact that I liked Journey was an example of my varied musical interests in the early '80s. My appreciation of music styles went far beyond New Wave, punk, rock, and "classic rock." I was also becoming increasingly aware of jazz music and the legendary drummer Buddy Rich. And I loved musicals and was still getting regular doses of *The Sound of Music* and *Fiddler on the Roof* from my parents on the family stereo. Musicals were like theatre mixed with music, and that wasn't too far from what Bowie did. But perhaps most of all, outside of Bowie and the New Wave revolution, I developed a rabid interest in the Toronto band Rush. My real devotion to Rush would begin at Tom Rivington's house in 1981.

I have this theory that the first time you really listen to an artist or band, you can intuitively sense what your relationship will be to their music for the rest of your life. Usually. You will know deep inside whether you like them or whether their music is not for you. You will even know in that moment if you're going to become a real devotee. Your gut will know this, no matter how many friends give you their opinion. You will know it, no matter how many times you say things like, "I wasn't so sure about Madonna ... but she's really grown on me ... now I really like her." It's not true. You always knew. And eventually the chickens come home to roost, and you will hate or love or be indifferent to Madonna. But you'll usually know how you feel from the first minute you really listen. That is, if you learn to trust your gut.

It's like the way mothers know about girlfriends. The first time your mother meets your new girlfriend, she may have no information about this person, but somehow she always knows if the girl is right or not. Mothers are natural arbiters of people you want to date. Or people you think you want to date. Or people you want to take on a date but are trying to do it in a way that won't be considered a date so they won't say no. Mothers are arbiters of those people. My mother was always able to do this. She probably knew that Dana Verner was going to break up with me when she met her for the first time at my birthday party in Grade 5. She knew it wasn't right. She knew this, even though she said, "Dana seems like a very nice blond girl." I could tell by the way my mother said things. Your mother has the antenna with girlfriends. And, in the same way, we all have that with music.

But the antenna will only work when you're actively listening. You have to really experience the artist for an inaugural time. So, I'm not talking about a song you might hear when you're walking through a mall. You're not really listening then. Or when your father says, "I don't understand thees punk music, why you are playing thees so loud?" He's not listening. Or when you're tapping along to a catchy melody that comes on with an ad on TV. That doesn't count, either. I'm talking about actually sitting and listening in a focused way and giving something a chance. Like when you're alone in your car and a new artist comes on the radio and you somehow opt not to turn the channel but to listen to this new song and decide what you think. Like that. After that first time, you know.

I knew I would become a devotee of Rush the first time I heard them at Tom Rivington's house in the fall of '81. I mean, I'd heard Rush songs in passing on the radio before that. But I first *really* heard Rush at Tom Rivington's house. It was after school in the beginning of Grade 9, and we were upstairs in his bedroom with Pete Hickey. Tom Rivington handed me a pair of large headphones plugged into his stereo and said, "I've got something you're going to want to hear." Tom Rivington was often right. This time, he was very right. And that moment would lead me to a Rush-related pilgrimage in the summer of 1982.

Tom Rivington had good headphones. They were large. In 1981, people only really wore headphones that were attached to their stereos. The Sony Walkman with portable headphones was invented in 1979. It would catch on very quickly over the course of 1982, but it wasn't really commonplace yet in '81. Things are very different now. Everyone wears headphones these days. Always. Have you noticed that? Well, maybe you haven't noticed that, because it's so obvious. Saying everyone wears headphones is like saying everyone has a mouth. Obvious. People wear headphones nowadays walking down the street, or driving a cab, or while they're working out, or when they're in bed, or when they're on the subway. People wear headphones attached to their iPads and their BlackBerrys and their video games. Much of the time these days, people wear "earbud" headphones that go right inside their ears, so you can't even tell that they're wearing headphones. You've probably been in the back seat of a taxi and thought the driver was speaking to you, but he was really speaking to a person that existed inside his headphones.

Now imagine there was a time before everyone wore headphones. Imagine a time when headphones were only attached to stereos. And if they were big headphones, they were considered better. And if the stereo was also big, it was the best. Then imagine yourself putting on those headphones for the first time, and they're pretty loud and it's a live Rush album and you hear Neil Peart's remarkable and protracted drum solo from "YYZ" recorded at the Montreal Forum in the spring of 1981. Well, here's the thing: in that moment you will freak out (in the good way) and stand a good chance of becoming a lifelong fan. For me, it was both.

Rush came from Toronto, and in the '80s they were the kings of Canadian rock. They could play their instruments better than anyone else in the business. Well, actually, they could play their instruments faster than anyone else in the business. But many people agreed that this meant better than anyone else in the business. Rush had started out in the early '70s as three guys with long, stringy hair and moustaches and strange, flowing outfits that looked like wizard robes. Back then they played heavy rock songs that weren't really very popular, and the wizard robes didn't seem to help. But by the early '80s, Rush had become three guys with long, stringy hair and no moustaches and no wizard robes. And by 1982, they had hit songs and they could fill arenas with their fans. Rush were loved for their musical precision and impressive solos. Later, they would become known as purveyors of "math rock." In the '80s, everyone in Canada was aware of Rush. Even my Persian-Canadian father knew Rush. He would call them "The Rush," just like he said "The Dan Hill." By the time I was in my mid-teens, I had become very interested in Rush, and my father would tell people this: "Yes. My son. He ees a big fan of The Rush!"

But I didn't know all this about my Rush fandom in 1981. And I didn't know I would become a devoted Rush follower in the midst of my adoration for Bowie and New Wave. I didn't have a sense of this until one afternoon at Tom Rivington's house.

Tom Rivington was tall and had longish, straight hair that parted in the middle. He was only a few months older than me, but he was one of those guys who always seemed wiser than the rest of us. Imagine Deepak Chopra when he was twelve years old. Deepak Chopra is a prolific book-writing spiritual guru who has published more than fifty volumes. Now, imagine him at twelve. He was probably disproportionately wiser than kids who were a few months younger than him, right? He would probably declare things like, "Grape Crush drink ... I do not think that is a good idea," and everyone would agree that Grape Crush was not a good soda-pop idea because young Deepak Chopra said so. Then, after that, no one would drink Grape Crush. Well, Tom Rivington was like Deepak Chopra, except tall and white and with long, straight hair that parted in the middle.

Tom Rivington's dad, Mr. Rivington, was a Scout leader with our 2nd Thornhill troop and wore a Scout uniform, even though he was an adult. Mr. Rivington wore the shorts of the Scout uniform too. He was a large round man, and his adult Scout shorts needed to be extra-extra-large. Mr. Rivington was a very good man. Everyone knew that the adults who wore Scout uniforms cared the most about scouting. They were also probably the best at using the Coleman stoves on camping trips. My father was the treasurer of our Scout troop for a while, but he only wore suits. My father was a professional engineer. In Iran, professional engineers wore suits, just like my father. On rare occasions, my father would dress more casual and put on a dress shirt with a sweater. But my father would never wear the Scout uniform with the shorts—even if he didn't require the extra-extra-large size like Tom's dad. People could probably tell that my dad was not as good with a Coleman stove.

Tom Rivington had a really big JVC home stereo in his bedroom. It took up a whole section of the wall next to his bed. It was the best stereo of any of the Thornhill kids I knew. It was even better than something Davey Franklin would have had. In the early '80s, if your stereo was big, it was good. If it was really big, it was even better. Tom Rivington's JVC stereo featured a number of rectangular metal units stacked on top of each other. Each unit had a series of flashing lights next to the knobs. Sometimes, when Toke or Pete Hickey and I were at Tom Rivington's house, we would close his bedroom door and turn off his bedside lamp, and we would watch the flashing lights while the music played. We would all be very impressed. And we knew it was an excellent stereo because it was the size of half a fridge. And the speakers came up to our waists.

You see, in 1982 things were better if they were bigger. Now, things are better if they are smaller. For example, in the early '80s, large cars were considered better than small ones. Everyone agreed this was true, except the Europeans. At least, that's what my father said. The Europeans liked smaller cars, but no one else did. My father had a very large Buick. When he first got the Buick, he proudly commented on how big it was. "It ees one of the biggest cars! It ees very long! It ees longer than the Cadillac car!"

My father was sure he had a very good car because it was so big. And bigger things were better.

The same was true of muffins and doughnuts. In the '70s and '80s, everyone preferred to eat large muffins. And if you got a big doughnut, you were lucky and you were happy. We knew about doughnuts in Canada, because Canada is the country with the highest doughnut consumption rate in the world. That is a fact. Canada also has the most doughnut shops in the world. Another fact. And Canada invented treats called butter tarts. Fact. They were also large in the 1980s. By large, I don't just mean popular, but actually significant in size. But even our biggest doughnut chain, Tim Hortons, started making smaller doughnuts called Timbits, and by the 1990s they were all the rage, because they were smaller. Now, coffee shops sell mini-muffins as well, because they are better, because people want smaller things and people will get less fat with smaller things.

I have made a short list (or shortlist) of items that were once considered better if they were bigger but are now considered better if they are smaller:

- stereos
- cars
- computers
- phones
- doughnuts

As you can see, there were many items that were considered better if they were bigger in 1982. Before everyone had personal computers, the bigger they were, the more impressive they were. The first computers were the size of a bungalow. Those were really good computers. Now, everyone wants a tiny computer that they can put in their pocket.

All this attraction to big was also true when it came to Rush. Rush were bigger than most bands. And the fact that Rush were bigger meant that they were better. It's not that they had more members than other groups. They didn't. But they had big amps and big stage shows, and Neil Peart had the biggest drum kit on any stage. Rush had songs that were longer than other bands' songs, just like my father's Buick was longer than most other cars. Rush were only three guys, but they had a BIG sound. Nineteen eighties big. So, when Tom Rivington gave me his large headphones and cued up the music on his giant stereo to the big drum solo in "YYZ," he knew I would be impressed. And what I heard blew my mind. I mean, it was actually blowing my mind with the volume, the drum riffs, and the impressive sonic array of noises being piped into my ears.

Soon after my experience at Tom Rivington's house, I became a true Rush fan. I started by buying the new live album at the time, *Exit ... Stage Left*. I continued collecting Rush records with *Moving Pictures* (1981) and then *Permanent Waves* (1980) and then *2112* (1976). I worked my way through Rush's back catalogue the same way I'd done with Bowie, and with the Beatles in Grades 7 and 8, and with the Clash in '82. I took regular trips to Sam's or A&A on Yonge Street in downtown Toronto to buy these albums. In the early 1980s, the act of buying music was itself a testament to how much you appreciated and wanted the records. It was no simple task. These days, you might hear a song you like, and so you click a button on your computer and it ends up in your collection. You click this button on your tiny computer, because smaller is better. The item you buy is now so small it's only a few words on your screen. It's not even plastic or vinyl or anything. But in 1982, you had to *want* the music badly enough to put in the time.

Let me explain for those of you who weren't around what it was like to buy music back in the day—back in the '80s. (I'm qualifying this as "back in the '80s" because I realize that "back in the day" can also refer to the 1970s, the 1990s, or the 2000s, depending on whether you're really old or not really old.) For each Rush album I ended up buying—not to mention my increasingly bulging Bowie back catalogue—I had to make significant plans in advance. First, I would need to earn the money for an album by working at SAVCO Pet Food and Supplies. I would greet people at SAVCO by saying, "Welcome to the largest retail pet food outlet in North America. Can I help you?" That was what I was expected to say. My job at SAVCO was to shovel mounds of dog kibble from twenty-kilogram bags into two-kilogram bags and then seal them and label them. I did this for hours. Initially. This was before I graduated to the more glamorous role of dog-food sales clerk when I was fifteen. That was a big promotion. Not everyone got elevated to dog-food sales clerk. That really became my job. And I counselled people that if they fed their dog too much of a cereal-based product he could grow up to have a less shiny coat and a dark attitude. But anyway, with the money I earned from shovelling dog food, I would have enough to buy a record album. Singles had fallen out of favour in the 1980s, and it was all about buying the full record. It was all about having the full album experience, man.

Once I earned enough money, I would go "record shopping" with Toke or Murray. This involved actually leaving the house. Nowadays, you might just press that button on your tiny computer at home to get the music you want. You might buy music while you're actually doing something else. For instance, you might choose to press the button and buy the music while you're taking a bath. That way, you are buying music and getting clean at the same time. But in the '80s, we had to leave the house with specific intent to get an album. We would take a Thornhill Transit bus to Finch subway station and then a thirty-minute subway ride to Dundas station on the Yonge line. Then we would walk to Sam the Record Man and into the magical den of new vinyl and cassettes.

Sam the Record Man was massive. It was three floors of musical bliss in the heart of downtown Toronto. Walking into Sam the Record Man in the early '80s was like witnessing one of the wonders of the world. It was a drug emporium for a pothead. It was a candy factory for a kid with a sweet tooth. It was filled with every kind of record and cassette from every genre and era you could imagine. For me, it was like Niagara Falls.

Niagara Falls is a tourist site about ninety minutes from Toronto that adults consider very impressive. My parents would take us on a family trip to Niagara Falls each summer, and sometimes, when relatives from other countries like Iran or England visited us, we would take an obligatory trip there. We went to Niagara Falls because the falls were a natural wonder and were really big and had hosted many daredevils who went over them in barrels. But I never totally understood what we were doing at Niagara Falls. My parents and relatives would all look at the falls and say things that suggested they were awestruck.

"Wow. I could just stand and witness this for hours," my mother would say. "Don't you love this, honey? It is just so breathtaking."

"Yeah. It's good. We saw this last year," I would reply.

"The water, it ees never stopping! It ees creating energy!" My father was also very impressed with Niagara Falls. Always.

He was an engineer. So my father would explain that the falls were a source of atomic energy. Or something like that.

But I never totally understood the magic of Niagara Falls. It sure was big, but I usually felt like we were just standing and looking at water. That was because we were just standing and looking at water. It's as if you stood and watched your tap. Now, imagine the tap was really big and no one turned it off. That was Niagara Falls. Was that really interesting to look at after thirty seconds? I never understood it. But Sam the Record Man was wondrous. I could stare at the offerings in Sam the Record Man for hours and hours. I imagined what it would be like to own everything in Sam the Record Man— even those Bowie rarities on vinyl from Europe. I could not get tired of seeing these things. If I'd had lots of money, I would have bought Sam the Record Man before I bought Niagara Falls. For young teens who were into rock music in 1982, Sam the Record Man was our Niagara Falls.

Of course, there was also a purpose to every visit to Sam the Record Man. Once I was inside the glorious emporium, I would need to find, say, the Rush album I was looking for and bring it to the counter. This involved rifling through all kinds of other vinyl records until you identified the one you were seeking. It was probably easier to ask a clerk to help, but that would not be cool. Rifling through vinyl was cool. Then, assuming I found the Rush album I wanted, I would bring it to the counter and pay for it. I would almost always have the exact change counted out in bills and coins, including tax. I knew what I was getting into here. And after I'd paid for the Rush album, the person at the counter would put it in a plastic bag to confirm I was not stealing it as I left the store. Then came the hardest part, another thirty-minute subway ride and trip on the bus before I could get home and put the record on the stereo. On the subway, we would always peel off the plastic shrink wrap and look at the artwork and read the liner notes. Then at last, after a round trip of a few hours, I got to put the new album on the turntable in my room. It was all a lot of work, but there was nothing more gratifying than the journey to buy a new record, and then actually—finally—getting to spin it.

Why am I giving you this detailed account of purchasing a Rush album? I'm doing so because it really felt like an investment to get music in 1982. Not just an investment of money, but of time and energy. Listening to the music became a reward for all the work you had put in. It's like we appreciated music more in the 1980s when it wasn't available to us at the push of a button. And then we would play it on our big stereos with large headphones.

Throughout Grade 9, I solidified my interest in playing drums and becoming good on the basic four-piece drum kit by spending countless hours practising after school in our music room, Room 273. Amongst drummers in our high school, the standard to shoot for was very clearly Neil Peart of Rush. He set the bar high. Learning to replicate every riff by Neil Peart was the goal of any aspiring drummer worth his salt. All the drummers in the music room learned to play the song "Tom Sawyer," which had been released the previous year. If you wanted to be a real drummer, you learned "Tom Sawyer."

Everyone was judged by how well they could play "Tom Sawyer." I had gotten my job playing drums in the Thornhill Community Band because Don Margison had seen me playing "Tom Sawyer" in the music room after school and told his dad, Mr. Margison, that I was a good drummer. I wasn't as good a drummer as Don had suggested. But I knew how to play "Tom Sawyer."

In Grade 9, we had a battle of the bands called Rock Nite at the Thornlea gymnasium. The bimonthly Rock Nite was organized by an intimidating Grade 12 student named Hussein. Hussein was quite gruff. And he wielded a lot of power. He was tall and burly and he wore a leather jacket the way Toke's brother, Mitch, did. Hussein would select from the best high school bands and, if selected, they got to play at Rock Nite. Almost all of the bands that took the stage at Rock Nite played cover songs. You always knew who the drummers in the audience were at Rock Nite, because they would stand right in front of the stage with their arms folded and stare intently at whatever drummer was playing. The stare would become even more pointed when each band inevitably attempted to play "Tom Sawyer." I wasn't good enough to play Rock Nite for most of Grade 9, and I didn't even think I was good enough to stand in front of the stage with the other drummers with my arms crossed. But I practised "Tom Sawyer" in the music room. Don Margison thought I was good. I aspired to play "Tom Sawyer" by Rush onstage one day.

I was having some trouble in this period reconciling my growing New Wave status with my appreciation for Rush. Rush fans were not very New Wave, even though the band had started to integrate synthesizers and were trying to move in a more progressive, keyboard-based direction. My friend Shael Risman, who was also a drummer and played in our Grade 9 band Urban Transit for a while, saw Rush live at Maple Leaf Gardens in November of 1982. He told us the next day that a Canadian New Wave band called the Payolas had opened for Rush and had been booed by the Rush fans. Shael said everyone gave the Payolas the finger and started screaming, "Fuck off, Payolas! Rush!" I had liked the Payolas before this. They were New Wave, and I had seen a simulcast of their concert at the Masonic Temple on Citytv. A simulcast meant that you could watch the concert on TV at the same time as it was being played on CHUM FM. That way, you could hear the music in stereo—which was especially good if you had a big stereo.

The Payolas had a song called "Eyes of a Stranger." It was a bit of a hit, and it would be on the soundtrack for the film *Valley Girl* the next year. That was more of a preppy film. But in '82, the song was really New Wave. And it featured "eyes" in the title. There were lots of songs about eyes in the early '80s. I'm not sure why.

I have made a short list of songs about eyes that were released in the beginning of the 1980s:

- "Bette Davis Eyes"
- "Eyes Without a Face"
- "Private Eyes"
- "Eyes of a Stranger"
- "Eye of the Tiger"
- "She Blinded Me with Science"

As you can see, there were many songs about eyes in the early '80s. But the Payolas' "Eyes of a Stranger" was definitely one of the best. I had decided I liked the Payolas. But I wondered if I'd have said so if I were there when they opened for Rush. Shael Risman had been pretty clear that everyone had screamed, "Fuck off, Payolas! Rush!" It didn't sound like the Rush fans would have appreciated me very much if I'd cheered for the Payolas. There were still clear divisions between rockers and New Wavers in 1982. Rush may have been gravitating towards New Wave, but their fans were not. And New Wavers still didn't really understand Rush. I was stuck in the middle.

For some of the aforementioned reasons, I had a keen sense that Wendy was not really very impressed with Rush. I had this sense because I had seen Wendy making a face when her brother mentioned Rush once in the hallway at Thornlea. I'd remembered this and made a mental note not to talk about liking Rush in front of Wendy. Wendy was a fan of the Beat, and the Human League, and the Clash. Rush were not cool to her. But it also made sense that Wendy didn't like Rush because she was a girl. Girls didn't like Rush. You might think I'm making a generalization. But I'm not. No girls liked Rush. Well, maybe there were some oddball girls who had decided to follow Rush, but for the most part Rush was a guy thing. Just like wrestling in gym class or playing Dungeons & Dragons, Rush was the domain of young men and boys.

Here is a short list of things boys liked in 1982 that were not as appreciated by girls:

- Coleco tabletop hockey
- Dungeons & Dragons
- wrestling in gym class
- Gobstoppers candy
- Rush

As you can see from this list, being a devout follower of Rush was not a way to win Wendy's heart. But even Wendy couldn't deter me from my appreciation for Rush. They were musical heroes of mine, and to worship them I would have done whatever was required of me. I was also fourteen. When people get older, they have less patience for worshipping their musical heroes. It's not that they don't appreciate them or love them anymore. It's just that increasingly they have things to do like getting a new filter for the furnace because a couple of times a year the furnace doesn't work very well and they don't know why and then they realize it's because the furnace needs a new filter and so then they have to get a new filter so that the furnace will work well again. They have things to do like that.

But when you're fourteen, you might camp out overnight to get tickets to see your favourite band. Or when you're young, you might drive or take a bus for hours to get a glimpse of your performing idol. When you get older, you start saying things that demonstrate that you no longer have the patience for such epic worship. Trust me. Listen to what older people say at concerts. They get frustrated when they have to wait. Even if they've paid a lot of money to see a band they think they love. "This is ridiculous. Weren't the Eagles supposed to be on right at 9 P.M.?" Or: "We've been here for at least thirty-five minutes now! I need to get up early and get a new filter for the furnace. This really isn't worth it."

See?

You might hear adults say things like that. These same people may have been willing to line up overnight for the Eagles when they were fourteen. An extra thirty-five minutes at the show would make no difference. But now they're tired.

And they may need to change the furnace filter. Of course, if you've never been a fan of the Eagles, it would never be worth it to wait for them. But when you're fourteen and a fan, it makes a lot more sense. And that's what led to the great Rush pilgrimage of 1982.

By the end of June, I had little in the way of an agenda for the summer months except to work at SAVCO and perform a small role in the Thornlea Theatre Troupe's outdoor production of *A Midsummer Night's Dream*. I also needed to call Wendy and confirm that she was coming to the Police Picnic, and then, assuming the phone call went well, go to the Police Picnic with Wendy in August. Still, my calendar for July was relatively free. Open season. That was about to change.

One afternoon as the school year was ending and summer was finally about to begin, I heard the doorbell ring. It was Toke. He was standing on the front porch, huffing and puffing, totally out of breath. He'd obviously rushed over with some urgency. Something was up. Toke had been running. Toke was a bit chubby. Toke didn't really run.

"Mitch just told me! ... It's ... they're coming!" It was near impossible to figure out what he was going on about. "... They're recording. Dat studio ..." More panting. "On Doncaster. Alex Lifeson ... dat guy ... ee's great!"

Toke was really out of sorts. But I could tell he was very excited.

"What? Who's coming?" I was trying to keep up. "What is it, Toke?"

"Rush! Rush!"

"Toke, slow down." I had to help Toke get a hold of himself. But with his mention of Rush, I was also feeling some excitement. "What is it you're trying to say? What's going on with Rush?"

Toke began to catch his breath and compose himself. He explained that Mitch had got word from an insider source that Rush was recording up the street at a place called New Media Studios (at least, that's how I remember the name) on Doncaster Avenue. I assumed this was a joke. But Toke looked quite serious. And he was panting.

It seemed inconceivable. Rush? Near us? The news was unlike anything we'd encountered in our quiet suburban hamlet. How were we to process the idea that one of our favourite bands was scheduled to record only a ten-minute walk away? But Mitch was pretty reliable. And Mitch had an insider source. So it must've been a reliable insider source. This must've been true.

When Toke had fully caught his breath, he explained that he thought we should keep the info about Rush to ourselves. He didn't even want me to tell Tom Rivington. Toke was very specific about who he thought deserved to hear certain choice headlines.

In the days that followed, Toke and I did some digging around and learned that the members of Rush were in fact going to be cocooning themselves at New Media Studios on Doncaster Avenue, just up the street from where we lived. By "digging around," I basically mean we asked Mitch about twenty times for more details. It turned out that Rush were not recording but were practising for their imminent world tour to support their forthcoming album, *Signals*. The word was that Rush would be at New Media Studios for most of July. Toke and I agreed we would not let this opportunity pass. Other than our shifts at SAVCO Pet Food and Supplies, we had found our sole mission for the first half of the summer of 1982.

We mapped out a plan that was admirably consistent. Starting at the end of the first week of July, and for every single day over the following three weeks, Toke and I would get up early and make the trip to New Media Studios in the hopes of meeting Rush. Toke would meet me at my place and we'd make our way there. I put gel in my hair and wore my black boots in the hope that, if I met the Rush guys, they'd know I was cool. And maybe New Wave.

To be clear, we couldn't get particularly close to the main doors of the building where Rush were practising. The entrance to New Media Studios was on a closed-off driveway where kids couldn't be hanging around. But the building backed onto a large field and baseball diamond that was at the far end of our old Henderson Avenue Public School. There was a four-foot wire fence between the parking area behind the studio and the field, where we could walk with impunity. Toke and I would go and sit by the fence each morning and peer through it from around 9 A.M. until dusk. We took shifts, always making sure one of us was present in case the other needed to go to the bathroom or run to get supplies. Our supplies included peanut butter sandwiches, Lolas, bags of nuts, and, on one special afternoon, some takeout burgers from the Golden Star bought with extra money my mother had given us for a healthy lunch.

Maybe the strangest part about our daily pilgrimage to meet Rush was our unwavering commitment. We didn't get discouraged when for the first week we barely even caught a glimpse of them. We saw sports cars coming in and out of the lot, but our view was obscured and we couldn't tell who was in them. But nothing deterred us. Nothing. In our Adidas bags, as well as supplies, we had vinyl copies of Rush albums. We wanted to be prepared if they agreed to sign our Rush records.

We never saw them. Not for the first week or two. And it didn't faze us. This was the devotion of two young guys sitting in a field, unconcerned with how long this wait might take. Impatience was for adults. This was about Rush. We were in it for the long haul.

By the second day we knew Rush were inside because we could hear them practising. This was very exciting. They seemed to play songs in twenty-minute stretches. They would practise one song and then stop. We would hear nothing for a while and wonder if they were still there. And then we would hear a loud bass, or Neil Peart's drums, or some heavy synth sounds, and we'd know that Rush were still inside. We were getting a free daily concert, if a bit muffled and disjointed. When they started playing, Toke would put his finger in the air and scream "Rush!" He never tired of this. Toke was consistent.

Most often of all, Toke and I heard Rush practising the song "Subdivisions." It would start with this heavy bass synth riff, and Toke and I would pump our fists in the air from outside the fence. "Subdivisions" had been released as a single in May. It was from the *Signals* album. We had heard it on the radio, but we hadn't paid a lot of attention to the lyrical content. In the middle of the song, Neil Peart's lyrics went,

> Any escape might help to smooth
> The unattractive truth
> But the suburbs have no charms to soothe
> The restless dreams of youth

Later, it would occur to me that Rush had been singing about us—kids trying to make sense of life in the suburbs. In some ways we were deep in the middle of that struggle to "conform or be cast out," as another line in the song says. But Toke and I didn't realize this at the time. It might have helped if someone had explained it to us. But no one did. And we really didn't know much about the song's meaning. And it sounded a bit muffled from outside the fence. We just knew it was the heavy new Rush song. And that we were getting an exclusive preview of the tour. Toke kept screaming "Rush!" with his finger in the air.

At times, during our days behind New Media Studios, other kids would come along and ask what we were doing. It was always at moments when Rush had fallen silent. We'd say we were just hanging out. Mitchell Toker's inside source was someone who worked at the studio, but other than Toke and me, it seemed very few people were aware that Rush were practising right there in Thornhill. This was our secret. The only unrealized part of our mission was actually meeting our rock heroes.

In the third week of our daily routine of listening to Rush from outside of New Media Studios, Toke and I saw what looked like a new two-door sports car parked close to the fence where we'd been sitting each day. This parking spot hadn't been used before. We stared at the car and wondered if it belonged to any of the members of Rush. We debated throughout the day who the car might belong to. Sure enough, at the end of that afternoon, a skinny guy with long black hair, dark jeans, and a black shirt came out from behind the studios and walked towards the car. Toke and I looked at each other and nodded.

It was Rush singer and bass player Geddy Lee. Geddy opened the car door, jumped in, and drove away. Geddy had walked near the fence to get to the car. We'd witnessed this. Now we'd not only heard Rush, we'd seen Geddy Lee. Our patience was starting to pay off.

For the rest of the third and final week that Rush were practising, we saw Geddy's car consistently parked at the fence. On the third day, he came out and very clearly spotted us before he got into his car. Geddy looked at Toke and me and then smiled and waved. He waved the way people familiar with each other wave. Like the way you wave to your neighbour across the street, someone you'd say hello to, and if you're not going to stop to speak to them, you still want to acknowledge them. He waved like that. And when you wave like that, it's usually a reciprocal exercise. You expect the other person to wave back. But we must've been a bit stunned. Neither Toke nor I waved back. Geddy got in his car and drove away. Toke was very upset that we hadn't reciprocated the wave with Geddy Lee.

"Ee waved at us and we didn't wave. Geddy Lee! And we didn't wave."

I wondered that night if we would ever forgive ourselves for not waving back at Geddy Lee—bassist extraordinaire and man with high-pitched vocals. Rock god. What if he thought we didn't care? What if he concluded we didn't know who he was? Or what if he thought we were not Rush fans and we'd been waiting for REO Speedwagon or Air Supply or some other preppy band? All of these possibilities were humiliating. But the following day, we had our chance to compensate. This time, we saw Geddy as he arrived. Once again he acknowledged us, sitting there at the fence, as he got out of his car. But this time he decided to speak.

"Hey, guys!" Geddy Lee said.

"Hey, Geddy," I replied.

"Hey, Geddy," said Toke.

Then Geddy Lee locked his car and walked into the studios.

It wasn't much. But it was a conversation. We had talked to Geddy Lee. It seemed a little uncreative that both Toke and I had said the exact same thing to Geddy Lee. "Hey, Geddy." You might think one of us would've gone out on a limb and said, "Good morning." Or, "Have a nice day." Or, "Have a killer day of rehearsal!" Or, "You rock!" But no such luck. And yet, we had spoken. This was progress. Just like when I first spoke to Wendy at the lockers and asked her to go to the Police Picnic. And that had turned out rather well. Or, I hoped it would. We heard Rush practising "Subdivisions" for the rest of the day, and Toke and I couldn't wipe the smiles off our faces. We had spoken to Geddy Lee. It felt totally unreal.

On the second-last day of Rush's practice time at New Media Studios, the unthinkable happened. At the end of another shift of sitting in the sun by the fence with our Adidas bags, we saw two men come out of the back of the studios and head towards us. It was Geddy Lee and a taller-looking blond guy. It didn't take us long to realize it was guitarist Alex Lifeson. Toke started whispering under his breath. "Holy shit! Holy shit! Holy shit!" We stood at the wire fence, the top of which came to our chests. We were both frozen as the Rush members approached.

Geddy Lee and Alex Lifeson walked right up to us. Geddy spoke first.

"See? These are the guys who've been sitting out here each day," Geddy said to Alex. Then he turned to us. "Right, guys?"

"Um … yeah," I replied. I had become very shy. No matter how long we'd been sitting outside the fence, we still hadn't adequately prepared for this moment. Nor was it really possible to.

"Rush!" said Toke. No one understood why he said that. He seemed a little bit in shock.

Now Alex Lifeson spoke.

"Well, that's really cool, guys. Thanks for hanging around. You want us to sign those?"

Toke and I had almost forgotten that we were holding copies of our Rush albums, *Moving Pictures* and *2112*.

"That would be really cool."

Before we knew it, Geddy Lee and Alex Lifeson had each signed their name on our Rush albums. Then they both got into Geddy's car and drove away. As they were leaving, Alex waved at us. We waved back.

After almost three weeks of a musical pilgrimage only ten minutes from our homes, Toke and I had met a couple of our musical heroes. Rush were better than just a big rock band. They were nice guys. My faith in music and my idols was never stronger. I wondered what kind of car Bowie would have driven into that parking lot. I wondered if he would have signed all of my Bowie records. I imagined he would.

"Dat guy … Alex Lifeson," Toke said. "Ee's great."

8

"ONCE IN A LIFETIME" — TALKING HEADS

Rock concerts can change your life. You have to trust me on this. They really can. They can also be boring. Just like REO Speedwagon albums released in the 1980s. Boring. So it is with concerts. There are concerts that are mundane, or predictable, or a waste of money. But sometimes rock concerts can change your life. And when they do, it's magic.

Wendy and I were still jammed in the middle of a sweaty crowd as afternoon turned to evening at the Police Picnic in August of 1982. Amidst the pushing and excitement, we'd somehow managed to maintain our real estate on the floor only about twenty rows away from the main stage. In a gathering of forty-five thousand fans at the CNE Grandstand, our positioning was actually pretty stellar. Not bad for an aspiring New Wave kid and a diminutive blond girl with a Bowie-like glow. I wondered if Wendy was impressed with how close we were to the action. I wondered if she credited me for our positioning. And I wondered if she was thinking of us as a team the way I was.

The MC guy had now returned to the stage.

"Okay, everyone, please be patient! Please, you guys. We'll be back in just a few more minutes with … Talking Heads!"

There was a roar of approval from the massive stadium of punters at the mention of Talking Heads. This must have come as some relief to the shell-shocked MC guy. He looked a little desperate. His job was to calm the restless crowd after the near mutiny that had just taken place, and simultaneously to get us revved up for the next act to hit the stage. Mind you, everyone knew the next band would go over better than Joan Jett and the Blackhearts. It couldn't get much worse in terms of audience reaction. The promoters were probably crossing their fingers, hoping the show would get back on track.

It had been almost forty minutes since the premature end of the Joan Jett set and the debacle that had cost me my red-and-blue Adidas bag. I was no longer in possession of my jean jacket or my new Walkman or my hair gel or my mix tapes featuring the Police and the Beat and Heaven 17. All of those items were gone forever. But Wendy had been really sweet. She kept giving me affirming looks. That is, she kept giving me affirming looks from underneath that longer bit of straight blond hair that flopped in front of her face and sometimes covered one eye. As I might have mentioned, she had a short haircut with a longer bit in front like Bowie. And she had sparkling eyes. And I now realized she had kind eyes. And I noticed she was smiling at me a lot, too. Maybe it was to inspire me to smile as well. This was nice. But it was also a bit of a surprise. Smiling was not always very cool. Not in 1982. It was very controversial to smile in 1982. Siouxsie, from

Siouxsie and the Banshees, would never be caught smiling. That wasn't very New Wave. Or punk.

To be clear, the non-smiling disposition was not limited to Siouxsie and her band, either. It was much more of a widespread epidemic. New Wave artists were considered to have more credibility if they were brooding. At least, that's what I'd concluded by the end of Grade 9. Smiling would undermine the idea that a New Wave artist's life was hard, and dark, and goth, and serious. Hardship was an important part of what it meant to be New Wave. It was essential to communicate pessimism at every turn. When you heard Phil Oakey from the Human League sing in 1982, did he sound like he was smiling? No. Of course he didn't. And neither did he smile in his videos. Smiling was superficial and preppy. Being preppy meant being well off and content and wearing bright clothes and having dodgy mainstream artistic interests. Preppies might regularly smile. Cool people did the opposite. The theatre students in 213 who were considered the real deal and only wore black didn't smile much. Well, they might smile if they had to play a role from another time period. That is, if they had to act a role from an era when people smiled. Like in the old days, when life was less serious and people didn't have thick eyeliner and synthesizers. But otherwise real theatre types didn't smile in 1982. Just like New Wave bands.

I have made a short list of New Wave acts from the early 1980s that featured members who would never be seen smiling:

- Siouxsie and the Banshees
- the Cure
- New Order
- Depeche Mode
- Duran Duran
- Ultravox

As you can see, there were many cool New Wave bands that refused to smile in 1982. None of these groups had members who were allowed to smile. Not at that time. They would look very strange and out of place if they smiled, because no one else did. Sure, there were a few exceptions. The English Beat were allowed to smile sometimes, because they were partly ska. Playing ska music meant they were happy. So that was an exception. They jumped up and down because they were so happy. And then there were some bands, like Spandau Ballet, that were originally cool when they didn't smile but then started to lose their credibility when they decided to begin smiling. As Spandau Ballet began to smile, they also became preppy and tanned and sang the saccharine and emotional saxophone ballad "True." By then they were no longer cool. Obviously.

But Wendy could smile. She made it okay. Wendy could smile without being uncool. It was actually very nice. And I knew that Bowie would smile on occasion as well. I had seen a vintage photo of Bowie smiling when he was onstage at Boston Garden in 1978 during his "Berlin" period. This was when he was making some very serious music about his drug addiction and beating his drug addiction. You'd think that Bowie would only be brooding at that time. He would have had good reason to brood. But even then, Bowie would smile sometimes. I assumed Bowie was above a lot of these conventions.

On the floor at the Grandstand, I was quite sure Wendy was smiling because she wanted to put me in a good mood after the Adidas bag situation. I could tell Wendy was attempting to be compassionate about my loss. But she was also pushing me to move onward and forget about it all for the sake of the rest of our night.

"It's just a bag, right?" she'd said in the aftermath of Forbes the punk launching my prized possession at Joan Jett. "It's not a big deal. Just stuff, right?"

I knew what she meant. And she was not wrong. It was probably more mature not to care about "stuff." But Wendy really had no idea how important my Adidas bag had been. It was a shock when Forbes had raised my bag above his mohawk head and thrown it at the stage. And now Forbes was no longer anywhere near us. He'd graduated to terrorizing other members of the audience. Forbes had enough punk cred to avoid repeatedly picking on the same kid.

Odd things can happen as a result of unforeseen events. Now that my Adidas bag was gradually becoming a memory, I was filled with a strange new sensation. I began to feel okay about no longer having it in my possession. It was not fun to lose my goods, but I wasn't as devastated as I thought I'd be. The Joan Jett incident had actually rendered me less freaked out about the whole day. You might think that was strange, too. You might think it's the opposite of what would happen. But in a way, I felt free.

Experiencing a loss can make you forget about putting on airs. Maybe that's what happened after I lost my Adidas bag. Or maybe it was a genetic predisposition to react calmly to catastrophe. My father had a knack for bringing calm to a storm. He could react with impressive composure when truly horrible things went down. When I smashed his Buick outside of Unionville High School a few years later, he had every right to scream at me, but he didn't. He had every right to be really angry, but he wasn't. Immediately after the collision, I was worried about what my father's reaction would be. I had totalled his Buick. And my father's Buick was big, and very long, even longer than a Cadillac. My father loved his big Buick. And bigger was better in the 1980s. But when I got him on the phone from the school office to explain that I'd been in an accident and that it was my fault and that his big Buick was now wrecked, he reacted with surprising serenity.

"You are okay?" my father asked softly after taking a breath.

"Yeah, I'm fine. But, Dad, the car ..."

"If you are okay, this ees most important theeng," my father said, calmly cutting me off. Then he added in a reassuring tone, "Don't worry about thees car. We can fix thees."

My father could be calm when we needed him to be. Maybe that had rubbed off on me.

It certainly was odd for me to be at peace without my long-time material companion—my Adidas bag. But this was exactly what transpired. Up until the late afternoon at the Police Picnic and the Joan Jett thing, I'd been self-conscious about the way I was looking and acting with Wendy. I'd been very focused on trying to be cool and anxiously hoping she'd like me. But losing the Adidas bag had somehow made me forget much of that—at least for a few hours. It was strangely liberating. It was like the way those Buddhist guys figure themselves out and learn what's important in life when they give up everything they own. The Buddhist guys have a revelation when disposing of their possessions. The Buddhists are really impressive when they do that. Or maybe it's the Hindu guys. Well, I can't remember which, but the point is, I was just a boy who had recently turned fifteen named Jian, standing at a concert and waiting with an older girl named Wendy for the next band to play. That's it—nothing more dramatic or less. And no more fake-leather baggage. Just like Buddhists. It was an inspiring realization. Not that I didn't still want to be Bowie. I did. Maybe I just wanted to be Bowie mixed with more of me now. Before the end of this day, I would have another revelation, too. I would discover something very magical. It was all about to happen. And I could not have anticipated what I was going to find.

During the prolonged break between Joan Jett and Talking Heads, I asked Wendy if she would like a drink. She told me she would like that very much, and I headed off through the crowd in pursuit of refreshments. I should explain that by "a drink," I mean a Coca-Cola. Actually, I mean two Cokes and some pretzels—the large kind. I know that "a drink" sounds like alcohol. That's why I said it. That would be cool. But this wasn't alcohol. And whether it was alcohol or not, I liked the idea of taking care of Wendy and showing her I could assume control. Besides, they didn't sell fancy foods and drinks at concerts in 1982. They only offered basic items like Coke and pretzels. Today, they might include sushi. Today, they might sell various packages of sushi rolls and sashimi at inflated prices at concerts. But we didn't know what sashimi was in the

'80s. Most of the fish you bought in a Toronto restaurant was cooked or fried back then. And you probably wouldn't buy fish at a concert. It would be odd to be carrying around fish at a concert in 1982. They just had pretzels at the Grandstand. And Cokes.

I still had some cash. Fortunately, I'd put money in the front pocket of my black jeans earlier in the day rather than inside the dearly departed Adidas bag. I'd done some calculations and was satisfied that I had enough to buy Wendy and me some non-fancy refreshments and pay for us both to get home on the subway. I was feeling more at ease now. I found the concession stands and got in line to buy the Cokes and pretzels.

I was standing just behind two goth guys with heavy eye makeup and black cloaks. It seemed strange to see goth guys buying pretzels. I'm not sure why. But you probably know what I mean. I think you do. You wouldn't really expect goth guys to eat. Or at least, you wouldn't expect them to eat concert pretzels. I don't really know what the alternative would be, but that was the image I had of goth guys in the summer of '82. Non-eaters. Maybe I thought real goths would have some rule confining them to consume only cool and gross things, like human blood or imitation human blood. I wondered about this as I stood in line at the concession stands at the Police Picnic. Maybe these guys were fake goths or young recruits on a goth apprenticeship program. Maybe that's why they ate pretzels. One of the goth guys had a Bauhaus T-shirt on, and he didn't look very happy—just like his heroes. Bauhaus was another band full of members that weren't allowed to smile.

I made my way back to Wendy with the drinks, pushing through punks and sweaty New Wave fans. I was experiencing a new excitement. I debated whether I should try to put my arm around Wendy during the next band's performance. It would be a big move. Maybe we were ready for that step. I wasn't sure how people made such decisions. But things seemed to be going well.

Coming back, I was reminded that our position on the floor was remarkably near the stage. As I approached the place where I'd left Wendy, I spotted the older stubble-faced guys in the cut-off English Beat T-shirts who'd been standing next to us earlier. Then I saw Wendy amongst them too. The stubble-faced guys were talking with her again. They were sharing a smoke. Wendy looked cool when she smoked. She looked intelligent and introspective. The main stubble-faced guy—who was very tall—was speaking with his face quite close to Wendy's. I figured he'd probably offered to light her cigarette. He'd also said something that made her laugh. Wendy's eyes squinted a lot when she laughed. It was like Bowie. The main tall, stubble-faced guy had his legs planted squarely on the ground and held his cigarette in one hand while he hooked the thumb on the other hand in his jeans like a gunslinger. He looked like a real man.

Our prime minister at the time, Pierre Trudeau, had also been known to stand like a gunslinger. He knew karate. I wondered what I would look like if I attempted to stand like our prime minister. I didn't think I'd be very believable as a gunslinger. I tried to imagine the way Bowie would stand if he were there. I adjusted my body and my expressions to appear more Bowie-like. I had actually started doing this over the previous year anyway. I carried myself based on images of Bowie I'd seen. New Wave was about the music and the culture and even the aesthetics, but it was also important to consider the way you held your body. At least it seemed so. I knew Bowie moved in an impressive way, but I had no idea he had practised this. I had no idea he had begun studying back in 1967 under the tutelage of Lindsay Kemp, an abstract mime who was also a dance instructor. I didn't know he had then learned how to move onstage and how to help reveal a song's meanings through movement and lighting. I knew nothing of any of this. I would learn it all later. I just knew that Bowie carried himself in a cool way. And whether that was New Wave or not, I'd taken to trying to physically copy what Bowie did.

There were many ways to look like Bowie by the early 1980s. Sometimes, I would lift my shoulders up and slightly bend my left leg like on the cover of the album *David Live*, recorded in Philadelphia in 1974. That was a more passive position, so I would do that if I was standing and waiting for someone. Or other times, I would scrunch up my face like I was about to sneeze, the way Bowie did in the video for "Fashion." I'd seen the video for "Fashion" on *The NewMusic* on Citytv. It was a song from his *Scary Monsters* LP, which had been released in 1980. I don't know why Bowie made that scrunched-up face in the video. He probably didn't have to sneeze. But the fact that he'd made that face meant it was cool. So I tried to do that, too. That's the thing about being a trendsetter. You can do anything odd and it will be cool. It will become something that others want to do. Maybe Bowie was aware of this. Maybe he had a laugh with his mates about the fact that there would be a fourteen-year-old boy copying that scrunched-up face a couple of years later just to look like him. Maybe. But when Bowie did these things, they really did look cool.

I truly had no resemblance to David Bowie, but I sometimes imagined I did. I imagined this even though his skin
was very pale and mine was olive brown, and being pasty-
white was part of being New Wave. But it helped that I was
skinny. I was really skinny. Just like Bowie. Mind you, I still
had more of a circular Middle Eastern face. I got that from
my father. Bowie had chiselled features. Wendy also had
chiselled features. Just like Bowie. I always wanted chiselled
features, but that physical trait would never be in my repertoire. I couldn't get much skinnier than I was, and I still had a
round-looking face. You see, along with being an olive-brown
colour, the cherubic face was another cruel trick God played
on Middle Eastern guys so we'd be destined to be less New
Wave. But at least my body was very thin. That was one way
I could be like Bowie.

I'm really not sure why I was so skinny in the 1980s. It
was my metabolism or something like that. That's what my
mother said. My mother was very helpful in explaining these
things. She would inform me that it was probably my metabolism or something like that, and then she would add some
helpful suggestions so I would know what I should aspire to as
an alternative to being thin.

"You should eat well and be active, honey. Then you will
look grand! You know, Umar has a very nice build. He's not
as thin as you."

My mother would say things like this. She would make
her point about how skinny I was by comparing me to Umar.
Umar was quite perfect in the eyes of my mother. Often, when
my mother wanted to make a point about how I could change
the way I was, or what I might aspire to, she would talk about

Umar. It didn't help that Umar seemed to have been blessed with a tediously pious disposition. It really wasn't fair. And Umar had a remarkable facility for doing adult-like things at an early age.

Once, when we were eight years old, Umar had single-handedly made hamburgers for both our families over at the Jans' house. My mother had been very vocal at the dinner table about how impressed she was when Umar came out of the kitchen with the hamburgers.

"Oh, my, look at that! Umar, those hamburgers look just lovely. You made all of those by yourself? Wow! Do you see that, Jian? That's just so great. Thank you, Umar."

That's what my mother said. As you can see, my mother couldn't compliment Umar's hamburgers without reminding everyone that I hadn't made the hamburgers. And in truth, it really was quite impressive that Umar had made us all hamburgers. He was eight. I never found out if Mrs. Jan helped him, but I don't think she did. I'd actually seen him in the kitchen with a pan in hand, cooking meat on the stove. And I really didn't know how to make hamburgers. And anyway, I was quite sure my mother's point had little to do with Umar and more to do with why I wasn't cooking dinner for guests. Umar was just like That Chris from across the street and all the other kids that were better than me at various things. None of this seemed very equitable when I was growing up. And I already knew I was thin without my mother having to point it out.

Besides, it was true that Umar had a nice build. He was more robust than I was, inasmuch as a kid can be robust. At the very least, I could still take solace in the fact that being skinny made me more like Bowie. I could hang on to that. Then again, even that claim wasn't entirely steeped in credibility. The tragic part about my lean frame was that I wasn't even skinny for the right reasons. Bowie had been gaunt because he was a drug addict and ate nothing but cocaine, milk, and red peppers for a lot of the 1970s. My skinny build had nothing to do with cocaine or anything glamorous like that. It was more that I was a fourteen-year-old asthmatic who seemed to get sick a lot as a kid. I also had allergies and I would sneeze often. This was bad. Mind you, by the '80s, sneezing meant looking a bit more like Bowie with the scrunched-up face as if he were about to sneeze in the video for "Fashion." There were some benefits to my downsides.

Back at the Police Picnic, I had returned to our place in the crowd. Wendy spotted me and deftly pivoted away from the stubble-faced guys to face in my direction. She threw her cigarette butt on the ground and smiled as I gave her one of the Cokes in a large red paper cup that said "Coke." Wendy and I then went about tearing into the two big pretzels. At one point, she playfully broke off a piece of my pretzel and threw it in her mouth. We both laughed. It was all very comfortable. There were moments when I forgot that Wendy was older and more experienced and cooler than me. It felt like she forgot that sometimes, too. Those were my favourite times.

We'd now resumed the wait for Talking Heads to hit the stage, and I had no idea what to expect. The anticipation in the Grandstand was palpable, and it was building. Wendy leaned in close and looked directly in my eyes.

"This is going to be rad. I know it. Their rhythms are really intricate."

I loved that Wendy used words like "intricate." She was very smart. I had heard that Wendy did particularly well in school. This did not surprise me. Bowie was smart, too. We watched the crew guys wearing laminates set up the stage. And then, finally, the members of Talking Heads made their appearance.

THE MOMENT TALKING HEADS hit the stage at the Police Picnic in 1982, the course of my life was altered forever. That is a fact. You might think I'm being dramatic. You might think that statement is what they call hyperbole. It's not. Talking Heads were *that* important.

That moment—and the set of music I was about to witness—would lead to big changes in my future. It would lead to years and years of Talking Heads music being played on repeat on my stereo, in my car, on my headphones, and in my head. It would lead to buying every single one of the Talking Heads albums on vinyl and then updating them with CDs and then digitally with each new decade. It would lead to learning and covering Talking Heads songs in various bands and musical incarnations. It would lead to attending a concert tour the following year that would be filmed to create the second-best rock movie of all time. It would lead to forming a band in my teens with a name as close as possible to "Talking Heads" with the secret intention of being placed next to them in the racks at record shops. It would lead to using their music as the theme to a national radio show I would host many years later. And it would lead to recording a version of "Psycho Killer" with my touring group in the late '90s that would appear on our live album and become one of our standout show closers.

From the moment Talking Heads hit the stage at the Police Picnic in 1982, I was transported.

I had never seen or experienced anything quite like Talking Heads. Ever. All of a sudden, it was as though there were a hundred people onstage. I barely knew where to focus my attention. There was a cool blond woman playing bass. There were brilliant percussionists. There was a curly-haired guy who was very animated on rhythm guitar. There were black people and white people. There were women and men. There was a stage full of humans and everyone was grooving. From the moment they started playing, all the performers moved like the music was joyously deep in their bones. And at the centre of it all was a tall, thin guy with an elastic body that was contorting in ways I had never witnessed. He was like a rubber man. He was also somewhat androgynous. And then he started singing. Or speaking. Or announcing. And his words were profound. And weird. And funny. And he captured my attention like no one had beyond Bowie. And he had the same first name as Bowie. David. I was transfixed. I looked over at Wendy after the opening song. She was staring at the stage with her mouth half open. She was transfixed as well.

I would later learn who all these people onstage were. I would learn that they had emerged out of an art school on the east coast of America in the 1970s. Talking Heads were based in New York City and were almost more of an art experiment than a band. The cool blond woman on bass was Tina Weymouth. She was known for her minimalist art-punk bass lines combined with funk-inflected riffs. She would go on

173

to form the band Tom Tom Club with her spouse—who was also the Talking Heads drummer—Chris Frantz. Tom Tom Club would then write and record the infectious song "Genius of Love," which Mariah Carey would later reinterpret and record as "Fantasy," with which she enjoyed a major hit. The animated guitarist who was jumping around onstage was a guy named Jerry Harrison, who also played keys. He had been a founding member of one of the most influential bands of the '70s, the Modern Lovers (whose "Pablo Picasso" would later be covered by Bowie on *Reality*). He would go on to produce bands like the Violent Femmes and Foo Fighters. The other musicians onstage were rhythm makers, synth players, backup singers, and another electric guitarist. When I did a proper count, I decided there were nine people onstage in all. Or maybe the number was ten.

In the middle of all the action stood David Byrne, the lead singer and guitarist. He was the man with the elastic body. He was the kind of person that important critics would forever after call "an enigma." David Byrne was wearing grey pleated dress pants and a white fitted shirt with a collar that was buttoned all the way to the top. He was rake thin, and his jerky motions made him look like a puppet on a string. I would later learn that he had worked with the master producer Brian Eno, just like Bowie had in the late 1970s. And that he had the same creative adventurousness.

By the end of the second song, David Byrne was undoubtedly in charge of the stadium. Everyone was following his lead. And Talking Heads seemed to have it all. World-beat poly-rhythms, enough percussion to fill a drummer's paradise, futuristic synth sounds, chanting vocals, elements of disco and funk grooves, a punk rock urgency, and David Byrne as the ringmaster. It all combined to create something stunning.

The whole production of the Police Picnic show was bumped up a notch at this point, too. Talking Heads hit the stage around dusk, and the lights had been turned on and were splashing over the electrified performance area. I was awestruck. The happenings onstage were trumping anything in my life that had come before. It suddenly felt like nothing mattered but what I was witnessing. My Adidas bag, the Joan Jett incident, the intimidation by the older punks, my insecurity around my dream girl … all of it was left behind. This was not what I'd expected. I'd expected the Police Picnic to be about being with Wendy. I'd expected the highlight of the concert to be the Police. I was quickly realizing that my new focus was Talking Heads. That is, as well as being with Wendy. Experiencing this moment with her next to me made it all the more magical.

"I can't believe how good this is!" I screamed at Wendy over the music, even though she was standing so close that her shoulder was intermittently touching mine.

"I know!" Wendy replied with her own version of full volume. "This is so rad. I told you! I told you!"

We were now jumping up and down to Talking Heads' third song in their set. It was a tune called "Once in a Lifetime." I recognized this song from a video I'd seen on *The NewMusic*. Music videos were just starting to become commonplace and were only seen in Canada on shows like *The NewMusic*. In fact, *The NewMusic*, a weekly show based in Toronto that aired on Citytv with hosts J.D. Roberts and Jeanne Beker, had been a pioneering program in this regard. MTV had launched the previous August in the United States, and the Canadian music video channel, MuchMusic, would not be on the air until 1984.

With the appearance of MTV, and especially after the release of Michael Jackson's video for "Billie Jean" in January 1983, videos became mainstream and everyone started making them. Music videos very quickly transformed into an obligatory part of the business. As early as 1982, crappy bands began feeling like they had to make videos. These videos were usually crappy. Of course, artists like Madonna and Michael Jackson and Duran Duran would go on to shoot world-famous videos that were a major boon to their careers. But before then, it was largely more artistic acts that made short films to accompany their music.

Bowie had done this. And so had Talking Heads. And no one who'd seen Talking Heads' 1981 video for "Once in a Lifetime" would forget David Byrne's performance as a bespectacled marionette. This included hitting himself in the head each time he repeated the refrain at the end of the song chorus. Now the video and the marionette were coming to life on the stage in front of us.

"Once in a Lifetime" appeared on the Talking Heads record *Remain in Light*. That album would later be considered one of the best of the '80s. It brought with it progressive synthesizer sounds mixed with the influences of "Afrobeat" from Nigerian bandleader Fela Kuti. Eno had introduced Fela Kuti's music to the members of Talking Heads in the late '70s. "Once in a Lifetime" had a propulsive and hypnotic beat as its template and featured David Byrne speaking over top of the drum and bass groove in the verses. Much of what he was saying in the song was posed in the form of questions. And in the lyrics he would tell you that you might ask those questions as well.

David Byrne would do all this in his speak-sing style throughout the song. And when he delivered those questions onstage at the Police Picnic in 1982, it was as though David Byrne was speaking to me. And to a certain extent, he really was. Then, at the chorus of "Once in a Lifetime," Byrne began singing the refrain along with a number of the band members singing backup behind him. He was holding his arms up high in the air like President Richard Nixon before he'd gotten on that plane in disgrace in the 1970s. And then David Byrne would hit his head repeatedly. It was just like the music video, but even better. In the *Toronto Star* the next day, there was an enthusiastic review of the Police Picnic with a black-and-white photo of David Byrne in his white collared shirt with his arms in the air. The caption read, "David Byrne—kinetically involved." I repeated those words. Kinetically involved. I'm still not sure exactly what that meant. But it sounded just right. I cut the photo out of the newspaper and stuck it on my wall. It stayed up there for years.

As I've noted, David Byrne's elastic body was at the centre of the spectacle. I have made a short list of some of the physical positions that David Byrne contorted himself into during the Talking Heads set at the Police Picnic in 1982:

- man being punched in stomach
- man with arms in air like preacher (or Nixon)
- man slapping self on forehead with right hand
- man bending backwards in "camel pose"
- man speaking to talking hand
- man intensely shaking like a vibrator

As you can see from this list, there was no shortage of physical gestures in David Byrne's action repertoire. It was captivating. Wendy and I were now fully immersed in the Talking Heads experience. It felt like the whole stadium was moving under the influence of the music and sermons of David Byrne. The songs were magical. And the music was infectious. But well beyond the intoxicating sound emanating from the stage, it was clear that Talking Heads and Byrne were also about something else: theatre. Between the band members' animated performance and David Byrne's actions, it all felt like a real stage show. And this was not just any regular theatre … it was experimental theatre. I'd found another element to draw me to my new favourite band. And I'd found it with Wendy at my side.

9

"DO YOU REALLY WANT TO HURT ME"
— CULTURE CLUB

Wendy and I were no longer simply at a rock concert. By the middle of the Talking Heads set in August of 1982, we were witnessing a theatrical stage show. And it was brilliant. Really. You might think this is misty-eyed nostalgia. It's not. A band of New York City art school graduates had elevated the Police Picnic and the entire CNE Grandstand into a wild performance space.

The first rule of achieving cool is to position oneself in proximity to cool. And I had Wendy. Wendy had already known about Talking Heads. She'd been a fan. She had specifically mentioned them as the group to see when I first asked her to the Police Picnic as we stood in the second-floor hallway at Thornlea. That was back in June. I had been scared to talk to Wendy then. But I did. And here we were, two months later. I thought about how young I had been in June. I'd been naïve. I didn't even know anything about Talking Heads back then, except for identifying them with that song at a party that sounded like they were saying "fuck" in it, even though they weren't really saying "fuck" in it. I hadn't put it together that I'd seen the "Once in a Lifetime" video and been captivated. Talking Heads were more sophisticated than the standard band that might end up on a Grade 9 New Wave mix tape. I'd missed out on them until now. But Wendy had known all along. She'd been spot-on. That part was no surprise.

It made sense that Wendy would've already discovered David Byrne and his magical crew in Talking Heads. She was older. She was cool. She was the female Bowie. But with Talking Heads now onstage, I had little time for embarrassment about my former ignorance. I wanted ownership. I'd found my new favourite band and they validated my own curious mixture of interests. They were alternative but still popular. They were rhythmic but melodic. They were strange, but proof that strange didn't mean bad. They were like Bowie. Especially David Byrne. Just like Bowie, David Byrne would have had trouble fitting in on any given day in Thornhill. He was artsy and odd. And Bowie was odd. And knowing this gave me confidence. Their existence meant I wasn't weird. Or rather, that I might be weird, but that it was okay. Or that it was acceptable to want to be weird.

Wendy and I kept stealing glances at each other and smiling as Talking Heads powered through their set, gaining strength with each new song. It was as if we were sharing something very personal, even if we happened to be sharing it with forty-five thousand others as well. The dramatic flair of Talking Heads was tapping into our mutual interests. Theatre was something Wendy and I had in common. We were both involved in 213 at school. Theatre had become a big part of my life and had led to a challenging test of my identity only one month earlier.

I had experienced something of a true theatre debut. It hadn't exactly been pretty. And I still wasn't sure how much Wendy really knew.

MY TWO MAIN PASSIONS in the early '80s were music and theatre. Well, I also liked politics. And I liked Persian food. And history. And hockey. And girls. And maps. And soccer. But my main passions were music and theatre. It was the theatrical nature of much of New Wave music that brought those interests together. It's no surprise that I gravitated towards it. And no one embodied that creative blend more than Bowie. Bowie, in his chameleon-like style as a performer, practically *was* theatre. But when Talking Heads hit the stage at the Police Picnic, I learned that David Byrne and his bandmates were ambassadors of theatre and much more, too. This wasn't just rock. It was art.

In the summer of 1982, I celebrated my first foray into professional theatre. Okay, maybe that's a bit of a lie. It was professional inasmuch as performing for fewer than seventy-five people a night in the outdoors and having only eight lines might be considered a professional theatre gig. But people had to pay to see the show. They had to pay five dollars. Or something. And when people pay for anything, it's professional. Right? And anyway, no matter how professional you might've thought it was or it wasn't, it was an important experience. I'd concluded that theatre was in my bones. And this was a major step up-market from performing the role of the pharaoh in *Joseph and the Amazing Technicolor Dreamcoat* at Woodland Junior High in Grade 8. This was my real stage debut.

In the spring of '82, my Grade 9 schooling became

devoted entirely to the Theatre Troupe program based out of Room 213. This elective was a full trimester of theatre and music that was part of Thornlea Secondary School's fine-arts focus. It was quite revolutionary. Or at least we considered it to be. In Theatre Troupe, students spent all day every day doing acting exercises, reading plays, creating docudrama scenarios, and listening to New Wave music and Neil Young. We would do this for three months straight. Only this. In retrospect, it couldn't be anything but a formative experience.

The lights were kept low in 213. Even in the morning, when students first arrived. You might wonder why. But this was a no-brainer. Dim lighting was theatrical and demonstrated depth. In Theatre Troupe, each day was an adventure in drama and introspection. Everyone was very serious and eager to illustrate their passion. Between workshops and rehearsals, important things would be muttered amongst the Theatre Troupe students. Things like, "The world is totally fucked." This was a necessary demonstration of emoting, because the inhabitants of 213 were so artistic. And as well, the students were all very deep and cared a great deal about the world. That is, everyone cared about the world except when they didn't care about the world because things were just too heavy and "totally fucked" to spend time caring about it.

Also, as part of a worldly outlook in 1982, everyone in 213 hated Thatcher and Reagan. It was important to hate them. I wasn't entirely sure why. Neither of them was Canadian. But I knew that cool 213 students said Thatcher and Reagan had contributed to the world being fucked. So we all hated them. This was obligatory. On a personal level, I did remember that Margaret Thatcher had taken the milk away from schoolchildren when I was a little kid in England. One year in the '70s, we arrived at school to find there was no more free milk, which had been a staple of English education. Then everyone started saying, "Thatcher took our milk away!" I was unsure how this one woman had single-handedly taken all the milk. And I may also have thought her first name was Thatcher. But as I grew older, I understood that she'd taken our milk away because she was a Conservative. That's what Conservatives in Britain did. I knew she was not very nice to school students. And there was no more free milk. And she probably wouldn't have liked the artsy types who hated her in 213.

One other essential tenet of the Theatre Troupe experience was sex. That came with the territory, too. Sexual cross-pollination seemed to be part of the burden of being a dedicated theatre student in 213. This was not mandated by the teachers, of course, but developed quite naturally amongst those enrolled in the program. Almost all of the students dutifully obliged in the sex part. I was a novice in this area, but eager to learn. The truth was, I was generally too intimidated to act on anything with the older Troupe members. Not yet. That was all way beyond me at this point.

Despite my insecurities and confusion, I knew I wanted to be part of the Thornlea theatre scene. I knew music and theatre were my passions. And that Troupe was cool. And I knew that my sister had done theatre, and she was cool. And so I had angled to convince my parents to let me enroll in Theatre Troupe by getting through the full list of my obligatory math and science and history course requirements in the first two-thirds of the school year. Despite covering the educational bases, I knew my father would still be unhappy with the academic diversion of a full trimester of only theatre and music. He'd made his position clear. But I remained resolute. My father never really understood Theatre Troupe.

"You are going to be playing weeth only thees acting all day?" he said.

"It's more than that, Dad. We're learning about the world and life and struggles. We're doing docudramas, too." My replies were generally delivered in a patronizing tone. That was important. It demonstrated that I was ridiculing his mistaken ideas.

"The world? You are learning all of thees by doing thees acting?"

My father was never convinced.

You see, to my father, Theatre Troupe sounded unproductive and even destructive. My sister had done theatre at Thornlea, and she had managed to be a brilliant academic student in addition to her foray into fine arts. But my father still didn't get it. And he had been much harder on her when it came to 213. She had broken ground by mounting the first artsy insurrection in the Ghomeshi family. By the time I was angling for acting roles, my father had resigned himself to accepting it, but he still wasn't very pleased. In his eyes, Theatre Troupe was tantamount to kids spending their school days in a playground or the mall. It was heretical. This was not how strong vocational futures were built for middle-class Iranian boys. But he was wrong. Theatre Troupe was not akin to hanging out in a playground. It was more about *imagining* hanging out in a playground (or maybe the mall). I was going to be an actor.

The thing is, my father simply wasn't as deep as the introspective theatre students of 213. Theatre Troupe students understood hardship and worried about the world being fucked, and also what to wear when worrying about the world being fucked. Oh sure, my father may have gone through some tough times himself. He may have lost his own dad at fifteen and raised his six younger siblings with my grandmother in Iran. He may have single-handedly carried on the family business while putting himself through school and university in Tehran. He may have struggled to become a top engineer and make a good life with his wife and kids in England and then Canada, where he had a heavy accent and was sometimes treated with disdain. He may have lived through all of that. But what did he know about real hardship? He didn't understand a difficult life the way middle-class teenage theatre students at Thornlea did. We had perspective. And we had songs by the Cure. And we listened to music by bands that didn't smile. We knew no one had it as tough as us. Maybe that's what heavy New Wave eyeliner ultimately meant: life is hard.

Finally, my father and my mother reluctantly agreed to let me enter the Theatre Troupe program.

Mind you, that was not the end of the debate about my future career with my parents. It took a couple more decades for my father to truly accept my artistic interests. In university, I formed a band with Murray and Mike Ford and Dave Matheson, also former Thornlea theatre students. We called ourselves Moxy Früvous and started out as street buskers, performing in zany costumes. We would put on mini-shows on street corners and pass a hat around for tips, in the tradition of jugglers or fire-breathers. I would try to explain the concept to my father.

"Dad, it's called busking. It's street performance. There is a long and distinguished tradition of busking around the world. People love buskers. We're making art!"

"Yes," my father replied. "We have a name for thees in Iran as well. Eet is called begging."

You see, my parents really wanted me to be a doctor or an engineer. Don't blame them. It's not their fault. It's in the manual for immigrant Persian parents. It took many years for my mother and father to accept that such vocational aspirations would not be realized when it came to their son. It was near devastating for them. Middle-class Iranians believe there is nothing more honourable than for their kids to become engineers. Somewhere, sometime back in the old country, there was a decree that engineering was the noble profession. I can't tell you when this happened. I wasn't there. But I know many brown families that seem to adhere to the same handbook.

And honestly, the pedestal upon which engineers are placed feels a little out of whack with contemporary society. The doctor thing might be understandable. Doctors make a fine salary and save other humans. They are important enough that they wear white lab coats. But I never quite got the engineer thing. Not that there's anything wrong with engineers. There isn't. But they don't wear lab coats. Or save humans. Or make good music that kids can be inspired by. Still, the real rock stars in Iran have not been movie stars or footballers or politicians, they've been engineers.

I have made a short list (or shortlist) of occupations that most middle-class Iranians would like their kids to pursue:

- doctor
- civil engineer
- businessman
- mechanical engineer
- general engineer

As you can see, three of the top five occupations that Iranian parents seek for their kids are related to engineering. My father was an engineer. But it really wasn't for me.

As I got older, the windows gradually closed on all of these occupational possibilities for me. I just wasn't interested in the maths and sciences as much, even though I did pretty well in those areas. And to their credit, my parents were ultimately liberal enough to allow me to pursue my passion. They gave me their blessing to enter Theatre Troupe in the final part of Grade 9. This was a significant turning point for me. To tell you the truth, notwithstanding some silly moments, it was in Theatre Troupe that I got much of my greatest high school education. It was in Troupe that I truly learned to question everything. The news. History. Ideas. Traditions. Laws. And this questioning came in very handy. I would later learn that questioning everything is called "critical thinking." It helped me get top marks in political science and history courses in university. My father probably would not have guessed that in 1982.

I was the youngest in Theatre Troupe and one of only a few Grade 9 students enrolled. I remember it being hard to get into. I'm not exactly sure that it was, but that's how I always thought of it. Maybe it was because other students would say things like, "No way! You got into Theatre Troupe?" In reality, getting into Theatre Troupe largely required signing up to be in Theatre Troupe. That was mostly it. Mind you, hardly any Grade 9 students were accepted. My sister's status as a theatre star helped my position.

At the end of May 1982, it was announced that some of the members of Troupe would be doing a run of performances of Shakespeare's *A Midsummer Night's Dream* at an outdoor gazebo stage in Markham. The shows were scheduled for the end of June and early July. The news quickly became a hot topic amongst the Thornlea artsy crowd. Many of the cool older 213 students who were regularly clad in black and smoked were to be cast in the main roles. I auditioned and was proud to earn a part as one of the "mechanicals." The mechanicals are the amateur players in *Pyramus and Thisbe*, a play within the play in *Dream*. It wasn't much. But I was in. I was to perform the role of Tom Snout, the tinker.

My casting as Snout paid immediate dividends. It led me to new levels of access within the elite circles of 213. At rehearsals after school as well as in class, I was now in regular proximity to the likes of Alexa Fotheringham and Mary Daniel and Mike Farnell. They were all three or four years older than me. They were all friends with my sister. And they were all real-like actors who smoked and wore black. I'm not actually sure that Alexa smoked, but she probably did. She had long dark hair and she was serious and she was a good actor. That meant she probably smoked.

Most important, it was easier to meet my New Wave aspirations once my days were occupied in the theatre room. I no longer had gym class, where I might have to endure teasing from that Lacoste-wearing preppy Joel Price. He had beaten me at wrestling. And I didn't have to hang out near the rockers in science classes or the yearbook types in the second-floor hallway. Bowie would have been out of place in phys. ed. or math class, too. I was gradually marching closer to my Bowie-tinted goal.

Being the youngest and having a small role in the big Theatre Troupe show meant I was often at rehearsals but not paid much attention to. This suited me well, given that I was quite intimidated by all the thespian talent around me. In *A Midsummer Night's Dream*, Snout has very few lines, and his most significant contribution is to transform into the wall that separates the gardens of Pyramus and Thisbe. The two lovers whisper to each other through Snout's fingers, which are meant to represent a chink in the wall. My scenes added up to about five minutes of stage time. I think. Maybe seven minutes. There was no way to sugar-coat the limited nature of the gig. I was playing a tinker playing a wall. I know. It's not the type of experience that self-esteem is supposed to be built on. But then, it wasn't the limited nature of the role that would become an issue for my confidence, but the outfit I would be asked to wear.

Since Thornlea Theatre Troupe's outdoor staging of *A Midsummer Night's Dream* was a "professional" production, everyone had cool Shakespeare-like costumes. The actors wore boots and brown mesh and scarves and belts over the kind of pirate-type shirts Wendy's brother wore. Paul wore pirate-type shirts because he was older and an emerging professional actor. I'm still not sure why theatre people were supposed to wear boots and baggy trousers tucked into the boots and pirate shirts onstage. I suppose that's what Shakespeare himself wore, and serious actors were supposed to look like him. The more you looked like Shakespeare, the better an actor you were. That must be it. It's like how an aspiring classical musician must benefit by looking a bit like Mozart. Or how an aspiring prophet would be wise to look like Moses. And so, everyone had these very fine costumes, including all the guys playing the mechanicals. Everyone, that is, except me.

It seems the production team of Theatre Troupe's *A Midsummer Night's Dream* were one outfit short when it came to the mechanicals. While the other guys wore the pirate tops with big belts and boots and theatre pants, the only piece the costume people had for me was a giant mauve-coloured collarless shirt. To be fair, I really did have the smallest role in the play. Anyone else with a limited role was multi-tasking and playing other parts in the show as well. Not me. I was a natural to be the guy who ended up without a real costume. The mauve shirt I was given was procured in a dramatic frenzy backstage. It was on the day of the dress rehearsal that the slight dearth of costumes was discovered, and the costume people were improvising.

My mauve shirt had no buttons, just a V-neck, and it was quite billowy and wide. I was very aware of being the youngest in the cast and, given the limited nature of my role, had the least leverage to launch any sartorial complaints. The shirt I was to wear was also very long. It was far too large for my body. And it had no collar. It came down to my mid-thighs. I really don't know why a tinker would wear this outfit. But this was Shakespeare. And I assumed it was important for me to wear this frock rather than a New Wave T-shirt and jeans. Besides, I was in no position to decline the "costume."

But it got a bit worse: there really was no appropriate belt for my mauve shirt, so it just flowed down over my body with my skinny legs peeking out. I had been given black "theatre tights" to wear underneath (there were no proper trousers left, either) and a pair of black slip-ons that everyone called Chinese slippers. The reality was, it looked like I was wearing a dress. But not a fancy dress like a girl wears to the prom. Not one with bows and nice stitching. More of a dress like Jesus used to wear. Or the old Greek guys when they were thinking up excellent philosophies. Or what those traditional Saudi men might sport when they were on their way to pray. But actually, not even like that. It didn't look as cool and acceptable as any of those. This wasn't like a robe or an Arab *thobe*. It was more of a long-sleeved maternity dress. Except, no, it was really more of a minidress. I was performing in *A Midsummer Night's Dream* with the cool 213 crowd wearing an unbelted mauve minidress. On the night before our first performance, I asked Nancy, the nice costume girl—also a student at Thornlea—if she thought my outfit was a bit odd. She replied, "Don't worry, this is theatre!" She was trying to help me out. She assured me that no one would really notice. I would soon learn that Nancy was wrong.

Each evening, when I came out to deliver my lines as Tom Snout playing the wall, I would hear the audience snicker. I tried to convince myself they were snickering because of my comedic turn as Snout, but I had a good sense that it was also due to my inexplicable mauve minidress. To accompany the costume, I was wearing quite heavily applied theatre makeup. In sum, along with my gelled and dyed hair, I probably appeared much less like a tinker and more like an innocent young drag queen. I don't think being a drag queen was in the original script for Snout the tinker. I did my lines as Snout with an English accent. This was comfortable, because it was what I'd grown up with. But the accent just made me stand out even more. My exit line as the wall was the zenith of my performance.

Thus have I, Wall, my part discharged so;
And, being done, thus Wall away doth go.

Some people in the crowd would cheer a bit and laugh when I left the gazebo stage after delivering the final words of my big moment. I took little delight in the reaction. I was very self-conscious about my lines. And I was madly self-conscious about my minidress.

Still, given that no one was saying anything explicit to me about the costume, I held out hope that the laughter I was generating had to do with my comedic timing. *A Midsummer Night's Dream* has comic moments, after all. It's meant to be a farce. I was simply part of that, right? Surely my outfit just fit the bill. But I was getting hints that my attire was not going unnoticed. During the first show, one of the Theatre Troupe leads, Donna Davis, bumped into me backstage and said, "Is that your costume?" She asked me this with a note of concern in her voice. She said it as if to suggest there had been some kind of mistake. I nodded. This was my costume.

Toke came to our second night and barely spoke to me afterwards. This was odd for my best friend. He mumbled something about it being very much "like theatre and all dat," and I chose not to pursue any further explication of his critical thoughts.

But things really took a difficult turn when my father and mother came to see the show on our third night. After the play ended, I emerged from the backstage area (which was actually an indoor gymnasium near the outdoor gazebo) to find my parents waiting to say hello. My father was wearing a very proper suit and looking quite sheepish.

"Yes, hello, Jian." My father always spoke to me quite formally in public, even if no one was listening. "Eet was nice play," he said. He seemed to want to leave it at that.

"Good job, honey!" my mother chimed in exuberantly. "You were great!"

My mother punched the air when she said "good job," the way you do when you hit a home run or find out your teacher is sick and your class is cancelled. But I wasn't sure about her enthusiasm. My mother was always polite, just like the way she would say "This is great!" when the Polish people next door gave us Christmas baskets we didn't need. I knew she was likely embellishing for my sake.

"Oh ... well, thanks, Mom. Anyway, thanks for coming, you guys."

I didn't want to spend too much time talking to my parents. I had spotted Mike Farnell and Tom Howard both looking at me with my family. I wondered if these older actors would think I was less cool if I were speaking with my parents. I prepared to make my escape to the backstage area. Just when I thought I was home free, my father felt the need to speak up.

"Tell me," he said, audibly enough so that anyone in the vicinity could hear him, "why you were wearing thees dress in the play?"

My father could be very blunt sometimes. I don't think he

wanted to hurt me. It was, after all, a pretty good question. I was playing Tom Snout. A man. So why was I wearing a dress? Or rather, a shirt that looked like a dress. But it wasn't what I needed to hear. Not right after the show. Not with other people around. I lashed out with my reply.

"It's not a dress, Dad!" I shouted in my father's direction. "It's a costume! You don't understand Shakespeare. I'm sorry … if … you don't have Shakespeare in Iran!"

I turned away from my parents and darted across the gazebo to get my Adidas bag so I could take the bus home with some of the other cast members. I was feeling humiliated. Was being in the theatre scene really worth all this? I had tried to defend myself. But my father was right. It was more of a dress—and not a very pretty dress or an intentional one. Even worse, I had heard Wendy was coming to one of the performances of *A Midsummer Night's Dream* with her brother, Paul. I prayed she wouldn't make it. I never found out if she did. I surveyed the audience each night and never saw her. But either way, she didn't mention it now at the Police Picnic. Maybe Wendy had come to the play and decided not to mention the Jesus minidress. Maybe she was being sensitive to my feelings. Again.

With my higher-pitched voice and the impromptu mauve dress, I had inadvertently assumed a genderless look in our Theatre Troupe production. I had just turned fifteen in early June, and being seen as anything less than an adequate male was not entirely comfortable for me. I was already self-conscious about being skinny and one of the lousier players on my hockey team. Then again, gender ambiguity was all strangely apropos if you were New Wave. It made some sense to appear in drag. Albeit unwittingly in this case. New Wave culture was very much intertwined with androgyny and gender reversal. And this had become my forte. After one of our performances, Mike Farnell's friend saw me in the communal changing area and bluntly asked me if I was gay. I wasn't sure if it would be a good thing or not to tell this guy I was gay. Maybe he was gay. Maybe he would like it if I were gay too. I said no. But I wasn't entirely sure. And nor would I have thought it a bad thing to be gay. Maybe the makeup and the mauve dress I had to wear as Tom Snout were a message sent from above. I certainly liked Bowie. He was a man who sometimes dressed like a woman. And I was smitten with Wendy partly because she was like Bowie. I was obsessing over a girl who reminded me of a man who dressed like a girl. These were confusing times.

At the Police Picnic I saw that my newest role model, David Byrne, was also genderless in many ways. As Wendy and I watched him on stage, it dawned on me that he was a man who was comfortable in his skinny body and with not being particularly muscular or macho. What you need to know is that the early '80s was a period when many artists were challenging traditional ideas about masculinity. This was especially true in New Wave culture. If men were expressing themselves as tougher guys in rock bands like Van Halen, New Wave music was about the exploration and celebration of androgyny. Guys were wearing skirts and makeup and streaked hair. At the epicentre of all this was the lead singer of a band called Culture Club. He was an enigma in 1982. We would later find out his name was Boy George.

You know all about Boy George. First of all, you know that's his name. George. Boy George. You know he was a guy

who wore makeup and played with themes of gender stereotypes in the early '80s. You know him as a gay man now. But
we didn't know who he was in 1982. More importantly, we
didn't know *what* he was.

The debut Culture Club album, *Kissing to Be Clever*, was
released in 1982. It featured the hit song "Do You Really
Want to Hurt Me," which was the third single released by the
band in England but the first to come out in North America.
Culture Club had an appealing pop sound that was a mixture
of New Romantic synthesizers and old-school R&B and soul.
They were a very good group that would be unfairly judged
more for their image than their sound—although that image
was very much cultivated by the band. And as you also likely
know, they would go on to have several international hits in
the 1980s, and Boy George would become a widely recognized star before fading away. But we didn't know him in the
beginning.

For many in my circle of kids, our first exposure to Boy
George was the video for "Do You Really Want to Hurt
Me." The singer was unlike anything we'd seen before. This
person was in a white, genderless outfit, with long hair, heavy,
feminine makeup, and a cute hat. The singer had luscious lips
and a girlish pout and danced around through the video in
a slow and seductive way. The whole subtext of this music
video was that the singer was on trial for looking and being
different.

I have made a list of characters' reactions to the androgynous lead singer of Culture Club in the video for "Do You
Really Want to Hurt Me":

- judge shakes his head
- old man loses his monocle
- horrified young couple stops kissing
- shocked woman removes sunglasses
- arm wrestlers lose incentive to win
- woman falls off diving board into pool

These were all reactions to the gender-ambiguous lead singer of Culture Club in the video for "Do You Really Want to Hurt Me." It was a powerful and effective statement. The video was sending up our own reactions to this curious person. Especially given that we didn't know who it really was. I had a few debates with Toke about the lead singer of Culture Club in late summer of '82.

"Dat is totally a chick. It's an ugly chick."

Toke could be quite direct sometimes. Just like my father. He was convinced the lead singer of Culture Club was a woman.

"I think it's a guy, Toke. His voice is more like a guy's, too." I was not really sure myself. But it was important to maintain a debate.

"No. It's a girl. Dat's a girl's voice. A chick!"

The debate went on for a couple of weeks. Remember, this was before Google or Wikipedia. Arguments couldn't get settled by asking your iPhone for help. Now, you might just say to your smartphone, "Is that a chick?" and you'd get an informed response instantaneously. But we didn't have that in 1982. We had unanswered questions that could linger for days and wouldn't be resolved by *Encyclopaedia Britannica*. And in this case, even a lot of the New Wave kids at school didn't know the answer. It wasn't until one afternoon at Toke's house, when his older brother, Mitch, heard us discussing Culture Club, that he told us the lead singer's name was Boy George and that he was a man. Toke remained suspicious. But Mitch was usually an authority on these things.

The example of Boy George very much represents the way the world was changing for me with music and theatre in 1982. Questioning sexuality—including my own—was part of my routine, along with wanting to be Bowie. And I was not alone. Lots of the students in 213 were gay. Some of them were gay sometimes and not other times. One of the New Wave girls at Thornlea, who was a year older than me and dressed like John Taylor from Duran Duran, had told me she wished she was gay. It was odd for her to be disappointed that she was straight. Wider society's intolerance for homosexuality ran deep at the time. But in the New Romantic milieu, being gay or bisexual was almost coveted. I had a good sense that I was ultimately oriented towards a sexual attraction to women. And I certainly only fantasized about girls. But there was something liberating about sexual orientation not being a big deal. That was what New Wave music and 213 were teaching me. And in Wendy I got to be attracted to a beautiful female and still be devoted to Bowie.

My adoration of Bowie was related to the fact that I felt like an outsider. Bowie was the champion of the outcasts. At the end of Grade 9, I attended the commencement ceremonies for the graduating class at Thornlea. It took place in our school gym. I was there because Theatre Troupe members had a small role in a theatrical number to honour the graduating students, and I was also singing in the Thornlea Vocal Group.

The highlight of the event was a touching duet by Mike Ford and Dani Elwell. Mike had been dating my sister and was the coolest person I actually knew. He was five years older than me but still hanging out at high school. He was in theatre and also in music. He carried around an acoustic guitar and played in the hallways. He had a beard and Coke-bottle glasses. He was widely revered for his creative talents and encyclopedic knowledge of essential trivia. He would go on to play in Moxy Frûvous with me.

Dani was one of the prettiest girls at Thornlea. But she was also super New Wave and punk. She was like a gorgeous version of Siouxsie from Siouxsie and the Banshees. Dani wore a black leather jacket and big black scarves and crimped her hair. I was in awe of her, and she could sing, too. She had played bass in a Toronto punk band called the Babyslitters when she was only fifteen.

Mike and Dani ended the commencement ceremony with an acoustic guitar medley that concluded with David Bowie's "Changes." In "Changes," Bowie had written lyrics about children being spat on as they tried to change their reality. The words in the song suggested that young people were self-aware and "immune" to the influence of the mainstream adult world.

Hearing Mike and Dani sing "Changes" was one of the most beautiful experiences I'd ever had. It was probably partly because I was in awe of them both. But Bowie's lyrics also moved me. I always took "Changes" as a message from Bowie to all those who saw themselves as outcasts or outsiders. He understood us. He had written that song—albeit a decade earlier—for us. Bowie was more than a rock idol. He was a role model for those who felt they were different. Whether that meant differences of sexuality, gender, artistic choices, attitude, or race, I felt like Bowie understood me.

BACK AT THE POLICE PICNIC, Talking Heads had now launched into a frenetic song called "Life During Wartime." Wendy and I were bopping up and down along with what seemed like everyone else at the CNE Grandstand as well as the band onstage. My connection with this creative band was becoming more profound with each passing minute. I marvelled at how it was even possible that a rock group so infused with my own interests could not have occupied my stereo and my life before now. At the point in the song when David Byrne sang about changing his hairstyle so many times he didn't know what he looked like, I turned to Wendy and smiled. She smiled back. The fact that I was experiencing all of this with Wendy beside me was taking it from memorable to dreamlike.

By the time Talking Heads launched into their final song, a cover version of Al Green's classic "Take Me to the River," I was overwhelmed. It's a strange sensation, the moment when you discover your new favourite band. It's like the feeling of love at first sight with your fantasy partner. Or it's like being told you've won your school's public-speaking contest for your epic speech about the Montreal Canadiens' Guy Lafleur and you're only in Grade 5 and you've beaten all the kids in Grade 6, too. Yes. It's like either one of those two things. There is a sense that you will remember the moment forever. There is also the awareness that it will never get this good again. It may never again taste quite as good as it does the first time. But I can tell you, my devotion to Talking Heads began that day in August of 1982 and never abated.

The summer after the Police Picnic, I would go to see Talking Heads perform outside again, but this time headlining at the Kingswood Music Theatre for their "Stop Making Sense" tour. The tour featured an outstanding theatrical stage show with three giant screens displaying iconoclastic messages. The concert began with David Byrne in a tight white jacket that would grow throughout the set until by the end he was in a giant oversized suit. The oversized suit performance is now the stuff of legend. That tour was shot and made into a movie by Jonathan Demme. It's still one of the best concert films of all time.

In 1983, I formed a band named Tall New Buildings with Murray and John Ruttle and some other musician friends I'd met. Unlike the Wingnuts and Urban Transit, this group was our first to play outside of school and get some real exposure, even though we were all in our mid-teens. We had a minor New Wave hit on the alternative music station CFNY and some other radio channels for a song I wrote called "Fashion in Your Eye." And our videos got played a bunch on MuchMusic in the following few years. I would often get asked where the name Tall New Buildings came from. I would tell interviewers how I liked the name because it suggested modernity and was futuristic and it was somehow related to Toronto's growing skyline. But the truth was that I liked the name Tall New Buildings because I knew our records would come immediately after Talking Heads in the sales bins at record stores. If you were rifling through Talking Heads albums at Sam the Record Man, at some point you would hit Tall New Buildings. That was the theory. And it worked. Any type of proximity like this was something to jump at.

In the mid-90s, I would discover a new band that would achieve favourite status in my life and remain there to this day. They're called Radiohead and they're from the UK. I don't think there has been a better band in the world than Radiohead over the last two decades. Interestingly enough, Radiohead got their name from a song called "Radio Head." That song is from a 1986 album entitled *True Stories*. That album is by a band called Talking Heads.

When Talking Heads exited the stage at the CNE Grandstand on August 13, 1982, I was physically and emotionally exhausted. Wendy and I were both drenched in sweat. It wasn't until after they'd gone that I realized I'd been laughing out loud for much of the Talking Heads set. I was giddy. I was giddy like a schoolgirl or a young man in a mauve minidress. I would have been concerned about my less than manly disposition except that Wendy seemed to be high on the same energy. Besides, things couldn't really have gotten much better. Losing my Adidas bag felt like a lifetime away.

When the Police hit the stage mid-evening for their set, there was little question that they owned the headliner billing. The lighting and the sound and the staging were more ostentatious and glamorous than they had been for all the other bands combined. The Police were the superstars. And there was no doubt they sounded good. Sting was in fine form, playing coy and teasing the audience between songs. He had blond, straight hair with a long bit like Wendy's. He jumped up and down and hit all those high notes that I'd not been able to reach when I'd sung "Roxanne." Andy Summers bounced around the stage like a Muppet on guitar. And of course, I was transfixed by Stewart Copeland's stellar drumming.

Mind you, for all that they were trendsetters, the Police certainly had a lot of hits. Despite their New Wave synth sounds, there was something uncomfortably commercial about the Police. They had increasingly become mainstream pop stars. I wondered why they were allowed to have massive successes with their songs but Joan Jett was not. I wondered if it had been fair that the entire crowd had turned on Joan Jett as a sellout. Forbes the punk had thrown my Adidas bag at Joan Jett because she was such a sellout. Yet the Police were now staples of pop radio as well. In fact, they were much bigger than Joan Jett. It didn't entirely make sense. But the Police were still cool. They were still considered New Wave. Their art was still suspected to be real. The audience roared with delight.

Watching the Police was not a letdown. That would be an overstatement. But there was nothing that any band could have done to follow the magic of Talking Heads on this day. Wendy and I maintained our position near the front of the stage and we sang along to all the familiar songs and high-fived with the stubble-faced guys, who were still next to us. The Police were good. We stayed until the encores were done. During one break in the set, Wendy leaned in to me and whispered, "This has really been a great day." She smiled, and her eyes squinted like Bowie's eyes would.

On the subway ride home, Wendy and I didn't say much to each other. We agreed that Talking Heads had been the best band on the bill, and we joked about the Forbes incident. After Eglinton station, the crowded subway car emptied enough for us to share seats next to each other facing the direction of home. Wendy and I were both looking straight ahead. I was tired. I wanted to rest my head on Wendy's shoulder. I wanted to curl up into her or have her rest her head on me. But I couldn't. I became very self-conscious.

I thought about how long it had been that I'd wanted to spend time with Wendy. I thought about how I'd spent most of the year hoping she would notice me in the Thornlea hallways. I suddenly became very intimidated by the thought of doing anything that Wendy might consider uncool. I wondered if I'd see her much during the new school year. I wondered if we'd continue to become close friends.

When we got to Finch subway, we walked up to the round-about where Wendy's brother, Paul, was waiting to pick her up. We were there about half an hour later than we'd said we would be, and he didn't look happy. Wendy offered me a ride, but I told her I'd be fine taking the Thornhill Transit bus home. I was a bit scared that Paul would be angry if I came along.

"I guess I'll see ya when I see ya," Wendy said with a smile. Her eyes twinkled. She was really very pretty. And cool. And she was genuinely nice.

"Yeah … back to school soon, eh?" I said.

It was an odd thing to say in that moment. Much colder than I'd intended. I regretted my words as soon as they came out of my mouth. That was the best goodbye I could say to the girl I'd thought about for months? I suddenly felt very young and awkward. But then something quite unexpected happened.

"Well, I hope I get to see you soon, Jian. Thanks again for bringing me along today. It really was rad."

Wendy then moved towards me and got up on her toes and

threw her arms around my skinny shoulders. She kissed me on the right cheek. I felt her lips touching my skin. It felt like they lingered there. It felt magical. It was slightly more than a peck, but still somehow very graceful. It was pretty much as good as a kiss on the cheek could get. Wendy slowly pulled away, smiled at me, and then turned and ran to her brother's car, where he was waiting.

The Police Picnic had turned out to be a lot more than a concert. It was a coming of age. I felt like a man, no matter how much eyeliner I'd worn. In one long and eventful day, I had been kissed by my dream girl, forever lost a prized possession from my recently departed youth, and forever gained a new favourite band that would see me into adulthood.

10

"EBONY AND IVORY"
- PAUL McCARTNEY AND STEVIE WONDER

I had always wanted to be a rock singer.

I'd done pretty well with the Wingnuts and our big gig at the Woodland Junior High gymnasium in Grade 8. I'd certainly deduced that girls fancied rock singers. And so I imagined that if I became a good rock singer, I would probably get Wendy's attention and affection.

The good news was that a few months before I summoned up the courage to ask Wendy to the Police Picnic, I began to receive some notice for my vocal abilities. The less than good news was that this modest vocal triumph did not really come from singing. It was about speaking. In the middle of Grade 9, I started doing the morning announcements at Thornlea Secondary School. It was a job for a nerd. I was that nerd. Actually, no, I was more. I was an aspiring Persian-Canadian New Wave singer with newly acquired hair gel ... and also a public-speaking nerd. This was the first time I became identified for my voice.

The morning announcements were roughly five minutes in

length and involved holding a microphone close to a cassette deck that was playing the national anthem and then telling everyone that classes were to begin. We didn't have digital music players in the early '80s. We had clunky portable cassette decks left over from the '70s. They would make loud whirring sounds when they were rewinding. And we would hold a microphone close to the cassette-player speaker for the audio to be heard over the school PA system. If you're a teenager reading this now, you probably think the whole exercise sounds prehistoric. That's because it was. Sometimes, describing the way we lived in the early 1980s is akin to telling the story of being a pioneer:

"Yes … we survived with these large-knobbed cassette players, children. And we used shiny tapes in plastic cases that moved quickly in circles and often broke. And also, we learned how to mash up peanuts and butter in order to make peanut butter for food."

Okay, maybe I have no idea how you make peanut butter. We never did that. But the point is, clunky Thornlea tape-deck technology was the only option at the time. It was all very antiquated.

The morning announcements were a thankless endeavour but a big step into prominence by my standards. And I'm still not really sure how I got this odd morning gig. Somehow, I took the place of our vice-principal and his moustache. The vice-principal, who had a very prominent moustache, had been holding down the morning announcements duty for the first few months of my Grade 9 year. He had a temper that could spring up like burnt toast. Word had it that he'd become frustrated one morning when the "O Canada" tape was not cued up properly, and he had spent several minutes "live on the air" trying to rewind the cassette and begin it at the right place as everyone listened over the school speakers. When he finally started the anthem, it was somewhere in the middle, at the "... in all thy sons command" part. Some students later claimed they overheard the vice-principal with the moustache curtly say "Oh, fuck it" over the PA system. I don't really know if he said "Oh, fuck it." It wouldn't be something a vice-principal was supposed to say to an audience of students. But whether he said "Oh, fuck it" or not, that day proved to be his breaking point. So in early 1982, I began as the voice on the school speakers every morning.

My job was to greet the student body and introduce the national anthem and then read a list of meetings and events for the school population. After a few weeks at the mic, I started adding a "thought for the day" to end the announcements with. This element became my favourite moment on the job. My thought for the day was usually something benign, like an affirming declaration from Gandhi or John Stuart Mill or one of the popes. You know those quotes. You see them at the beginning of important movies, or at the end of important movies, or when someone dies, or in the books of quotations that sit on top of the toilet at your friend's house. You see these kinds of quotes on Twitter now when everybody is writing #RIP about something. They are words that are universally considered very wise and significant. These are quotes I knew to be non-controversial and likely sanctioned by the school authorities.

"All good things which exist are the fruits of originality."
—John Stuart Mill

See? Who would ever disagree with that? It's very important sounding, right? And no one has issues with a proclamation that includes "good things" and "fruits of originality." So I used that one once. But does it really add to your daily knowledge about life? No, it doesn't. This is an example of a benign quote. Nice fancy words that ultimately add nothing. But then once in a while I would slip something different in. I took pride in imagining myself a rebel in this way. And on two occasions I used a Bowie lyric as the thought for the day. That was when I was being subversive.

Once, I used a Bowie quote from the song "What in the World" on the album *Low* about being out of control and in the mood for love. I'm pretty sure that was the only time the chorus of "What in the World" has ever been used as an inspirational message for the morning announcements at a high school. I cunningly recited this lyric over the loudspeakers at Thornlea knowing that the vice-principal with the moustache would never have done so. Maybe I wasn't entirely sure what being in "the mood" really meant, but I imagined that Bowie would think I was cool for using it. Being subversive at the time didn't mean Malcolm X or Trotsky quotations. Not from where I stood at the mic. The future of change was Bowie. "What in the world can you do, I'm in the mood for your love" would later become my graduating quote in the Thornlea yearbook in 1986.

The thing is, I thought of the morning announcements as some sort of performance. I thought of them like a mini-concert with a large audience. Thornlea was a school with almost two thousand students. This was no small crowd hearing my fledgling baritone. But very few others considered the announcements to be cool. No popularity came from being the kid who informed everyone that schoolwork had to begin. And it's not as if girls would like a guy because he did the morning announcements. Not even the nerdy girls. There has probably never been a heartthrob in history who attained heartthrob status based on his prowess doing morning announcements at a high school. So it was a losing proposition overall. But I was good at it. And one time, when Paula Silverman found out I was the voice, she told me I sounded "sexy." And she wore short shorts. And her compliment made me feel good, because I figured I was like a broadcaster—a "sexy" broadcaster. And being a broadcaster seemed cool.

Most important, the morning announcement job was largely anonymous. A bunch of my classmates knew who was behind the voice, but I never said my name over the PA, and few students saw me making the announcements from the principal's office, even though the walls all had windows. I took some comfort in my anonymity. I could perform without being judged. It didn't matter that I was brown or New Wave or not New Wave enough. But this was a contradiction, too. I didn't actually want anonymity. I wanted to be a rock star. And being a rock star meant being seen. It meant singing in front of Wendy and crowds who could witness it. And that meant trying to come to terms with who I was. And that's why the Harbourfront concert in the spring of 1982 was so pivotal. And that's also what would lead to a duet that brought a good deal of uncertainty about my identity.

You see, I was confused in Grade 9.

I know. That part isn't a particular revelation to you at this point. But there were times when I couldn't quiet the voices in my head. The voices would remind me I was a fake. An imposter.

You might think this sounds familiar. You might contend that all kids in their early teens go through feelings like this. And I appreciate the solidarity, but you'd be wrong. It's a thing that benevolent people say:

"Oh, all teens are messed up and trying to figure it out."

Or:

"Yes … it's a challenging time for anybody."

Just like that. That's the kind of thing well-meaning people say. They say this to make kids feel better about being imposters so that they don't swallow turpentine or harm small dogs when they become adults. But not all kids struggle with this equally. It's easier not to feel like a fake if you have a perfect nose and straight blond hair. That's a fact. Or at least, I was always sure it was. I was sure that Wendy never felt like a fake. That's one of the reasons she was almost perfect, like Bowie.

For me in 1982, the voices in my head were a reminder of my ongoing life as an imposter. The voices would also point out that I wasn't who I was made out to be in song. And this would lead to a most unfortunate onstage experience before the end of Grade 9. It wasn't about how I sang. My singing didn't really suck. The point was, the quality of my singing was *not* the point if I wasn't sure who I was. I was confused.

I WAS NERVOUSLY WAITING at the side of the stage at Harbourfront Centre in downtown Toronto in the spring of 1982. The second-last song of the show was coming to an end. There was a small set of steps leading up to the area where I would soon be standing in the spotlight for the finale. My eyes were trained on those steps. I was about to make my major singing debut. I was fidgeting. I had my hands focused north of my forehead, where I was trying to sculpt the gel that kept the front part of my hair standing up so the tips could then come flowing down in an arch. That's the way the guy from Ultravox had his hair. He was New Wave. I was never quite sure how to get that right.

This gig was what I'd wanted. I was supposed to be excited about my debut. I mean, I had been onstage before. I wasn't entirely a rookie. As I've told you, I had played in the Wingnuts, and we had done our big show at the Woodland Junior High gymnasium at the end of Grade 8. I had performed the role of the pharaoh in *Joseph and the Amazing Technicolor Dreamcoat* there as well. And I was now the main drummer in the Thornhill Community Band, and we had performed the theme from *New York, New York* with featured tap dancers at our Christmas concert at the community centre. The tap dancers had worn sparkly jackets and little shorts that exposed their long, tap-dancing legs. But I hadn't really done an official show on a big stage. Not as a singer. I was two minutes away from my turn to step up. I would be holding a microphone of my own. And I would be performing two solo verses of a famous song.

The plan was for me to close this landmark show in a duet with the most talented singer at our high school. Our music teacher had wanted a boy and a girl to perform together, and I had been selected for the guy part. I had nothing close to the pipes of my singing partner, but she was a girl. And because she was a girl, it was acceptable that I wasn't technically as good as her. Boys never sing as well as girls. Not usually. Have you

213

ever noticed that? They don't. That's because female vocalists can sing the way Mariah Carey or Beyoncé does. They have dizzying multi-octave ranges and engage in vocal gymnastics. Guys, on the other hand, they just have to be able to warble like Bob Dylan or Jay-Z. They can rely on their personality and "musical integrity." Women sing better. That's why, in most musical duos, the man plays the lame supporting role. Just look at Sonny and Cher. Or Rihanna and Drake. Or Kermit and Miss Piggy. Or Captain and Tennille. I'm not even sure if Captain sang at all when Captain and Tennille did their hit song "Love Will Keep Us Together" in the '70s. And if he did, he wasn't as good as Tennille. Guys never sang as well as women. That is, except for Bowie. His voice was always as good as a girl's voice, except it was much deeper. Usually.

For the Harbourfront finale, it didn't matter if I was a vocal master. I simply needed to hold my own. I just had to get up there and do my best in front of the enthusiastic crowd. That's what Bowie would do. That's what Bob, the music teacher, had said to do. If only I could sing the lyrics like I meant them. If only I could really believe I wasn't a fraud. If only my entire identity wasn't bound up in performing one side of a crappy pop duet.

I knew what I was supposed to do. I was supposed to exude confidence. I was supposed to act like a star. But memories of being the oddball were flooding back to me. I'd always been the oddball. I wanted so badly to be accepted. But who was I trying to *be* in this song? I wasn't sure. It was like when the nice gay guy sings "Who am I anyway?" in *A Chorus Line*. People usually have sympathy for the nice gay guy at that point in the show. But in the musical, he's struggling with being gay and insecure and needing to present himself as something else. That was just like me. Except in my case it was a different shade. For me it was about being ethnic. And there's a grey area when it comes to brown. The song I was about to sing was forcing the issue. I was confused.

MY JOURNEY TO THE GRAND Harbourfront stage in May of 1982 began with countless hours spent in the school's music room as a member of the Thornlea Vocal Group. By the second month of high school, I was doing whatever I could to pursue my musical dreams. Beyond attending to core subjects and spending time and energy in Room 213, I would occupy the Thornlea music room. It was a large rectangular space with graduated floors and a parade of instruments sitting on various shelves. In the middle of the room stood an upright piano and a drum kit with some guitar amps. It was a high school rock-music version of McDonald's Playland for kids. Before and after the regular school day, any number of aspiring musical stars would hang out in Room 273 and exploit the instruments. This was where I did my time on the four-piece school drum kit with fancy Zildjian cymbals learning to play "Tom Sawyer" by Rush. There were always drummers and rocker guitarists and their followers hanging out in the music room. Everyone generally had long and greasy hair and wore faded jean jackets. This was cool.

You might think the music students would have had a lot in common with the theatre group in 213, but there was actually little crossover. The music and theatre crowds were largely a divided lot. The 213 students were artsy and introspective. They were also punk and New Wave. The music room was populated by rockers, aspiring pop singers, and orchestral instrumentalists. I straddled both communities. I never really saw Wendy hanging about the music room area. She was part of the theatre scene. By the end of Grade 9, I would know to spend more time around Room 213, even beyond my class requirements in Theatre Troupe. The 213 crowd was where I might encounter Wendy. I had my priorities.

The main music teacher at Thornlea was a man named Bob Leonard. He was a hip guy in a "jazz cat" kind of way. Just as with the theatre teachers in 213, the liberal origins of our high school meant it was okay for students to call Mr. Leonard by his first name. So he was Bob. On most days, Bob wore a brown jacket with suede elbow patches and blue jeans or brown corduroys. He dressed the way a rumpled musician of the 1970s would dress if he was trying to appear "grown up." Bob had facial hair and glasses and a very nasal voice. He said "sure" a lot. In fact, he began and ended almost every sentence by saying "sure." But with Bob's nasal voice, this trademark word of his sounded more like "shoo-er." Bob was also very nice and quite gentle. So, for example, if Bob wanted to order you to be at a class on time, at his most forceful he might say, "Shoo-er ... well, please make shoo-er to get there on the hour, please ... shoo-er." It was a strange vocal tic to go along with his genial nature. Maybe "shoo-er" had been part of 1970s jazz-speak when he was young. I'm not sure. But it was Bob. And most students had great affection for Bob. He cared about music. And he cared about us. And Bob always made me feel like I belonged. I didn't usually feel ethnic or oddball when I was around him.

Bob spent most of his time sitting at the upright piano in 273. He would teach classes, lead the school orchestra, and conduct the choir and the band from his perch at the piano. He was a very good piano player. But we'd also heard he had been a fine drummer as a student at Humber College. He seldom got behind the drum kit at Thornlea. On the only occasion I witnessed him picking up the sticks, it was clear he still had the chops. Bob was a jazz drummer in the Buddy Rich tradition. That meant he held his left drumstick in the cross-position on the snare drum. This was another reason Bob was cool.

It was positive being in the presence of Bob. He seemed to exist in a perennially jovial state. I only once saw Bob get angry and lose his temper. We were singing "Africa" by Toto in Vocal Group when I was in Grade 10, and one of the rhythmically challenged singers was tapping offbeat on the top of the piano while Bob was playing. I could see that Bob was getting angry at the tapping. Midway through "Africa," Bob suddenly stopped playing and slammed the piano cover down over the keys.

"If you're going to tap along, make sure you do it in time!"

Bob was steaming mad. He didn't even say "shoo-er." I'd never seen him like that. And it didn't make sense that a normal person would become so bothered by a rhythmic transgression. That's when I knew he was a real drummer. He was badass about rhythm. That's when I knew Bob was one of us.

In November of 1981, I saw a posting outside the music room inviting students to join the Thornlea Vocal Group. The group comprised a small collection of the best singers from different grades at our school who would get together and work on songs to be performed at school assemblies. Bob was the leader of the group and the teacher in charge. I just assumed that no other secondary institution had an official vocal group like ours. We were an arts school, after all. I later learned that in other places such groups were referred to as "glee clubs." That never really made sense to me. Singers aren't always filled with glee. They can be quite morose. But joining the morose club probably didn't have the right ring to it. School board trustees and advisors would likely not want to hear about a morose club. So it was the Thornlea Vocal Group. That seemed like a much more appropriate name. And Vocal Group wasn't easy to get into. Or rather, it was easy to get into, but it wasn't easy to build up the guts to ask to be involved.

By December, I started attending Vocal Group practices in the music room. I'd been tentative about joining for fear I wasn't good enough and had approached Bob for his advice after school one day. He was as encouraging as ever.

"Shoo-er … you'll fit in just fine in Vocal Group … shoo-er," Bob said. "Oh, you should do it. Shoo-er."

I was one of the youngest and skinniest in the group, and I tried to sing quieter on some days so that no one would hear me. That way, I wouldn't stand out. Most of them likely didn't know I had been in the Wingnuts and sung "The Jean Genie" the year before. And none of them really knew I was the guy that did the announcements each morning.

Thornlea Vocal Group assembled for practice in the music room two or three times a week. There were about fifteen core members, and many of them were older blond girls who had perfect noses. Most blond girls with perfect noses want to be pop stars. At least, at some point they do. They assume that because they have blond hair and perfect noses they are more likely to become a star. This assumption is based on the fact that they actually are more likely to achieve stardom with their perfect noses and blond hair. So they decide to focus on becoming celebrities. That was definitely true at Thornlea. Everyone took things quite seriously, and everyone also wanted to be a great singer, like Irene Cara from *Fame*. This may explain why we ended up doing a lot of songs popularized by Irene Cara from *Fame*. *Fame* was a movie that had become a TV show that had become a musical. It was about trying to achieve fame by singing and dancing. The message of *Fame* was that you had to work hard for fame, and that if you work hard you would get fame. Maybe. And also that working hard meant breaking into song and dance on the desks of your classroom at any random time.

In Vocal Group, the song "Out Here on My Own" from *Fame* had become one of the staples of our repertoire. I had taken a descending harmony at the chorus section of that ballad for my contribution in the group. It's the part that features the lyrics about closing your eyes so you can be with that special someone. I closed my eyes when we sang that part to show I was serious. Serious singers often closed their eyes. I'd seen Bowie closing his eyes in the black-and-white video for the song "Wild Is the Wind." Sometimes, closing your eyes and looking forlorn made the listener realize you meant what you were singing. So I closed my eyes often.

In Thornlea Vocal Group, we also did the song "Fame" from the musical *Fame*. And we regularly worked through a version of a tune called "Higher and Higher" that Rita Coolidge had made popular in the late '70s. We didn't do any New Wave songs. I once brought in a song by the Cure, but Bob didn't seem to think that was appropriate. Real singers didn't do New Wave. Except for Bowie. But we didn't do any Bowie.

Here is a short list of songs we performed in Thornlea Vocal Group in 1982:

- "Fame" (from *Fame*)
- "Out Here on My Own" (from *Fame*)
- "What I Did for Love" (from *A Chorus Line*)
- "Higher and Higher"
- "I Sing the Body Electric" (from *Fame*)

As you can see, there was a lot of interest in singing songs from *Fame*.

The Thornlea Vocal Group's gigs were limited to playing on the school grounds, at first. That changed in the spring of 1982. In March, we were told about the biggest show to be booked in Vocal Group history. Bob announced that we would be doing a concert at Toronto's Harbourfront Centre in mid-May. It was huge news. The concert was to be creatively called "The Thornlea Vocal Group in Concert at Toronto's Harbourfront Centre!"

The Harbourfront gig was scheduled to last about forty-five minutes and was open to the general public. It wasn't clear why any member of the Toronto general public would want to make it a priority to see an amateur high school vocal group sing a forty-five-minute concert featuring various selections from *Fame*, but that didn't matter. We knew this was a major show for us. And we knew there would be parents and other students in attendance. Bob suggested we would do seven songs from our Thornlea Vocal Group repertoire as an ensemble, plus a version of "Out Here on My Own" that would be led by Debbie Drew singing the Irene Cara solo bit at the front. Debbie Drew was a fine young singer who was only in Grade 9 like me. She had been singing the solo part of the Irene Cara ballad since we'd started practising it. Everyone talked about how the Harbourfront concert was going to be Debbie Drew's "big break." No one really explained how performing for a few parents and peers would amount to a big break. But this was a public concert. That's what was important. And finally, Bob also declared that he wanted the show to end with a co-ed duet as the finale. Bob revealed that he had recruited Kim Richardson to sing with us. This was another major coup.

Kim Richardson was too good for the Thornlea Vocal Group. I don't mean she was pretentious. I mean she was really too talented to be wasting time with the rest of us. While she would graciously come and sing with us at some practices, she didn't need to be there. Kim Richardson was a year or two older than me, and she was the best singer at Thornlea. She may have been the best singer in Canada. She may still be. Her mother is a famous jazz and theatre singer named Jackie Richardson. I would later become very close friends with Kim and know her mom as Auntie Jackie. Kim had a tremendous gift. She could've sung any kind of music she wanted. But Kim liked to rock.

Kim was a fan of Van Halen and had pictures of the band members all over her locker. Van Halen were a rock group that insisted on wearing tight spandex and leather outfits to go with their monster guitar and drum riffs. Van Halen usually looked ridiculous. Sometimes they wore bandanas over random parts of their skin-tight clothing. This never made any sense, but it was high fashion in the '80s. These sartorial transgressions were balanced by the fact that Eddie Van Halen was a brilliant rock guitarist. And the band undoubtedly had a facility for writing catchy rock-pop songs. Kim loved Van Halen. She dressed in leopard-print clothing and tight pants the way the Van Halen lead singer, David Lee Roth, did. Kim was tall and had really, really big breasts. When she wore her tight Van Halen T-shirts, her breasts were emphasized, and it was hard not to look at them, even though it was not right to be looking at them. Kim started a band with three of the better rock musicians from Grade 12 at Thornlea and they called themselves MARZ. The name consists of the first letter of each member's last name.

Here is a tip for you about naming rock bands: Every band in the world thinks about naming themselves using the first letter of each member's last name. It's like a reflex. It's the first thing most bands think of, because most bands are usually a bit stupid. But then very few bands actually do it, because it's a bit stupid. The band can end up being called "GMALST" or something. That's hard to market. But MARZ did it, and it sounded cool. Kim was the *R* and Paul Zammit was the Z. Paul was a Jewish kid with a giant Afro, and he was a meticulously good drummer. Everyone called him Zammit, which even sounded like the name of a good drummer. MARZ was the best band at Rock Nite at the Thornlea gymnasium. Hussein, the head of Rock Nite, was also a drummer, and he made sure to program MARZ to perform last, because he knew Kim and Zammit were the best.

In MARZ, Kim Richardson sang all kinds of rock hits by Rush and Van Halen and Heart. You will note that two of those three bands I've just mentioned had male singers. Kim Richardson was a girl, but she sang those songs. In the early 1980s, it entirely made sense that a good female singer would need to handle rock songs sung by male stars. That's because rock men had entered a strange decade where singing with high-pitched voices became the norm. Geddy Lee from Rush was a part of this rock tradition whereby male lead singers needed to sing as high as possible. I was never sure why or how this began. In the 1960s, rock-band guys sounded more like men—like Mick Jagger or Jim Morrison or John Lennon. But by the late 1970s, credible male rock singers needed to wail like sopranos or hyenas. (Maybe it was some kind of throwback to castrato opera singers of earlier centuries, who would sing high because they'd had their testicles cut off. Or maybe the castratos had their testicles cut off in order for them to be able to sing high. I can never remember which came first. But anyway, it was an awkward and curious development in the 1970s and '80s, especially because I'm quite sure these rock lead vocalists retained their testicles. I think.)

Here is a short list of male rock singers who sounded more like high-pitched female rock singers in the late 1970s:

- Geddy Lee (Rush)
- Steve Perry (Journey)
- Rik Emmett (Triumph)
- Dennis DeYoung (Styx)
- Nick Gilder
- Roger Hodgson (Supertramp)
- the guy from the band Boston

As you can see, some of the most popular rock singers of the late '70s were men who strained their vocal cords to sing in a high-pitched way. This meant Kim Richardson could easily handle the male parts, and she did so with aplomb. But then, Kim's most captivating turn was performing a song called "I'm Gonna Follow You" by Pat Benatar from her album *Crimes of Passion*. Pat Benatar was very sexy and wore tight leggings just like the members of Van Halen. She also wore jackets with shoulder pads before most people did. I'm pretty sure Pat Benatar never heard Kim singing her song. That's probably a good thing. Pat Benatar was one of the best singers in rock. But Kim Richardson was a better singer than Pat Benatar.

Back in the Thornlea music room, Bob had recruited Kim Richardson to sing the female part in the duet that was scheduled for the Harbourfront finale. In mid-April, Bob began our regular Vocal Group practice by announcing to the whole group that he had chosen me to sing the male part in the duet. Some of the Vocal Group members clapped. It was a great distinction for me. That is, it was a great distinction for me even though there were only four other guys in Vocal Group to choose from. Actually, one of the four was a science teacher named Mr. Sanderson, so I'd really only beaten two others. Still, this was a major accomplishment for a Grade 9 student with a mediocre voice. I was probably the first Middle Eastern kid to get to do a solo in a duet with Thornlea Vocal Group. It felt like I had finally arrived. The only remaining question was what song we were going to sing.

It wasn't until three weeks before our big Harbourfront concert that Bob announced the song that I was to sing in the duet finale with Kim Richardson. The duet had not really been a priority at the practices, because it didn't involve the whole group until the end refrain. Finally, with some fanfare, Bob revealed the song that would close the concert.

"For the duet finale, I've chosen … shoo-er … 'Ebony and Ivory'! Shoo-er. It's going to be fantastic!"

Some of the Vocal Group members clapped to be supportive.

Bob had a big grin on his face. It made sense that he had chosen that particular song. It was rising in the charts and was pretty much ubiquitous on the radio. "Ebony and Ivory" was a hit. But it was with the selection of "Ebony and Ivory" that my stunning singing debut started to take a pale turn.

"Ebony and Ivory" was a duet written and performed by Paul McCartney and Stevie Wonder. It had become a number-one pop single after being released in March. It was about a black person and a white person coexisting in perfect harmony. To underscore this harmony, it was a recording of a black person and a white person who coexist throughout the tune. It was all very sweet. And it was also one of the worst songs in history.

It seems almost inconceivable that Stevie Wonder and Paul McCartney could come up with a song as horrible as "Ebony and Ivory." Both are musical icons that already had rich histories of writing stellar classics. They are two of my heroes. I had always wanted a voice like Stevie's. His *Fulfillingness' First Finale* from 1974 is one of the best albums ever recorded. And as I've already told you, McCartney was always an idol of mine. Still is. Long before I truly discovered how revolutionary the Beatles had been, I immersed myself in McCartney and Wings recordings, and some of them were among my all-time favourite songs. I'd learned to play "With a Little Luck" on guitar in Grade 8. But here's the dose of reality: both of those legends have had unfortunate moments in their careers when they created excessively candy-coated pop. This new duet took things to the next level of saccharine.

Let me explain "Ebony and Ivory" in scientific terms. Try this experiment at home. Pour a medium-sized coffee and then put seven large sugar cubes in it. Then quickly empty the coffee and keep only the wet sugar cubes. Now consume the wet sugar. Presto. You have an empirical example of the nature of the "Ebony and Ivory" duet (and some wasted coffee). Between the sweet melody and the earnest sentiment, the song was never easy to listen to. Or perhaps it was too easy to listen to. It became a giant hit. But that didn't make it any better. It is surely one of the most annoying duets of all time.

To provide some context, I have compiled a short list (or shortlist) of the worst pop duets of all time:

1. Gwyneth Paltrow and Huey Lewis, "Cruisin'"
2. Paul McCartney and Michael Jackson, "The Girl Is Mine"
3. Paul McCartney and Stevie Wonder, "Ebony and Ivory"
4. Bono and Frank Sinatra, "I've Got You Under My Skin"
5. Rob Lowe and Snow White, "Proud Mary"

As you can see from this list, one of the few duets worse than "Ebony and Ivory" is another Paul McCartney duet called "The Girl Is Mine." That song has a nice melody but similarly crap lyrics that defy any logical defence. In the main refrain of that song, Paul and Michael both sing that the "doggone" girl is his. Besides the absurd nature of the lyric, it's hard to imagine a girl who fancies both Paul McCartney and Michael Jackson. What kind of diverse taste does this doggone girl have? It doesn't make any sense. "Ebony and Ivory" was only slightly better. It featured a strangely literal video with Stevie and Paul sitting on giant piano keys and then dancing and high-fiving each other. It was all very embarrassing for two musical greats. The upshot is that it still belongs on a list with Rob Lowe singing out of tune with a cartoon Snow White character at the Oscars.

But anyway, I don't mean to mislead you. It wasn't the quality of "Ebony and Ivory" that was the problem in terms of my performance at Harbourfront in May of 1982—not at all, actually. It wasn't how silly or banal the song was. You see, there's something you need to know about Kim Richardson beyond what I've told you. Kim was one of the best singers around. I've told you that. She was a dear friend and had distractingly large breasts. You know that, too. But there's one more thing. Kim was black. That is, she still is black. And she was black in 1982. Why is that relevant? Well, when it came to deciding which one of us was going to sing the Ebony part of "Ebony and Ivory," it was quite clear what direction we would take. Kim was Ebony. Obviously. But that left me. And the song wasn't called "Ebony and Olivey." Or "Ebony and Browny." My only option was to play Ivory. And so it was. I was to sing Paul McCartney's part of the hit song that would close the Harbourfront concert. The song was about racial harmony. And I was charged with the responsibility of representing all white people. I was to do this onstage.

It may be a testament to Bob and the Thornlea Vocal Group's progressive thinking in 1982 that they cast an aspiring New Wave brownish Persian kid as the Ivory part of "Ebony and Ivory" at the Harbourfront Centre. It might even look good to the audience in a diverse city like Toronto. On the other hand, people might say things like, "Isn't that nice … they've got the Paki boy singing the Ivory part." That's probably what Jim Muffan, the angry hockey player, would say. Or maybe people wouldn't notice at all. But I noticed. It was too complicated to go from being teased as a kid and isolated in the locker room and regularly called a terrorist to pretending it was natural being Ivory onstage. But nor could I give up a glorious opportunity to achieve the acclaim and acceptance I so badly wanted.

Maybe this was another colourful example of the paradox that was me in 1982 and beyond. I was a terribly sensitive and insecure soul who wanted to be accepted. I wanted to fade into the woodwork. And yet I never shied away from putting myself out there in some form of potentially masochistic public adventure. It's like I needed to keep proving to myself as much as to others that I wouldn't succumb to judgment. So, as much as I feared being disliked, I created the conditions where I might polarize reaction. I shared my opinions and did the announcements. As much as I wanted to fit in, I would elect to wear purple eyeliner and pointy boots. As much as I wanted to be part of the group, I would set myself apart by becoming the student class president or the team leader. I was fearful of disapproval by my peers, or my cool sister, or the older theatre students. But I was even more scared of giving in to that fear. So I would soldier on and pursue my passions—sometimes recklessly toying with the implications. Maybe not all that much has changed as I've gotten older. For most of my life, people have assumed I'm a confident guy with a Teflon exterior. That you could say anything about me—or to me—and it will just wash away because of the strength of my ego or character. That's pretty much the opposite of the truth. But criticism has never fully prevented me from pursuing my goals or what I believed in. I somehow wouldn't let it. I guessed Bowie wouldn't either. Oftentimes, I was stupid to put myself out there. It's hard to tell, when it came to "Ebony and Ivory," if I was being stupid in May of '82.

When the moment finally arrived, I climbed the steps at Harbourfront Centre as my name was called and joined Kim Richardson onstage for the finale of the Thornlea Vocal Group concert. We stood together in the spotlight. Kim was dressed in a leopard-skin Van Halen dress. She was taller than me in her heels. I wore tight black pants and black pointed boots and as much hair gel as I owned. The audience politely clapped and Bob nodded to us from behind the piano and began the opening refrain of the song. I took a deep breath and tried to look confident. Kim was smooth and calm—ever the pro. I tried to follow her lead. We began singing.

Kim: "Ebony"

Me: "and ivory ..."

There was some clapping from the crowd, the way people clap because they recognize a song. I don't know why people do that. It's not like we'd written it. And we were only a couple of lines in. But it was exhilarating nonetheless.

Together in harmony, we sang the living together in harmony part. We sang about being side by side on a piano keyboard and then we reached the high notes at the end of the phrase that asks the Lord why we can't live together. (As you can see, much of the song involves living together or wondering if we might live together or if we can live together.)

As we entered the first verse I took the first line of my two solo verses about there being good and bad in everyone. Kim responded with an obviously more impressive voice about how in order to survive we must learn to give each other what we needed.

I would give you an actual transcript of the song and the parts that Kim and I sang, but I can't, because it would cost too much money for the rights and it would make my publisher angry, and then this book would be in trouble. Yes, even the lyrics to the worst duet in history require a mountainload of money to reprint. If we meet in person sometime I can sing you my parts. Like, privately.

But the point is, the song went off relatively well, I suppose. It was probably all very sweet. A cool black teenager and a confused brown younger teenager singing about being black and white. I had eased into the song about halfway through our performance. I got used to hearing the echo of my voice being blared over the speakers with no stage monitors. I got comfortable with sharing my half of the centre stage with a dear friend and one of the best singers I knew.

At the last part of the song, the whole Thornlea Vocal Group returned to the stage and sang the refrain about ebony and ivory living in perfect harmony. Kim and I stood at the front, singing along and doing a two-step dance the way Sonny and Cher would have done, if Cher had been a tall black woman with giant breasts and Sonny had been a skinny Middle Eastern kid. I tried not to look into the crowd for fear it would throw me off. I focused on Kim. And Bob. And the ground. And the lights. And the music stands to the side. And then it was over. Mercifully. Triumphantly.

When we finished the song, Kim and I hugged onstage the way men and women who do duets hug at the end of songs. No couple has ever done a duet without hugging at the end. This communicates that you're happy and moved and feeling very close, even if you're not. I was probably holding tightly onto Kim more out of relief than anything else. The audience cheered, and Kim and I waved appreciatively. It was, for all intents and purposes, a winning moment. I'd soldiered through the song and been made to sound better by singing alongside Kim Richardson.

But there was no way to fully embrace what I'd just done. I'd been miscast. And the point is that there was no part that existed for me at all. I had gone along with the Ivory casting and hoped no one would notice. And to be fair, no one really said anything. But I noticed. And so a confused ethnic kid with New Wave clothing and brownish skin earned applause for playing the role of Ivory at my biggest concert to date. I started to think of it as a character that I was playing. That's right. Maybe I was increasingly just a character. That's what Bowie had done for most of his career. Maybe it was okay.

The Harbourfront concert was over. Wendy had not been in the audience, and that was gratifying news. Being a rock singer was cool, but performing the role of Ivory wasn't. There were some messed-up sides of me that I decided Wendy simply didn't need to see. And in the end, most of the time, winning the affections of a doggone girl was what was important.

11

"THE THINGS THAT DREAMS ARE MADE OF" - THE HUMAN LEAGUE

"We're totally going to get caught!"

I was getting anxious and whispering far too conspicuously in Murray's direction. He was characteristically calm. It's little wonder we joked about him being Mr. Spock.

"The worst that can happen is they kick us out," he said. "Stop stressing. Remember how badly you wanted to see this."

We were furtively squatting inside the Imperial Six cinema with our eyes fastened on the screen. I kept turning around and searching the theatre to make sure no ushers were about to bust us. We weren't supposed to be in there. We had snuck in. And now, in the middle of 1982, I was witnessing full-frontal on-screen nudity for only my second time.

The star of the film was a sexy young actress named Nastassja Kinski. I couldn't really figure out the plot. I had deduced it was something about a mysterious woman with a cool short hairdo who was also a ferocious black cat—a panther or leopard or some kind of rabid feline—and unrelated to that, her lips were often wet. That was the storyline, as much as I could understand. The movie was called *Cat People*, and Bowie had worked on the soundtrack and sung the title song. This was the "erotic" film of the year that everyone was talking about. It wasn't rated X. It was just restricted and labelled "erotic." I decided "erotic" was the name adults gave to an X-rated movie that they wanted to see in public without feeling creepy. Besides, this film had a major Bowie connection. It was credible.

I was too nervous to actually be aroused by the occasional lurid activity happening onscreen. But I saw this as an opportunity for education. It was all about sex. I was committed to discovering more about sex. And I wanted to be old enough to watch *Cat People*. And this film had Bowie's voice attached to it. That meant he approved of it—a Bowie-sanctioned movie. Nastassja Kinski looked a bit New Wave. And I had increasingly become preoccupied with girls. Thankfully, this had nothing to do with Wendy. Besides, as I found out in the new school year, Wendy had moved on.

WENDY HAD A NEW BOYFRIEND in September of 1982. And it wasn't me.

I learned this because I was a sleuth. I had cunningly garnered this information on the down low on our second day back at Thornlea Secondary School. It was all very savvy. I'd overheard Donna Davis chatting with another girl near Room 213, and I'd read between the lines to conclude that Wendy was no longer single.

"Wendy has a new boyfriend."

That was what Donna Davis said. It was obviously an ambiguous statement open to interpretation.

"Yeah, I heard that, too," her friend replied. "She's off the market."

Okay, fine, maybe it didn't involve much sleuthing. Maybe that crushing conversation was overheard with absolute clarity. But it was only one clue about Wendy and her new man. How could anyone be sure? I was just going on a feeling. But then I saw Wendy with her new paramour and any doubt evaporated. That happened the next day. Wendy was walking down the hall on the second floor at Thornlea accompanied by a tall, preppy blond guy. My heart dropped. I told you, I had a feeling.

I recognized the new man immediately. His name was Joe, and it wasn't too much of a stretch to call him a man. He was entering Grade 12 and widely known at school as a track athlete. He was tall and white and handsome in a tall, white-guy way. And he was preppy. He had a button-down pink shirt on and khaki pants. And now somehow Wendy looked preppy, too. She still resembled Bowie. But she looked like an awkwardly healthy Bowie with a tan. Or something. Or not. Maybe she didn't look preppy at all. Maybe it was just my imagination compensating. I couldn't explain what my Bowie girl would want with this guy cut from a Benetton ad. That is, other than the fact that he was tall and handsome and blond and an athlete. Apparently, Joe played acoustic guitar, too. He was tediously perfect.

I hadn't spoken to Wendy since our magical day at the Police Picnic and the kiss on the cheek I received at the Finch subway roundabout. It had seemed inappropriate to call Wendy again right after our date. We had agreed to go to a concert together, but she hadn't committed to anything more.

Phoning her after that would have been much too overt a nod to my intentions. I wanted Wendy to know that I liked her without letting her know how much I liked her. It's like when John Ruttle wanted to ask Valerie Tiberius out on a date to see Journey without it seeming like he was asking her out. You had to be tactical about these things. After the concert, I'd decided to wait three weeks for our next encounter when school began again. I hadn't pictured it going like this.

Wendy spotted me as she walked towards where I was standing at the end of the hallway. I was now in Grade 10. She was in Grade 12.

"Hi, Jian!" She smiled warmly and looked into my eyes as she approached. Her Ralph Lauren boyfriend was at her side. "How are you?" she said. "How was the end of the summer?"

"Oh ... hi, Wendy." I tried to act cool and relatively uninterested. "Yeah, it was fine."

I was staring at the blond guy and couldn't seem to stop. There was a pause. Wendy could likely tell I was distracted by his presence.

"Oh, Jian, this is ... Joseph." Wendy turned to address the blond guy. "Jian is the one I told you about. Jila's younger brother that I saw Talking Heads with."

Ouch. I was now back to "Jila's younger brother."

"Of course," he said. "Hi, Jian."

Joe sounded like a man. He had a deep voice. If he'd been doing the morning announcements instead of me, everyone would probably have thought he was a teacher. And there was something annoyingly precious about the way Wendy called him Joseph. *Joseph?* His name was Joe. He was a jock. He probably wasn't that smart. And there was no way he understood Talking Heads like I did. I was quite convinced this Joseph would not be talking to me if it hadn't been for Wendy. He probably made fun of artsy guys. He had chiselled features and his blond hair was parted on the side like a baseball player's. Calling him Joseph was obviously an attempt to suggest some sophistication. It wasn't working. I didn't like this Joseph—even if he was being nice.

An uncomfortable silence descended upon the three of us. Wendy smiled and said they had to be going to class. Joe shook my hand as if we were signing a peace treaty. It occurred to me that I had never really asked Wendy if she had a boyfriend. I'd never been specific about investigating her status. Maybe they had been dating all along. Maybe he had been away at a place where older tall white preppy guys go while Wendy and me attended the Police Picnic. Or maybe they weren't dating at all. Maybe he was just a new acquaintance. But then, Donna Davis had called him Wendy's boyfriend, and the other girl had added, "She's off the market." Either way, it was disappointing. I thought Wendy was New Wave. If not me, I thought she'd end up with a cool punk guy or a mod or someone into ska. It seemed strange to see her so comfortable with a preppy jock. I wondered if I'd been wrong about Wendy. Or maybe I was wrong about Bowie. Would Bowie forgo potential punk girlfriends and boyfriends to date Loni Anderson? No. A thousand times no. It made no sense.

Wendy was letting down the team. If Wendy was rejecting me after our special day at the Police Picnic, what pretty blond girl would ever accept an ethnic, artsy, skinny guy as her boyfriend? None. And besides, if someone cool like Wendy was ready to bypass all the fine New Wave candidates to date a poster boy for preppiness, what hope was there for anyone in the alternative world? I was angry with Wendy. I wondered if I should be angry with Bowie, too. I stopped listening to Bowie. I changed the channel when the "Fashion" video came on TV the next afternoon. My boycott of Bowie lasted three full days. But only three days. If Wendy and I were breaking up, she couldn't have him—even with her Bowie eyes.

It wasn't entirely bad. The truth is, seeing Wendy with another guy was strangely liberating. It sanctioned a whole new world of carnal possibilities for me. It allowed me to follow my libido with no reservations. You see, as you know by now, Wendy had been a tremendous romantic aspiration for me. She had been the role model for what I wanted as a partner. She was someone I saw myself buying hair gel with and blasting the Cure in shared headphones with. But Wendy had never really been a sexual fantasy. Not once. I really didn't want to have sex with Wendy. I wanted to *be* with Wendy. And in my early teens, those were two very different desires.

Sometimes you could have a dream girl and not want to have sex with her. I don't mean you'd necessarily refuse to have sex if the opportunity arose. It's not that you'd hate the idea of having sex with her. It's not like your dream girl was lying on a bed and saying, "Let's have sex now, please. I'm ready. Take me now, take all of me …" and you recoiled and ran away. It's more that you'd just never really considered sex with your dream girl. The stakes were too high. It was even more understandable if you'd never had sex, like, with anyone. And especially if you'd never had sex and were a bit unsure about the whole process.

I'd never fantasized about full-on physical intimacy with Wendy. That idea was much too intimidating. She was cool and smart and classy. Prurient intentions would have soiled the dream. Not that dreams didn't occur. Just with other protagonists. If there was one thing I was definitely interested in by the time I hit Grade 9, it was sex. And girls. Any girls. And now my heart had some sort of free pass.

I didn't actually know a lot about sex in 1982. I was fourteen when the year began and I hadn't had sexual intercourse and I was a bit unclear on all the mechanics. I had kissed a number of girls since Dana Verner in Grade 5, and I had gotten to third base with Kim Inglewood by Grade 8, but it was all very clumsy. Kim Inglewood and I had stripped naked at her house, and I had pursued a forensic fascination with her chest. I stared at her breasts with a mixture of excitement and curiosity and then tried to caress them in a seductive way that would turn her on. I had no idea what I was doing. I remember looking up to see a befuddled expression on Kim Inglewood's face as she stared at me staring at her naked breasts. I had done my best with my caresses. I'm not sure she really enjoyed it. Kim Inglewood and I never really said that much to each other. But I liked her. Or at least, I liked her breasts. And we were both trying to stumble our way into intimacy. I later told Pete Hickey and Toke about getting naked with Kim Inglewood, and Toke said, "Whoa!" and Pete Hickey added, "You're the master!" I had felt secure in my fledgling manhood for a brief moment during that conversation. But I was no master. I was thirteen then, and I had no idea what I was doing. Part of the problem was that I didn't have the benefit of pornography. That might have helped.

We didn't have porn in the 1980s. I mean, we had pornography, it existed, but it was virtually inaccessible to kids. This was a real liability. Without porn, how were we supposed to learn how sex was done? Of course, pornography was often sexist, exploitative, patriarchal, and full of the wrong messages about human relationships and intimacy. But even so, it could have served as a handy tool for seeing how this foreplay and intercourse thing happened.

In the early '80s, porn was still mostly to be found in those seedy old theatres where lonely middle-aged men in trench coats would go and do horrible things. That was what we were told. These men did horrible things with trench coats on. I don't really know if all of these men wore trench coats. But that was the word on the street—by which I mean, the word from our parents. The dangerous porn men wore trench coats. Maybe wearing a trench coat sent a signal to others that you were interested in watching pornography. Then you could identify your fellow porn-lovers. Of course, wearing a trench coat may also have meant that it was a rainy day. And certainly, no credible spy would operate without a trench coat. Wearing a trench coat meant all three of these things in the '80s.

Trench coats had become cool in some circles by the time I hit Grade 9. Simon Le Bon, the lead singer of Duran Duran, wore a trench coat when they opened for Blondie in Toronto in the summer of 1982. I saw Duran Duran with Murray at the CNE Grandstand just a few days after the Police Picnic. We had actually gone to see Blondie, but this new band called Duran Duran was there in support, and they had synths with arpeggiators and lots of hairspray. Duran Duran played the song "Night Boat" near the beginning of their set, and Simon

Le Bon stalked around the stage looking mysterious in a trench coat. Simon Le Bon pulled up the collar at one point to cover his face to his eyes. He looked like a secret agent. That is, a secret agent with very masterfully applied frosted tips in his hair. I decided that wearing a trench coat must also be New Wave. That meant trench coats were cool.

I have made a short list of the kinds of people who might wear a trench coat in the early 1980s:

- spy
- person in rain
- seedy adult-film attendee
- Simon Le Bon
- subway flasher

As you can see from this list, if a New Wave spy wanted to watch porn on an overcast day in 1982, we know what his outfit would be. But the point is, I didn't have a trench coat. And I wasn't an adult. And experiencing pornography took effort. It was frustratingly challenging to see anything pornographic if you were under eighteen. And even if you were of age, you really had to out yourself if you wanted to watch it or buy a dirty magazine at a corner store. It was all near impossible for a suburban Iranian-Canadian kid in Thornhill.

Of course, things are very different today. Today, everyone can watch porn on personal computers. You know it. Now you can watch extreme hardcore porn even when you don't mean to. Now you might type "light bulb" or "squirrels" or "nice pond" into your computer and you will be transferred to a hardcore adult site. You don't even have to search for "porn" or "sex" to find porn and sex, even though that might be easiest. Now everyone has seen everything. There is porn that includes ankles or headbands or triple penetration or aliens or bearded men. And you can be a teenager and watch all of this and be exposed to all different kinds of sex. But we didn't have that in the 1980s.

To be clear, I'm not suggesting that all fourteen-year-olds should be watching all cyber-porn. Hardly. There is material that really should be seen by adults only. But the option exists now, and it's easily accessible. And if you watch it, you may learn some tricks about how people have sex. Possibly. I can tell you, I didn't know much about this stuff when I was a teen. My sexual skills were embarrassingly novice. And outside of some well-meaning but ineffective sex ed. classes, I had little help in understanding the mechanics of it all. I remember wondering how I was supposed to contort my body in order to get my penis inside another person. It was all very confusing. In the absence of more graphic sex ed., at least some pornography could have helped me with some visuals to consider.

Having said all this about porn, some manner of dirty images did exist back in the day. We may not have had helpful hardcore materials on video and online, but we did have *Playboy* and *Penthouse* and *Hustler* magazines. Or at least, Benny Travers did. And he would share some of the best of it.

Benny Travers was a freckle-faced redhead who lived on our street in Thornhill and was one of the more prominent kids in our scene. He was in Scouts and had gotten lots of badges, because his father and brother and other brother had also been in Scouts. He had acquired a bunch of old *Hustler* magazines from a retired neighbour who had been selling them on his driveway as part of a garage sale. Word had spread about the old neighbour who was liquidating his stock of adult magazines, and we all took turns visiting the garage sale and getting a glimpse of the dirty materials lying plainly on a table next to some used cups. Only Benny had the courage to ask the guy if he could buy the porno magazines, and for this Benny was our hero. He told us the retired garage-sale man had chuckled and given him all the dirty magazines for a couple of dollars. That was a good deal, even in the late '70s. Benny was two years older than me and already the leader of the kids on the street. But now he had elevated his status. Benny also claimed two Penthouse books when he made his garage-sale acquisition. Benny became a high roller with important commodities the rest of us wanted. And thus began an odd ritual amongst the boys in our area in the summer of 1978.

A couple of times a week, a number of us would gather at Benny Travers's house to sit for readings from one of his Penthouse books. It was called *Sex Takes a Holiday*. Toke, Davey Franklin, Pete Hickey, and me—and sometimes more guys from the area—would form an audience while Benny sat on the stairs above us in his parents' home and read the Penthouse stories out loud.

You probably think this sounds ridiculous. And I am aware that this must sound comical to any kid now. It must seem like some ancient, sad, horny/awkward ritual from another time. And it was. And it's entirely true. We would gather, and Benny would read these stories to us with thespian-like verve: "Ohhh … harder … do it to me hard … unnnn … I'm coming …"

Benny was a thirteen-year-old reading this stuff to a bunch of eleven-year-olds. I never quite understood what I was supposed to be experiencing when I listened to Benny read tales from *Sex Takes a Holiday*, but I know it was exciting. It was also illicit and somehow very wrong. That made it more exciting. Benny was royalty for a while in our circle as the proprietor of the used *Hustler* and *Penthouse* collections.

By the 1980s, we were much smoother about these things. We had gotten older and had graduated to watching nudity on TV thanks to *Baby Blue Movies* on Friday nights. *Baby Blue Movies* had originally begun in the 1970s as a publicity stunt for the independent Toronto TV network called Citytv. We also knew it as Channel 79. The visionary behind this new TV station, Moses Znaimer, had embraced the notion that late-night sex on television could be popular. Or at least that it would bring notoriety. The idea was that late on Friday nights, Citytv would air soft-core porn. It worked. It brought the station some attention, and the practice carried into the '80s before it was discontinued.

The possibility of seeing these movies on TV was not lost on us kids. Starting in 1980, I would host sleepovers at my place on Friday nights. I'd invite some of the boys over, and we'd lay sleeping bags on the floor of our family room and tell my parents we were going to sleep. Then we would turn on our console TV with the volume very low and quietly watch the movies on Channel 79 in our sleeping bags. Sometimes there was snickering. Sometimes there was silence. Sometimes there were other sounds. But the practice was clearly rewarding enough for us to do it on a few occasions. I really don't know who *Baby Blue Movies* was aimed at. The movies weren't very explicit, and the storylines were abysmal. In retrospect, they were probably for boys like us. I still don't know if my parents knew what we were doing. I assume they did. Sometimes my parents had the sense to let boys do their thing.

In 1981, a new and very unique film called *Quest for Fire* got wide release in theatres. It was an interesting, quality movie about prehistoric tribespeople discovering a source of fire for the first time. It was shot and performed with an attempt at cinematic authenticity, including grunting, hunting, and the skimpy outfits prehistoric people wore before we had Calvin Klein. All I knew about the film was that there were naked women in it. That's because in prehistoric times people ran around naked. I convinced my father to take me to see *Quest for Fire* on the giant screen at the University Theatre on Bloor Street in downtown Toronto. I was thirteen, and well equipped with arguments to sell my father on the idea.

"But what thees film ees?" my father said.

"Dad! It's a film about how the world started, and about fire and people in the beginning of the world!"

"Thees ees good film you want to see?"

"Yes! Yes, Dad. It's about history. You know how you like me to learn about history. It's like a documentary."

It wasn't a documentary. My father relented and took me to see *Quest for Fire* at a weekend matinee. I will not forget the feeling of my father glaring at me in the theatre when the first nude scene came on. I kept looking straight ahead. I could feel my father's anger. Or bemusement. I'm not sure which. I avoided making eye contact with him.

Either way, it was titillating to see *Quest for Fire*. Then again, it was also terrifying to anticipate what my father might say after the movie ended. We didn't speak much on the way home. Later that night at family dinner, my mother asked what the film was like. "Thees film ees full of the naked woman," my father replied. My mother said "*Vah-ee*" and gave a disapproving wave of her hand. I may have been a bit embarrassed, but I was glad I had experienced my first full-on, big-screen nudity.

Traditional ideas about what was sexy and my alternative cultural tastes didn't always match. For all the excitement, I found it difficult to reconcile mainstream "sex culture" with my New Wave aspirations. As much as soft-core movies and dirty magazines informed me about what I was supposed to consider desirable, I had trouble with some of the orthodox examples of what was sexy. Don't get me wrong, the first time I saw Ann-Margret in a rerun of the Who's *Tommy*, I was sold on sexy. That scene with her and the beans is mandatory fodder for excitable youth. And I don't remember a time when I didn't consider Brigitte Bardot or Farrah Fawcett attractive. But much of the pop-culture stuff never made sense to me. I didn't understand why Bo Derek had to put those beads in her hair. And I couldn't figure out why Jessica Lange acted so flakey when she was being sexy in the new version of *King Kong* when I was a kid. And when I went to see the movie *Grease* with my mother and sister when I was eleven, I was quite convinced Olivia Newton-John was much prettier before she got a perm and wore the black leather pants. All of this was the opposite of what I was supposed to think was sexy according to magazines and dirty movies.

Who knows what I would have considered "hot" if I hadn't been bombarded with pop culture throughout my youth. The idea of what you find attractive and what you're socialized to believe is sexy changes as you grow. When I was a little kid I used to watch reruns of *Gilligan's Island*, and I would wonder what all the fuss was about Ginger, the sultry actress on the island in the ball gown. Mary Ann was always more attractive to me in her little shorts and red shirt. Then, when I hit eleven or twelve, I started to understand the appeal of Ginger as the sex kitten. Mind you, I will forever have a thing for Mary Ann.

Even further, by the time *WKRP in Cincinnati* finished its run on TV in September 1982, I understood why everyone considered Jennifer Marlowe, the receptionist, to be a sexual bombshell. Loni Anderson played the role of Jennifer on *WKRP*, and she had bleached-blond hair and giant bosoms and tanned legs and high heels. But by my mid-teens, I was much less interested in Jennifer than I was in Bailey Quarters, played by Jan Smithers, who was a more peripheral character. Bailey was a brunette who wore glasses, and she was smart and quirky. If I were to fantasize about anyone on that show, I was more likely to focus on Bailey. She wasn't New Wave, but she was less mainstream and predictable.

I have made a short list of qualities that made Bailey Quarters, the reporter and ingenue on *WKRP*, sexier than Jennifer Marlowe:

- nerdy
- journalism grad (summa cum laude)
- Diane Keatonesque
- hard working
- intelligent
- environmentalist (Bailey even campaigned against nuclear power in one episode!)

As you can see, Bailey was quite impressive. And you might think I'm trying to take the high road by saying I liked the intelligent girl better. I'm really not. Bailey was very pretty, too. If you don't think so, you haven't seen the episodes where Bailey really lets her hair down and takes off her glasses. It's just that I always imagined I would have more in common with Bailey, and that made her particularly sexy. Similarly, I could look at the hot, blond Jennifer Marlowe cheerleader types at Thornlea and recognize that they were very attractive but be more drawn to the New Wave girls or brunettes or punks like Dani Elwell and Wendy. They were more in the category of Bowie, after all. And a girl named Paula Silverman was somewhere in between. Paula Silverman also helped me learn about sex.

I met Paula Silverman in typewriting class in Grade 9 at Thornlea. Between theatre and music and history classes, all of which happened on the second floor, where I was most likely to see Wendy, I would head downstairs to the lower floor of our high school to attend instruction in core subjects like typewriting. I'm not making this up. Typewriting class really existed.

We learned to type in typewriting class. Now you learn to type when you're two years old. But in 1982, we didn't have computers for everything. We had a separate class for computers. That's where we learned how to use a PET computer. The Commodore PET was first released in 1977 and discontinued in 1982. But not before we were taught to try to use it at Thornlea in Grade 9. It wasn't clear what we would ever be able to do on a PET computer. It was bulky and black and white and riddled with code and seemingly quite useless. But we knew it was important to learn. It was the future. On the other hand, in typewriting class we were taught where to place our fingers and how to type words without looking at the keys or the paper we were typing on. This was so we would be able to use typewriters until computers became useful. Then we could type on computers. It was an odd time of transition.

Paula Silverman was a very cute brunette girl who could type very quickly. That was impressive. She was one of the stars of typewriting class in Grade 9. But what was even more impressive to me was that she wore very short shorts to school each day. Sometimes she wore those flannel types of shorts that would bunch up and become even shorter short shorts. Paula Silverman was small and had nice tanned legs. Only one floor away but worlds apart from Room 213 and the New Wave crowd and Wendy, there was Paula Silverman in typewriting class. I was always very attracted to Paula Silverman. She was also a year older than me. She was somewhere between Bailey Quarters and Jennifer Marlowe.

You might want to know what exactly Paula looked like. You might be curious as to how I defined "very cute" in Grade 9. But I don't really have any pictures of Paula handy. And that's because we didn't take photos in 1982. Well actually, what I mean to say is, we didn't take photos of everything in 1982. And that includes Paula and me. Now everyone takes photos of everything. You've noticed this, right? Maybe you haven't because it's just become so ordinary. Now we all shoot photos of everything because virtually every gadget we own takes photos we can collect or delete or augment or send. So now everyone has become a photographer and everyone is eager to show photos on Facebook. Now people miss experiencing an event because they're busy taking photos of experiencing an event. Now people will take photos of entirely inane and uninteresting things because it costs nothing to do so. But that was not the case in 1982. We barely had photographs in 1982. Photos were an occasion and a situation and an aberration. We were too busy doing stuff to take photos. And even if we weren't too busy, photos usually required too much money and patience.

The 1980s may not have been that long ago, but photographic documentation was a century apart from now. If you wanted to take photos in Grade 9, you would have to start by owning a good camera. Not a camera that was part of your mobile device (we didn't have those either) but a separate camera camera. For this camera, you would have to buy film. The film might come in rolls of twelve or twenty-four shots, and it was expensive. Then, upon loading the film, you would have to make each photo count, given the expense and the limited number of exposures on your roll. After shooting the roll, you would take the film to a processing shop and pay more money and then wait a couple of weeks to see the photos. You would say things to the guy in the processing shop like, "Will these photos be ready by Wednesday?" And then the guy would say, "No ... they won't be ready for two weeks."

This is not a joke. Two weeks. Sometimes more. People would have aged by the time their photos were printed from their latest roll of film. That's how long it took. Men would grow beards in the time it took to develop film and get a set of prints. Then, inevitably, when you finally got the pictures, nine of the twelve photographs you received would be dodgy or blurry or ugly or unusable. So as you can see, it just wasn't an economically sage adventure for a kid in Grade 9 to be running around taking photos. Who had the time and money for that whole process? That's why I can't show you any shots of Paula Silverman.

But I can tell you that Paula was pretty and she wore makeup and she wore very short shorts. She also chewed gum all the time. Paula chewed gum the way those girls who speak while they're chewing gum chewed gum. It was a little annoying. But on the other hand, if you ever needed gum, Paula Silverman could supply you. And she was tanned. She was another white girl who always had a tan. Sometimes, she would tan so much she was dark brown. If my mother had been Paula Silverman's mother, she would have told her to stop tanning because she might become "black." But Paula wasn't Iranian, so it was okay to be "black." And she looked good with her tan.

Paula Silverman helped me learn the ropes when it came to some mutual sexual exploration in Grade 9. By "learn the ropes," I mean she allowed me to grope her. And she groped back. I don't know how it began, but about halfway through the school year Paula and I began meeting in a downstairs back lobby under the stairway at Thornlea. Our meetings would take place each day after school. The back stairway was where the rockers and stoners would generally hang out, and there was a giant rock outside the door so it was called the Rock. Paula and I would meet at the Rock at the end of school each day and make out under the stairs. We wouldn't really say that much to each other. And we weren't really close friends outside of our daily meeting. But we were both committed to our rendezvous at the Rock. And we didn't just make out. Paula would unzip my pants and fondle me while I made my way into her short shorts with my hands. With Paula Silverman, I learned what touching the inside of a girl feels like. This was a tremendous thrill. It went nowhere more than that. But it was genuine excitement.

But it wasn't enough for Paula. After a few weeks of our daily meetings, she wondered why we weren't having a relationship. It was a fair question, and she was a nice girl and she deserved an answer. I wasn't sure how to respond. I couldn't really tell her I was unavailable because I was interested in an older New Wave girl who looked like Bowie and rarely talked to me. That might seem odd. So I didn't really give Paula an answer. When Paula asked me if I would consider having sexual intercourse, I said no. I just wasn't ready for it. In retrospect, I was probably much too scared of the possibility. After a few weeks, devoid of a relationship or intercourse, my dalliances with Paula came to an end. But not before some education was found underneath a stairway at the Rock.

BY THE LATE SPRING of 1982, I had a new ambition to go with asking Wendy out and becoming New Wave. There was a film I needed to see. This film represented the intersection of two of my greatest interests in Grade 9: sex and Bowie. It was called *Cat People*, and it was definitely considered cool.

I first truly learned about the movie with the release of the *Cat People* soundtrack featuring Bowie's song "Cat People," written with producer Giorgio Moroder. It starts with a foreboding slow beat and then breaks into one of Bowie's most powerful and intense baritone vocal performances ever. When he starts with the haunting first line, it's as though his voice is going to burst out of the bottom of your speakers. It was a single that got some play on alternative radio.

I had also learned by the spring of 1982 that *Cat People* was an erotic thriller about a young woman's sexual awakening turning into horror when she discovers that her urges turn her into a monstrous black leopard. Nastassja Kinski played the role of the erotic leopard girl. She was a fine young actress, and she was regarded as one of the most beautiful people in the world. She'd started acting in her teens and had a relationship with the filmmaker Roman Polanski when she was just fifteen and he was forty-three. She was considered very sexy and was a big screen star. She was especially considered very sexy because the previous year she had appeared naked in a famous Richard Avedon photograph with a giant Burmese python. Kinski and the python were lying together. I'm not sure why lying down with a python was considered so sexy, but it was. First she was seen with a snake, and now she was a cat in *Cat People*.

I wanted desperately to see *Cat People*, to feel older and hear the Bowie music and see a naked Nastassja Kinski. When the movie was first released in April, there was much fanfare about all the sexuality and therefore little chance that any fourteen-year-olds would be able to get in. The film had a Restricted rating in Canada, which meant it was only for people over the age of eighteen. But after it had been out for a while, I convinced Murray to join me in a cunning plan. We would buy tickets to see another film at a multiplex playing *Cat People* and then sneak in to watch it. I became quite obsessed with the idea of seeing *Cat People*.

It was a nervous afternoon when Murray and I hit the Imperial Six on Yonge Street. Murray played it cool. The

Imperial Six was a famous movie theatre that featured six big screens. It was located across from the new Eaton Centre mega-mall. It turned out I had overestimated the dangers of our covert sex-film expedition. When we strategically bought our tickets for another movie, I fully expected the guy at the counter to say, "You boys aren't planning to sneak into *Cat People*, are you?" No such words were exchanged. The older guy at the counter barely even looked up at us. We dashed into the theatre playing *Cat People* at the appointed time, and I waited to achieve a new sexual awakening. We were in the clear. The theatre darkened. The movie began.

In the end, somewhat disappointingly, the movie wasn't all about sex. It followed an intense plot line that was decidedly less interesting to me than seeing Nastassja Kinski naked. I don't really remember loving *Cat People*. Maybe I didn't fully understand it. But either way, I spent weeks afterwards telling everyone I had seen it. It gave me credibility. And the fact that Murray and I had snuck in was badass. Maybe the best part of the film was when the theme song kicked in. That part included Bowie. There were still some things that were more important than carnal desires.

FOR ALL MY NAÏVETÉ about sex and girls, when I started Grade 10 in the fall of 1982, things were different. I was older and more experienced. Okay, maybe it had only been three weeks since the Police Picnic, but each new school year was like a restart, and I had become more self-assured. I had a new black briefcase to replace my long-gone Adidas bag. The briefcase was unquestionably more New Wave. I had also acquired updated pointy black shoes, and I was starting my new band, Tall New Buildings, which featured a drum machine. The drum machine telegraphed that we were a New Wave band and we were cool.

In the fall of 1982, I also started hanging around with a girl at school named Janelle. She was super-smart and did well in classes like science and math. She was also very sweet and played on the Thornlea volleyball team. She and I were both on student council, where I had joined as the head of social events. Janelle was half Asian and very pretty and very grounded. She was a couple of years older than me and was not really very New Wave. But she had a cute haircut like one of the Go-Go's. She wasn't really preppy. That was the important thing.

I was still hanging around Room 213, but I didn't see much of Wendy in the fall. Paula Silverman had been sexy but wanted to move far too quickly for me. Janelle was more patient with all my quirky needs. And she was really interested in my music. I made a mix tape for Janelle so she could become acquainted with more of the cool New Wave stuff I was into. The second side of the tape was all Bowie songs, with little descriptions I'd written for her inside the cassette jacket. Janelle told me she had started playing it on repeat.

12

"Let's Dance" - David Bowie

It's predictable, I suppose. It may not come as a big surprise to you that the most dramatic event in my life in the closing days of 1982 occurred with a Bowie song as the soundtrack. It somehow makes sense for that to happen, right? You might think I'm making this up. I'm not. It did.

I wish I could tell you something else. I wish I could inject more musical variety into this tale of a formative year. I wish I could answer those of you who've been thinking, "Look, you wuss, it's near the end of the book, where's the Def Leppard already?" Or maybe some of you are wondering why I've not given enthusiastic early '80s star Lionel Richie his due in these pages. In '82, he had an impressive Pharaoh-like moulded Afro that made him look like a black John Oates. Why haven't I talked about that? Or maybe I could've woven in some tales about Michael Jackson, too—he *was* the King of Pop. But that's not how it happened. I didn't gravitate towards Lionel Richie at all back in the day. Bowie provided the playlist for most of my young existence. And that was the case in the middle of

Grade 10. And that was the case following the most dramatic event of my life at the end of 1982.

"HOW ARE YOU GOING to make sure everybody's vote gets counted?"

The tone was very dismissive. One of the more conservative older members of the Thornlea Student Association (more commonly known as the TSA) was questioning the merits of my plan to have a big December school dance in the gymnasium that would involve some sort of countdown of the year's best music. I'd suggested this list would be developed according to an official poll of the student body. It was the third TSA meeting of the fall, and I was making bold promises as the new social director. I was sitting next to Janelle, whose presence was giving me assurance. I had no idea how to execute my plan, but that didn't affect my passion for it.

"I will personally ensure everyone at school gets a ballot and that we count the votes responsibly," I said with confidence.

This was bravado. I didn't know what I was doing. I was in Grade 10 now but still one of the younger reps on the TSA, and my experiment was quite audacious. I saw Hussein roll his eyes at the proposal. Hussein had moved into Grade 13 and was even bigger and more intimidating than he'd been the previous year. You may wonder what Grade 13 is. There's no such thing as Grade 13 now. It probably sounds funny. But I can explain. We had an added school year in Ontario in the 1980s. I'm not sure why. It came after Grade 12 and before post-secondary, and it was mandatory if you intended to go to university. It was some kind of extra lifeline for those who weren't ready to leave high school, and some kind of torture for those who were. Hussein was now in Grade 13, and in the TSA meetings he sat on top of a desk rather than in a chair. No one would tell him not to do that, because he was big and wearing his leather jacket. He probably considered my countdown dance a threat to the popularity of his Rock Nite. It didn't help that I was also the guy who had initiated a new coffee house series with live music called SWé. The name SWé was an acronym for "some wonderful entertainment." I thought of not telling you what it stood for, because it sounds so twee and makes me sound skinny and sensitive—which I was. But that's what it stood for. In 1983, Debbie Ngo would make a cool poster for SWé at my request that was like the cover jacket of Bowie's "Let's Dance" single but said "Let's SWé" instead. That was one of the lyrics in the song, too, but spelled differently. Smart stuff. It would become my favourite poster throughout high school. But SWé was somehow perceived as competition for Rock Nite—albeit with acoustic guitars. And Hussein didn't like that, either.

Still, I had a growing group of champions for my ideas. The dynamics at the TSA had shifted. The motion for my ambitious countdown event was carried with the support of Jane Decker and Janelle and a few others. Jane Decker was now a leader at the TSA, and despite the eyeliner incident a year earlier and my desire to tell her to fuck off the way Siouxsie had told us all to fuck off at her concert, she had become a good friend. She supported me during the TSA vote, but then after the meeting furtively asked me if I knew what I was doing. I assured her that the countdown dance would work. I convinced her of this even though I had no blueprint to follow. I just knew I had always been fascinated by lists. I had been making lists since I was a little kid in England.

Anyone who has ever known me well knows that I love lists. When we came to Canada, my father facilitated my interest in lists by giving me a book called *The World Book of Rankings*. The title handily referred to the fact that it was a book of world lists. It had lists like "Country with Most Oil Exports" and "Most Murders per Year, by City." I pored over the lists religiously, and tried to memorize parts of the book before going to bed each night. This may be an insight into my nerdy character growing up. While others were playing with model cars or fantasizing about girls, I was staring at international rankings in a book. Fast-forward to Thornlea a few years later, and this was my chance to compile an important list and have a popular event in the gym where a lot of New Wave music would get played. Besides, as much as I respected democracy, it may also have been the case that I intended it to be a cool list of New Wave songs regardless of the votes. Integrity at the polls needed to be compromised sometimes for the sake of a curatorial music policy.

Initiating my countdown event at the TSA was not inconsistent with a new bit of confidence I had in Grade 10. I was taking more responsibility around Thornlea, and I had the support of Janelle. She was quickly becoming a very beautiful presence in my life. And hitting the age of fifteen didn't hurt either. You see, the good news about high school is that, for the most part, over the course of your time there, things get better. That is, you get older. And as you get older and move into the higher grades, there are waves of young new recruits who enter the school and struggle to build their courage and get their bearings the way you once did. So you can look at the younger students and laugh at them, and then you feel better about yourself. That is what high school is ultimately designed for: laughing at others to feel better. And so, by Grade 10, I was no longer an insecure Thornlea rookie. No. I was more of an insecure sophomore with a year of high school experience and a briefcase instead of an Adidas bag. This was a big difference.

Aesthetically, I had also made progress by the fall of '82. My uniform was certainly more solid. For all that I'd grappled with a fledgling New Wave image the previous year, I'd made major strides in my presentation. My days with Toke and our Lolas from Mac's Milk seemed an eternity away. We were kids then … even if it was only the summer before last. Most of my clothing was now black, and my hair was longer and had more blond and jet-black streaks. I had a sleek black briefcase that I carried to school each day, and a few black shirts that I wore throughout the week. Concerts like the Police Picnic had taught me the look I was going for. And my involvement with Theatre Troupe at the end of Grade 9 had catapulted me into being considered one of the cool artsy students. This was important.

I was also honing my New Wave musical tastes in Grade 10 to include alternative rock and electronic groups like Gang of Four and Kraftwerk and Simple Minds. Simple Minds were a post-punk Scottish band with a charismatic singer named Jim Kerr who acted a bit like Bowie. No one could be Bowie, but Jim Kerr set a good example. I became a Simple Minds fan. Jim Kerr wore jackets with shoulder pads and black pants and black eyeliner. And he crouched when he sang. I was never sure why he did so much crouching. I assumed that's what the latest trendsetting New Wave singers did. I started crouching when I sang, too—for a while, anyway.

By mid-autumn, I was doing fairly well in school, I continued making the morning announcements and was in the Vocal Group as well as other extracurricular activities. A good portion of my time between classes was spent with Janelle. She was in Grade 11 and considered by many to be a great catch. She was definitely a girl that a lot of the boys had noticed. She was diminutive and sweet and had a natural beauty. She wore very little makeup except for a touch of eyeliner. She was graceful from being a ballet dancer as a kid but also a strong athlete. She was soft-spoken and well-grounded. She had been an exchange student in Europe and now spoke French fluently. She was also one of the top students at Thornlea. She was the kind of person that gets one hundred percent on a science test. Those kinds of people are usually annoying. But Janelle wasn't. Everyone liked Janelle. She was pretty much the whole package. And she was very nice to me.

My crush on Janelle felt strangely mature. I felt little of the nervousness and insecurity that had come with Wendy. On one of our first occasions alone in the hallways of Thornlea, I had spontaneously kissed Janelle on the lips outside the photography room. I remember her looking quite shocked and commenting on how I had some gall to do such a thing. I wasn't so sure where I'd found such confidence, either. But soon we were seeing each other regularly.

Janelle had a calm demeanour and was a good balance for my outgoing and neurotic personality. She was what others would see as an ideal partner. But we didn't actually become boyfriend and girlfriend in the fall. At least, I never fully acknowledged us that way. She asked me on a couple of occasions if I was her boyfriend, and I changed the subject. Maybe

Janelle was just too good for what I was ready for. She was not my sexual fantasy girl or ersatz New Wave role model. She was solid and real. That probably scared me. And Janelle really didn't have the background in punk or alternative music that I valued in a person. I needed to change that. I set out to try to educate her with mix tapes.

THE TRUE MEASURE of your affection for another human in the 1980s was in making a mix tape. It's different now. These days, you can throw together an iTunes playlist in a couple of minutes. You can make a playlist without caring very much. It's not so much of an investment. But in the '80s, the mix tape took time and consideration and creativity. The right amount of space left between songs on the cassette was not unimportant. The flow of the music was paramount. The choice of the material was key. And writing meticulous and artful liner notes was also a major element. The all-important title of any particular mix tape could make the difference between a regularly played classic and something that got tossed in a shoebox with other cassettes. Making the right mix tape was never easy.

One of my primary goals with Janelle was to instruct her about Bowie. This might sound like some kind of attempt at indoctrination. I assure you it was. I was on a mission to teach Janelle everything I could about my idol. I couldn't very well be attached to a girl who didn't know much about Bowie.

I called the Bowie mix tape "Scary Monsters Mix" as a nod to his 1980 album featuring "Ashes to Ashes" and "Fashion." Here is a list of the songs that appeared on Side A of the mix tape I made for Janelle in the fall of 1982, including the year Bowie released each song (as I outlined on the cassette liner notes):

"The Laughing Gnome," 1967

"When I Live My Dream" (*David Bowie*), 1967

"The Secret Life of Arabia" (*"Heroes"*), 1977

"Five Years" (*Ziggy Stardust*), 1972

"Cat People" (*Cat People* soundtrack), 1982

"Please Mr. Gravedigger" (*David Bowie*), 1967

"Karma Man," 1967

"Fashion" (*Scary Monsters*), 1980

"Speed of Life" (*Low*), 1977

"Breaking Glass" (*Low*), 1977

"What in the World" (*Low*), 1977

"The London Boys," 1966

"Wild Is the Wind" (*Station to Station*), 1976

As you can see, I wanted to include a lot of very early David Bowie on this mix tape, to demonstrate my credentials as a true fan and for Janelle to be aware of his beginnings. I also balanced things by taping "Cat People" and "Fashion," some of his latest work. I got some of the information wrong on my liner notes for Janelle. As a case in point, the gorgeous cover song "Wild Is the Wind" is from 1976, not 1978, as I had labelled it. But I didn't have the advantage of Wikipedia back then. And nor did anyone else. So details like this mattered less.

It made sense that I started the mix tape for Janelle with a quirky little song called "The Laughing Gnome." It went the furthest back for me. The first time I was introduced to

David Bowie was in England. I was five years old. I mean, I wasn't actually personally introduced to him, but I was made aware of his voice and his music as it emitted from the radio in our house. We lived in a house on a street called Beacon Close. Beacon Close was in Middlesex, a suburb of London. Middlesex was like the equivalent of Thornhill in England, but with less heating and more peas.

By the time I was five, my mother had taught me to record sounds that came from the radio by pressing the two top buttons on our new Panasonic tape deck. It was a portable tape deck that was also a radio. This device was a technological wonder. It could do it all. It was the cutting edge in the early '70s, and my Uncle Boyuk had brought it from America. Actually, he had brought it from another part of the world and then from America. My Uncle Boyuk always had the newest gadgets. He would get them from Japan or Germany and bring them to the United States, where he lived. Then he would deliver them as gifts to us in England when he visited. It probably would have made more sense for Uncle Boyuk to just send the gadget gifts straight from Germany to England, but it was more glamorous this way.

The Panasonic tape deck required alertness and quick reaction time. The way it worked was that you inserted a cassette into the player and cued it up to a blank part and then left it there. If something was on the radio that you really liked, you could then press "Rec" and "Play" simultaneously, and whatever sound was on the radio would transfer onto the tape. It took skill to do the double-press at the appropriate moment. You had to be physically ready for any possible taping opportunity. And so the problem was that if you were on the other side of the room—say, eating pistachios, or thinking about eating pistachios—you would have to run to the tape deck to catch the song just as you heard it come on the radio. This might explain why there is a generation of people walking around who don't remember the first ten seconds of most radio songs of the 1970s. Those parts just didn't make it onto their cassettes. But mix tapes were popular and became very much the norm. Of course, it was easier to make a mix tape when you were recording music that you owned on vinyl. But when it came from the radio, it posed athletic challenges to get to the buttons on time.

On one occasion, at the age of five, I accomplished the aforementioned taping mission with a David Bowie song. Actually, my mother told me to do it because she'd heard the song once before and recognized it when it came back on the radio. That was my introduction to Bowie. And I owed it to my mother. And once it was taped, it also became the first time I owned something by Bowie. Later, people would deem this kind of unlawful acquisition of music to be "piracy" or "stealing." But no one cared about that when we were young. You didn't really need the internet for illegal downloading back in the day. In the 1970s and 1980s, it was just called "taping stuff."

The song that I ran over to record was that Bowie ditty from the late 1960s called "The Laughing Gnome." Years later, it became the first song I put on that mix tape for Janelle. It features Bowie interacting with a laughing little gnome. I know. If it sounds a bit silly, that's because it is. The gnome has a high-pitched, helium-type voice that sounds like Alvin from the Chipmunks. I'm not really sure if this is the way gnomes sound. I've never heard another gnome speak. But I didn't question this as a kid in England.

"The Laughing Gnome" is an enjoyable and cute song that ends up with both Bowie and the gnome laughing quite hysterically. The whole thing sounds like a children's tune—which may have been regrettable to some, including Bowie himself. But I loved it as a kid. And given that I had recorded it on a mix tape my mother had started that also featured kids' performer Rolf Harris and the costumed band of furry creatures called the Wombles, I assumed for many years afterwards that David Bowie was a children's performer. I thought he just made kids' music. This might have led to a surprising encounter if I'd actually been introduced to Bowie as Ziggy Stardust doing cocaine and eating red peppers in the mid-'70s, but as a boy I didn't have much access to that Bowie.

My Bowie addiction continued through the 1970s as I discovered songs like "Young Americans" and "Space Oddity." Then my interest grew in the early 1980s, especially after the advent of video channels. In Grade 8, as I've told you, I ended up performing "The Jean Genie" with the Wingnuts, with little awareness, as a suburban, middle-class thirteen-year-old, that I was singing lyrics about a drug and sleaze fiend. By 1982, I played "Ashes to Ashes" at Thornlea with my older friend and mentor Mike Ford. I would then go on to use a Bowie quote as my final graduating words in the Thornlea yearbook, and all the time in between I would do anything and everything to try to follow in Bowie's footsteps. Of course, this ambition mostly manifested itself in embarrassing and unfortunate ways, but you already know that.

Janelle promised me in the fall of '82 that she would listen regularly to her new Bowie mix tape. Despite her predilection for more mainstream pop music, she told me she was becoming a big Bowie fan. This was important news for me. And the chances of some kind of future for us as a couple were growing more realistic.

BY EARLY DECEMBER, my countdown dance event at Thornlea was set to become a reality. I desperately wanted it to be successful, since I knew that if it wasn't, I would take the blame. Success meant a big crowd at the gymnasium. And fortunately, we got it. Whether it was the concept or—more likely—the desire to attend a blowout high school event before the Christmas break, students turned up in strong numbers. In fact, it became successful enough that I held sequel countdown dances for the next couple of years, and they grew in popularity to become part of Thornlea social lore. Voting to choose the most popular songs was held with good intentions each year, but the results would somehow end up mirroring my interests. I accept that this looks suspicious. I can report that the number-one song of Countdown '83 at Thornlea was "Let's Dance" by Bowie. I can neither confirm nor deny that any ballots were tampered with. I can only tell you that it was a fantastically correct outcome.

Janelle had become one of the main organizers of our inaugural countdown dance in the late fall of '82. A few folks from the TSA were involved and working very hard to put the event together, but it always felt like a partnership between Janelle and me. John Ruttle was an essential part of the logistics team, Jane Decker oversaw many of the details and coordinated with teachers and the administration, and my friend Daniel

Steinberg agreed to be the DJ who would preside over actually playing the top twenty songs of the countdown plus all the music in between. Daniel was a tech-savvy music fan who had a floppy New Wave haircut that made him look a bit like Alex Lifeson from Rush. He was a punk rock fan, and once, while the Clash were playing on the stereo in his bedroom, he gave me a private demonstration of how he could crush a beer can with his head. He was quite cynical about the world and would regularly greet me by saying, "Fuck you and hello." But Daniel was a friend and had acquired some fine turntables and DJ equipment. He was also a punk with a strange predilection for Phil Collins. His one condition for DJing was that I agree to let him end the dance with "In the Air Tonight" as the final song after the countdown had been completed. Phil Collins had released that song the previous year, and it was beloved. It was actually pretty cool and exhibited some masterful musicianship that can be found on the rest of his debut album. Phil Collins was not yet considered a sugary pop sellout. I agreed to Daniel Steinberg's condition to let him play "In the Air Tonight." Daniel also understood my love for Bowie and was committed to respecting it by spinning Bowie music at various points throughout the night.

The balloting for our schoolwide countdown was a little less rigorous than I had hoped. I did my best to distribute ballots, and a few hundred Thornlea students named some of their favourite songs. I tabulated the votes and compiled an official list that would encompass our high school's collective voice about the best tracks of 1982.

The gymnasium ended up looking quite impressive. We had the song titles and album covers projected onto a giant screen as the countdown progressed. The list would include "Freeze-Frame" by the J. Geils Band, "Down Under" by Men at Work, and "I Want Candy" by Bow Wow Wow. The number-one song of the year with the most number of votes turned out to be "Don't You Want Me" by the Human League. Like I said, the list just happened to be in line with my tastes.

When I secretly showed Janelle the full countdown list the day before the dance, she registered her support for the winner.

"I'm not sure I understand your list addiction," she said dryly. "But I'm glad it's 'Don't You Want Me' at the top. I like that song."

Janelle was also a big fan of Phil Collins, so his giant atmospheric hit was one that appealed to her as well. She was thrilled to hear that Daniel Steinberg had lobbied to end the night with that song. And it certainly was refreshing not to be bringing things to a close with the classic but ubiquitous Zeppelin song "Stairway to Heaven." Janelle and I agreed that if we weren't too preoccupied running the event, we should dance the final dance together. It would be a cool slow dance, after all. "You better save 'In the Air Tonight' for me," she said.

It felt good to have a plan with Janelle. It was reassuring knowing she was around and that we were in this together. I knew that while other guys would want to dance with her at this event, she'd be unlikely to give anyone else the chance. Even though we had not declared ourselves as a couple, it was clear to me that Janelle believed we were an item, and I wanted to respect that.

As it turned out, there wasn't all that much work for me to do once the event began. Things went quite smoothly. The gym filled with Thornlea students. Stashes of alcohol and pot covertly found their way into the dance. That made people happy. Things were generally fine and orderly. Exciting, even. At one point, Tim Matheson, the infamous and aggressive Thornlea punk who had spent some time in jail, accosted me on the dance floor and started yelling about the lack of Dead Kennedys music on the countdown. I tried to respond that it was the student body that had determined the list, but reasoning with him was never really a possibility. He soon got distracted anyway. I was grateful for this. I'm pretty sure Tim Matheson understood that it wasn't as empirical a list as I claimed it to be.

I spent most of the night overseeing things and dancing with John Ruttle and Janelle and Valerie Tiberius, amongst others. It seemed destined to be a fun and relatively uneventful evening. When I wasn't overseeing things or dancing, I was standing in front of Daniel Steinberg at the DJ booth. I was laughing out loud watching John kick up his feet to the music and do a comical routine with his lanky body. I watched the red-and-white light show animating the dance floor and the music. Our Thornlea gym looked as cool as I'd ever seen it.

"Hi, stranger."

I felt a tap on my shoulder. The voice behind me was familiar. The voice sent nervous energy through my body. I turned around. Everything stopped. I was momentarily stunned.

It was Wendy.

My heart dropped. I had barely seen her for weeks. I had never dared assume she might come to a silly dance like this. She was too punk. Or cool. Or something. But here she was, and she was smiling. Her eyes had the same twinkle I had seen at the Police Picnic. She looked exactly how she had the first time I'd seen her the previous year in Grade 9. Her blond hair swooped across one side of her face. She was wearing a black blazer with a tank top underneath. She was the coolest New Wave girl in the world. She still looked like Bowie. But somehow she was even prettier now.

"Wendy! Hi! Hello! I didn't know you'd come to this ..."

She shrugged and smiled again. "Yeah, why not? Hey, it's a cool event, Jian. Way to go. I like some of the music."

She was being sweet, the way she'd been when she stuck up for me against Forbes. I scanned the immediate area. She appeared to be alone. There were students I didn't recognize dancing around us. I leaned in closer to make sure she could hear me over the music.

"Well, um ... thanks for coming."

"How are you doing, Jian?"

"I'm great. Yeah, really great. Is your ... is Joe ... is Joseph here?"

"Joe? Ha! No ... we haven't been together since October. We were never quite right for each other." Wendy rolled her eyes. "Besides, he didn't have a red-and-blue Adidas bag."

"I have a briefcase now," I replied, much faster than I wanted to.

I wondered if she was making fun of me. I pulled away to assess. She wasn't. She laughed. We both laughed. And she was no longer with Joe.

"Wendy, it's really amazing to see you."

"Yeah, Jian. It's actually really nice to see you as well."

The countdown had progressed. Daniel Steinberg was now spinning "Tainted Love" by Soft Cell. The opening synth sounds were filling the spaces between our words. Soft Cell were quite high on the list. I pointed towards the speakers as if to say, "Check out this song." I knew Wendy was likely a fan, because they were New Wave and cool.

Wendy nodded to acknowledge the tune. Then she looked towards the doors at the back of the gym.

"Hey … I just need to hit the bathroom. I'll be back in a little bit, okay?"

"Yeah. Cool. Of course."

And then she was gone. I tried to compose myself and get some perspective. Wendy was probably at the dance with another guy. She'd been nice to me, but that was no reason to believe she cared about me any more than she did for any other arm's-length friend. I had spent a fair bit of time trying to clear Wendy from my mind throughout the fall. Surely the fact that she was making a cameo appearance at this dance and saying hello wasn't enough to revive my infatuation with her. She probably wasn't going to return. In fact, she definitely wasn't.

"Is she one of the girls from Theatre Troupe?"

Janelle was standing beside me and had likely witnessed my reaction upon seeing Wendy.

"Oh … no … she wasn't in Troupe."

"So, how do you know her?" Janelle's curiosity was perfectly natural but felt intrusive right at this moment.

"She's just … she's the younger sister of one of Jila's friends. Also, we went to the Police Picnic together in the summer."

"Oh … that's Wendy."

Janelle said this in a low, matter-of-fact tone. She nodded her head quickly. She knew exactly who Wendy was. It was the first time I sensed Janelle knew the extent to which I'd been crazy about Wendy. I thought I had hidden it. I'd barely mentioned her, but there must have been something about how I'd once explained our day at the Police Picnic. Janelle was smart. She hadn't spoken the words "that's Wendy" as a question. She said her name knowingly. I felt confused. But I didn't owe her any explanations. It's not like Janelle was my girlfriend. I had been clear about that.

Jane Decker swept in with another TSA member and pulled Janelle away to deal with something about photos for the yearbook. I told Janelle I'd see her when she was done and stood trying to make sense of the rush of emotions I had felt seeing Wendy. But why was I even thinking any more about this? Wendy had disappeared. Why was I so easily churned up? Then, just as I started to believe my own pessimism, I had another surprise.

"There's a massive lineup at the girls' bathroom. It's ridiculous!" She smiled and threw her arms in the air as she approached. Within less than ten minutes, Wendy had returned. She wasn't abandoning me at all. She was already back.

"There's no way I'm waiting!" she said. "Let's dance!"

Wendy grabbed me and dragged me to the middle of the dance floor, where a variety of punters were bopping up and down around us. The next song on the countdown was in full swing, and it was "Our Lips Are Sealed" by the Go-Go's. We started to do our full-on, arm-swinging New Wave dance on cue.

Wendy and I chatted loudly as we danced. We were both giggling a fair bit, and I felt energized and exuberant. She told me she'd been busy working at a bookstore after school. She asked about my sister, and my band, and my fall classes. She seemed truly interested. I realized Wendy had not changed from the caring older girl who'd attended the Police Picnic with me. Maybe I had projected all kinds of horrible qualities on her after seeing her with her older preppy boyfriend. Now her ex-boyfriend. Wendy was real. She was genuine.

And I was now more mature and more confident. Wendy and I stayed on the dance floor as the next song came on: "Just Can't Get Enough" by Depeche Mode. I started slapping my forehead like we'd witnessed David Byrne do in the summer. Wendy followed my lead and did the same. We laughed again. I was filled with excitement. It suddenly felt like little else mattered. I was with Wendy. It was like that magical feeling from our night at the Police Picnic. Maybe this was the way things were supposed to go. Maybe this was the way my year was supposed to end. Everything was happening for a reason.

"Rock the Casbah" by the Clash was the number-three song on the countdown. The crowd was a dancing frenzy. I asked Wendy if she wanted to get a drink. She agreed, and I led her under the stage, where Daniel Steinberg had hidden a cooler with beer in it. I opened a beer for Wendy, and we sat beneath the stage, watching the dance floor through the cracks, drinking and chatting with the Clash as our soundtrack. We didn't move for a few songs. I could have stayed there forever.

Daniel was now announcing that the big moment was here. The number-one song was about to be revealed. I grabbed Wendy's arm and we went back on the dance floor. Daniel was speaking into the microphone from his perch at the turntables.

"All right. Here it is, everyone. The number-one song of

1982, as voted by you ... 'Don't You Want Me' by the Human League!"

The song began with its immediately recognizable thumping bass and synthesizer groove. Wendy and I joined the crowd dancing to the top song. I saw Murray and some other friends also bopping up and down. We shouted the chorus at the top of our lungs and pumped our fists in the air. It all felt like it was meant to be.

The Human League song ended. The countdown was over. Daniel Steinberg informed the crowd that it was time for the final tune of the night and something about it being the last chance to grab that girl you'd been thinking about. As promised, we heard the opening keyboard notes and drum machine sample of "In the Air Tonight." Students started pairing off for a last slow dance. This was the finale I had been anticipating. But now that it had arrived, I suddenly wasn't sure what to do. Wendy was standing in front of me and looking a bit awkward. Maybe she hated Phil Collins. I avoided making eye contact. At the same moment I realized I had totally forgotten about Janelle. She had been my support for weeks. I could see Janelle approaching. This was the song she loved. This was the song we'd talked about dancing to. I didn't look at her. I didn't want to look at her. Out of the corner of my eye, I saw Janelle stop a few feet away from me. I turned fully towards Wendy. She looked up at me and extended her right hand.

"So ... you want to dance to this?"

I took her hand.

Wendy and I started slow dancing. I soon had my arms around her waist and was pulling her closer to me. I'd been silly to think Wendy might consider me too young and not good enough for her. This was all happening as it should.

I was ready to take the initiative. This was the guy that Wendy had been waiting to see. I had become the stronger version of me that she had desired. The new confidence I felt inspired physical action. I pulled Wendy closer to me and looked straight down into her eyes. The look on Wendy's face was curious. It seemed to suggest some confusion or hesitance or excitement. I couldn't tell which, but I sensed it was excitement. It must have been excitement. I pushed my lips into Wendy's and gave her a long kiss. I could feel her kissing me back. Phil Collins was providing the soundtrack.

The kiss felt perfect. It was as if it lasted an hour. "In the Air Tonight" had segued into the big section after the famous drum break, but I held Wendy close the whole time. The song was coming to an end, and I had my New Wave dream girl in my arms. My Bowie girl. For all the times that I was the outcast, this was the payback. For all my insecurities through the year, I was finally at peace with who I could really be.

The song was over. Wendy pulled away a little and pretended to fan herself with her right hand. "Well, I didn't really expect that!" she said with a laugh. She had a strange sparkle in her eye.

"There's a lot you don't know about me, Wendy. I've been wanting this for a long time."

Wendy giggled and bowed her head. For a moment, she looked like a little girl. I'd never seen her quite so shy.

The dance was officially over. Wendy shifted away from me slightly, but I kept my arm around her. She didn't move it.

The gymnasium lights were being turned on. We had gone

slightly over curfew, and now the staff and student council members were encouraging everyone to leave.

I looked at Wendy. "So, what now?" I smiled.

She was nodding slowly as if she agreed with the question. She smiled back at me, cocked her head, and looked into my eyes.

"Well, listen, for starters, I just have to get my coat. I'll be back in a minute, okay?"

She was holding my hand, and she softly squeezed it as she said this.

"Of course!" I replied. "I'm going to say goodbye to the guys and grab my stuff. See you in a sec."

She let go of my hand. I gave her another smile as we slowly parted. Wendy walked towards the back of the gym and into the hallway beyond, where everyone had left their coats. I turned and spotted Janelle by the exit. I looked directly at her. She had her coat and scarf on. I wasn't entirely sure what to do. I gave a little wave of my hand but got no response. She had an expression on her face that I'd never seen. It was devoid of emotion. No familiarity, no engagement, but no sadness, either. Nothing. The characteristic warmth I'd grown to depend on in Janelle was absent. There was no acknowledgment. I'm quite sure she saw me, but she hurried towards the doors.

I turned away. I thought about my kiss with Wendy. I could still taste her lips. I grabbed my briefcase and my long black coat from behind the DJ booth. I returned to the place where Wendy and I had been dancing. I waited for her there. I thought about where I might take her for a late-night snack. The gym was now almost entirely empty except for the cleanup staff. Daniel Steinberg was still playing music, but at a lower volume. He'd seen me dancing with Wendy. He was a New Wave comrade and had given me a knowing glance when I had her in my arms. I looked in his direction. He gave me a thumbs-up.

The coat check was probably backed up. It had been more than ten minutes. I looked back over at Daniel. He was putting on one last song for the staff and TSA members before packing up his stuff. He pointed at his turntables and winked. I heard the opening strains of a guitar line I knew well. It was "Wild Is the Wind" by Bowie. It is the most beautiful song Bowie has ever recorded. It's a cover tune. A slow song once performed by Nina Simone. It was the final track on the mix tape I had made for Janelle. It is exactly six minutes long. I stood without moving. "Wild Is the Wind" came to its soaring climax. I saw the students in charge of the coat check putting away the tables in the hallway. The doors were now closed. The song was over.

I waited.

AUTHOR'S NOTE

Dear reader,

This book is classified as creative non-fiction. Please take note of the "creative" part. It doesn't mean that this stuff didn't happen. It did. But it means, for example, that I cannot exactly remember all of the conversations that happened when I was in my early teens. Can you? I didn't think so. So, this is the story as best as I remember it. I don't claim it to be any more accurate than that. This is not an official history text.

The events you're reading about all occurred in 1982 or are based on events that occurred in the years immediately before or after 1982. All the characters in this book are real people or are based on real people. In any scenes with my parents and sister, it will be obvious to you that they are real people. In some other cases, the names have been changed to protect the non-innocent or because I couldn't get in touch with certain folks to make sure I could talk about them in this book. And finally—importantly—some of the characters are composites of a couple of people I knew.

1982

Fuzzy memories come with three decades of distance, but I've done my best to recount accurately the details of what occurred or the spirit of those details. My mother can confirm some specifics, such as the sheer amount of hair products involved in being me at the time.

Jian Ghomeshi

ACKNOWLEDGMENTS

Thanks to my dear mom and dad, who had to sit through the arguments and endure the growing pains and who always ultimately supported my ambitions and left turns. You are my true role models.

To my sister, Jila, who is forever the sage guide and smarter Ghomeshi sibling.

To my long-time agent and dear friend Jack Ross at the Agency Group, for continuing to be a co-conspirator and partner.

To Celeste Parr, who read all of this book before anyone else and let me know that I was on track and also let me know when I was not. You are a star.

To my trusted assistant, Ashley Poitevin—my rock—for her enthusiasm and commitment in helping make *1982* a reality.

To Lindsey Love and Stefanie Purificati, for being a support team that would be the envy of any boy. And to my best friends Andy Stochansky and Lisa Whynot, for believing and laughing at my stories so I could fool myself into thinking they were funny.

To my American agent, Marc Gerald, who inspired me to have the confidence to think I could do this and who helped me get the ball rolling on this idea.

To my fabulous editor, Diane Turbide, to my copyeditor, Alex Schultz, and to Nicole, Ashley, Beth, Scott, Justin, Lindsey, David, and all the amazing folks at Penguin Canada. From the beginning, you got it. I am forever thankful.

To Joe Goodman, for pushing me to remember that I like to push myself.

To the cast of 1982—Wendy, Murray Foster, Mike Ford, Ron Baker, Valerie Tiberius, John Ruttle, and all the friends named in this book—as well as the students and staff of Thornlea Secondary School.

To my dear old schoolmate Sue Fraser, for finding my Bowie mix tape notes and clearing up some foggy recollections.

To Dan Hill and the members of Rush, for very kindly granting me permission to reprint their fine lyrics in these pages.

To the staff and crew of the Sunset Marquis in LA, for hosting me and letting my creativity run in a rock 'n' roll setting. And to all my bosses and peers at CBC and Q, for letting me escape in various increments to scribble my stories.

To my fluffy, dutiful travelling companion, Big Ears.

And finally, my unending gratitude to David Bowie, for providing a lifetime of inspiration and impossible standards.

THE POLI

ENTRY SUE

OPENS AT 4

EXHIBITION

PRESENTED

FRI AUG

ENTER GATE

gate/aisle

42

sec/box

2

nt code

ER

4

ate/aisle

ILT
ion

S1

00
ce

OO

x

UL

ro